The Reconstructed Carmelite Missal

A. Carmelite Missal, fol. 68vo: Initial T introducing the introit of the Mass for the Dedication of the Church

THE RECONSTRUCTED CARMELITE MISSAL

*An English Manuscript of the late XIV Century
in the British Museum*

(Additional 29704–5, 44892)

by

MARGARET RICKERT

THE UNIVERSITY OF CHICAGO PRESS
CHICAGO ILLINOIS

THE UNIVERSITY OF CHICAGO PRESS, CHICAGO 37, ILLINOIS
W. J. Gage & Co. Limited, Toronto 2B, Canada
Faber & Faber Limited, London, W.C. 1, England

Printed by R. MacLehose and Company Limited

Contents

List of Illustrations

COLOUR

MONOCHROME

at the end of the book

LIST OF ILLUSTRATIONS

LIST OF ILLUSTRATIONS

Preface

THE reconstruction of the Carmelite Missal and the studies involved in the attempted solution of its various problems were begun in 1933 and cover a period of about sixteen years. Although the actual reconstruction was completed in 1938, publication of this monograph was postponed partly because of the war and partly with the hope that by some miracle further fragments of the Missal, especially the missing first part of the *Temporale*, might be found. Unfortunately, this hope has not been fulfilled. However, an additional scrapbook of cuttings has been discovered by Mr Neil Ker in Glasgow University Library, but on examination it was found to contain only further fragments of the parts already constructed.

During the war the two huge boxes containing the sheets of mounted cuttings, together with the unplaced fragments and all the working materials, were carefully stored away in safe places along with other British Museum manuscript treasures. And when in 1948 it was again possible for me to visit the Museum, everything relating to the Missal was exactly as I had left it ten years earlier. After a further consideration of the possibilities of adding to the reconstructed pages such of the many small unplaced fragments as could be identified, it was finally decided that the value of such additions would be incommensurate with the labour involved, unless at some future time the missing portion of the *Temporale* should be discovered.

From first to last, the project of reconstructing the Missal has been fascinating and at times most exciting. This has been due partly to the novelty and variety of the processes involved, and partly to the visible increase in the beauty which emerged day by day as more of the fragments were pieced together on the reconstructed pages. But the largest factor in sustaining interest throughout the laborious and often discouraging search for methods of establishing evidence for identifying unplaced fragments, was the unfailing help, encouragement, and appreciation shown by many different persons both in the British Museum and elsewhere, without whose active sympathetic support the reconstruction of the Missal could hardly have become a reality.

Among these many friends of the project, I can mention only a few, to whom I am indebted for kindness shown in special ways; Sir Sydney Cockerell, friend of all scholars and Dean of manuscript connoisseurs, whose keen interest in the reconstruction of the Missal was generously communicated to a number of his friends and thereby opened up contacts with specialists in various fields whose assistance and advice proved invaluable; the Trustees of the British Museum who, on the recommendation of the late Dr M. R. James (one of those who had become interested through Sir Sydney) officially expressed their appreciation of the work done on the Missal by presenting me with an honorarium; Sir Harold Bell and Dr Eric G. Millar, former Keepers of Manuscripts in the British Museum, and Mr A. J. Collins, present Keeper, and the late Dr Robin Flower, former Deputy Keeper, all of whom facilitated in every possible way the carrying out of the reconstruction; Professor Francis Wormald of King's College, University of London, former Assistant Keeper in the Department of Manuscripts, who, as a specialist in liturgies, was assigned from the Museum staff to supervise and check the reconstruction and who, as the work progressed, became an enthusiastic collaborator and himself contributed much important help on the project; Mr Longley, Mr Watson, Mr Edwards, and former and present members of the clerical staff of the Manuscripts Department, especially those who were called upon constantly to handle the enormous, heavy boxes in which the fragments and mounting sheets were kept, and whose patience and courtest never failed; Mr Reginald Seargeant, former technical expert in the Bindery of the British Museum, who, entrusted with the exacting task of inlaying the fragments on the mounts, displayed not only remarkable skill in the mounting but extraordinary intelligence and interest concerning the reconstruction as it progressed.

To Mr W. G. Constable, Director of the Fogg Museum, Boston, Mass., formerly Director of the Courtauld Institute of the University of London, and Professor John Shapley, formerly of the University of Chicago, I am deeply grateful for their unfailing support at a crucial stage of this work, both through financial aid in procuring photographs and in meeting other expenses connected with the research, and through their constant advice and encouragement. Grateful acknowledgement should be made also to the American Council of Learned Societies for a grant-in-aid to further the project, and to the Henry Bradshaw Society for paying for photostats of textual source material.

For the generous loan of textual material indispensable for the liturgical phase of the reconstruction, I wish to express my thanks to the following: the Rev. Claude Jenkins, Librarian of Lambeth Palace Library, and Miss Irene Churchill, Assistant Librarian, for the manuscript of the Carmelite Ordinal of Sibert de Beka; the Very Reverend Brocard Taylor, O. Carm., Prior of the Carmelite College of Pius XI at Rome, for a copy of the rare 1504 edition of the Carmelite Missal, and for permission to photostat the volume while it was deposited in the British Museum; the Chancellor of Trinity College, Dublin, for the manuscript copy of the Kilcormic Carmelite Missal and for permission to photostat it; the Master and Fellows of University College, Oxford, for the manuscript copy of the English Carmelite Breviary and Short Missal and for permission to photostat it; the late Dr Henry Guppy, Librarian of the John Rylands Library, Manchester, for the manuscript copy of the Carmelite Missal. To Mr Neil Ker who notified me of finding the most recently identified scrapbook of cuttings and arranged with the Librarian of Glasgow University Library for the book to be deposited in the British Museum for examination, I also wish to express my thanks.

Finally, among the many warm and stimulating associations resulting from the work on the Carmelite Missal will always be most gratefully treasured the kindly enthusiasm shown by one of the most learned of the modern Carmelites, the late Reverend Father Benedict Zimmerman, O.C.D., Prior of the Convent of the Discalced Carmelites in London. Besides allowing me to use some of his unpublished liturgical material, Father

PREFACE

Benedict was always ready with suggestions and assistance on points relating to Carmelite history and liturgy.

For permission to reproduce photographs of manuscript pages used as illustrations in this book, grateful acknowledgement is made to the officials of the various libraries and museums concerned.

The complex nature of the material contained in this book has involved many difficult technical problems in its publication, and I wish to congratulate the publishers and printers on their patience and skill in solving them so successfully. In work that has been done in successive stages through so many years, it has been impossible to recheck everything, and errors and inconsistencies will undoubtedly appear, for which the author, in the spirit of the mediaeval writer, can only ask indulgence, submitting this book 'with humble reuerence to be refourmyd wher men fynde offence'.

M. R.

On the Feast of the Patriarchs Abraham, Isaac, and Jacob
In the year of Our Lord nineteen hundred and fifty
University of Chicago

Introduction

In the catalogue of Additional Manuscripts acquired by the British Museum during the years 1861-75, numbers 29704-29705 are described as follows:

'Cuttings of Initial Letters and Borders, from a Latin Missal written and illuminated in England at the beginning of the XVth century. Two volumes. Of the initials forty-nine are of sizes varying from two to four and a half inches, and contain miniatures of great beauty; the remainder are in foliated designs. The character of ornamentation and painting and the gold grounds with punctured patterns closely resemble those in the Latin Bible, Royal MS. 1 E. IX[1], but the execution of the miniatures and designs of letters, as also the colouring, in the cuttings, are superior. Compare also Harl. MS. 7026, the borders and miniatures of which are painted by friar John Sifrewas, about 1400. Vellum; beginning of XVth century. Quarto.'

The emphasis in this description on the 'great beauty' of the miniatures and their superior execution and colouring as compared with the so-called 'big Bible' (Royal MS. 1 E. IX), itself one of the most sumptuous and imposing manuscripts of its period, leaves no doubt as to the quality of the cuttings. This was further attested by the continuous exhibition for over twenty-five years of selected fragments in the Grenville Library at the British Museum, and by the reproduction of some of the cuttings in all the important publications on English illuminated manuscripts[2] since the scrapbooks entered the British Museum.

Little is known about the history of the scrapbooks. On the flyleaf of MS. 29704 is the following pencilled inscription: 'Bought at the sale of Mr Hanrott's books who had cut out and arranged these illuminations in the two volumes. W. Tite.' In the lower corner of the back cover of each volume is a small label with Sir William Tite's autograph: 'W. Tite, Esq., M.P.'

The sales of Philip Augustus Hanrott's books took place between July 16, 1833, and March 22, 1834; the scrapbooks appear in Pt. II of the Sales Catalogue (Evans, Aug. 5, 1833, Lot 1525*), described as follows:

[1] For a discussion of this manuscript and also of Harl. MS. 7026 in relation to the Missal, see Chapter IV.

[2] See Herbert, J. A., *Illuminated Manuscripts* (London, 1911), p. 233, Pl. xxiv; Millar, Eric G., *English Illuminated Manuscripts of the XIV and XV Centuries* (Paris, 1928), Pls. 79–81; Brit. Mus., *Schools of Illumination* (London, 1922), Part IV, Pl. 3. A good, coloured reproduction of the initial containing Edmund the Archbishop teaching is found in E. S. Prior, *Cathedral Builders in England* (London, 1905), opp. p. 77. One of the finest of the miniatures, the Purification of the Virgin, was reproduced in colour for sale at the British Museum before the last war. More recently, another miniature, Saint Giles, was added to the series of uncoloured postcards on sale at the Museum. See also p. 18 note 3 below. In the most recent book, *English Art, 1307–1461*, by Joan Evans, Oxford (Clarendon Press), 1949, the Purification miniature is reproduced on Pl. 48a.

'Illuminations upon vellum, from ancient manuscripts. A very extensive collection of ·
Miniatures, Initial Letters, and other ornaments cut from ancient manuscripts, many of
them highly finished specimens, splendidly bound in two vols. morocco, gilt leaves.'
A notation in the catalogue shows that they were sold to Williams (a dealer?) for £28.10,
from whom, presumably, Sir William Tite bought them.

The Tite sales occurred between May 18 and June 6, 1874. In the Sales Catalogue
(Sotheby, Lot 1561), the scrapbooks are described thus:

'Illuminations. A collection of magnificent ornamentations, very richly illuminated
in gold and colours upon vellum, cut from Ancient Service Books, comprising 56 beautiful
initial letters[1] (each containing an exquisite miniature) above 1600 very large capital
letters, upwards of 400 other ornaments (consisting of borders, flourishes, etc.) and in-
numerable letters of gold, painted capitals etc. neatly mounted on tinted paper in 2 thick
volumes. Morocco, g(ilt) e(dged). Folio.'
The books were bought by Quaritch, as noted in the Sales Catalogue, and shortly after-
ward found their way into the British Museum.

The increased emphasis on the number, variety, and exceptional quality of the cuttings in the Tite Sales Catalogue as compared with the brief description in that of the
Hanrott sale, seems to indicate that the scrapbooks had found an appreciative owner—a
fact which is reflected in the much higher price fetched by them at the Tite sale. There is,
moreover, further evidence that the cuttings had attracted attention during Sir William's
ownership of them. In Additional 29704, pasted on the flyleaf which contains the inscription quoted above, are two letters concerning the loan of the scrapbooks in 1863 for an
exhibition at the Ironmongers' Hall, London, and the subsequent retention of the books
after the exhibition had closed, so that a study might be made of the miniature subjects,
which were considered exceptionally interesting.[2] An illustrated catalogue of the Ironmongers' Exhibition, published 1864-67, devotes a number of pages to the description of
the miniatures and reproduces four of them in colour.[3] In this description the statement
again appears that Mr Hanrott cut up the original pages and arranged the fragments in
the scrapbooks.

Supplementing these meagre facts about the history of the cuttings, their arrangement in the scrapbooks has yielded certain interesting items.

First, as to ownership: the grouping of initial letters on one page (29704, p. 139) to
spell two proper names, 'Philip' and 'Mai' (*sic*) (Pl. XXXIX), together with such combinations of letters as 'A.H.' and 'C.H.', suggested that the scrapbooks had been treated as
a kind of family autograph album. 'Philip A.H.' (fragments numbered 630-37 on the same
page) certainly referred to Philip Augustus Hanrott, either the owner of the scrapbooks or his

---

[1] Actually, there were only fifty-one historiated initials; the other five were not initials but fragments
of decoration containing figures. One more was contained in the scrapbook bought later, making the
present number of historiated initials fifty-two.

[2] The letter dated 17 July, 1863, contains the following statement: 'Almost every subject in the first
volume has been accurately described, in some instances correcting the pencil notes.' These pencil notes,
written under the miniatures in the scrapbooks, are not in the handwriting of P. A. Hanrott. See Add.
MS. 28653, pp. 174–8, containing letters written by him to Mr Burns, bookseller. Cf. also p. 19 note 3.

[3] *A Catalogue of the Antiquities and Works of Art, Exhibited at Ironmongers' Hall, London, in the
month of May, 1861.* Compiled by a Committee of the Council of the London and Middlesex Archaeological Society, with numerous illustrations. Parts II and III, London, 1864, 1867, pp. 245–53.

son of the same name; 'C.H.' could be Caroline Hanrott, wife of Philip Augustus, senior; 'M.M.H.' (the first *M* is actually an *E* turned on its side) could be Mary Magdalen Hanrott, his only living sister; 'I.S.C.' (the first letter really a paragraph mark used as an *I*) may have been Isaac (?) Cory, a cousin; and 'Mai' (the name presumably would have been spelled 'May' had there been a *y* in this kind of initial letter, which there was not) was certainly young Mary, second daughter of Philip Augustus, always known, according to family tradition, by this nickname.[1] Other pages with somewhat less varied 'signatures' were found in the same volume (29704), on pp. 140 and 155; and in 29705, on pp. 13, 48, and 172. On these latter pages the initials which appeared most often were the *P*.s, *A*.s and *H*.s. Page 140 (29704) showed a large, fine decorative initial *P* in the centre of a semicircle of small gold *M*.s.

In spite of Sir William Tite's statement that Mr Hanrott cut out and arranged the initials in the scrapbooks, it is difficult to imagine him, a highly respected, middle-aged, wealthy lawyer and a collector of fine books[2] deliberately destroying this magnificent manuscript, much less engaging in such childish 'busy work' as the arrangement of the cuttings indicates. Mr Eric Hanrott had a more plausible suggestion, namely, that it was May's idea to make up this series of family monograms, headed either by her father's name or (as is more likely) by that of her young brother, Philip. The large *P* mentioned above, then, may stand for this beloved brother's name and the *M*.s for herself: May's lifelong devotion to her brother is a matter of family record. The other *P*.s, *A*.s and *H*.s may stand for either the father or the brother or both. But if this evidence does point to the possibility that it was May who made the scrapbooks, it is certain nonetheless that Philip Augustus Hanrott senior must have known and approved the idea.

Second, as to the date of these two scrapbooks, the mounting paper used in both volumes is watermarked 1826. Moreover, the date 1827 is in the watermark of the paper of the flyleaves of both books, which may have been made up as blank books for this special purpose. It has been observed that it was Mr Hanrott's custom to write in his books,[3] but there is no indication in either of the scrapbooks of the provenance of the original manuscript.

Finally, there is evidence of three more scrapbooks containing cuttings almost certainly from the same manuscript. A small one was included in the same part of the same sale (as Lot 1764, 'octavo et infra') as the two volumes now in the British Museum; it was described in the catalogue as follows:

'Illuminated capital letters and ornaments from ancient manuscripts, mounted, and bound in a volume, morocco, with morocco lining, richly tooled, contained in a morocco case.'

[1] Most of this information about the Hanrott family was very kindly furnished by a great-grandson of the younger Philip Augustus, Mr Eric Hanrott, who became much interested in the history of the scrapbooks. Although his search of the few surviving family papers failed to yield any information about the British Museum volumes, an unforeseen result of his interest was the finding of another scrapbook in the family, which was subsequently acquired by the Museum. See p. 20.

[2] For the few facts known about Philip Augustus Hanrott as a book collector, see Seymour de Ricci, *English Collectors of Books and Manuscripts*, Cambridge, 1930, pp. 100 f.

[3] *Ibid.*, p. 101. Manuscripts in the British Museum which contain such inscriptions are Add. 11928, 11930, and 12031.

This volume, it is noted in the Sales Catalogue, was bought by J. Bohn for £5. Since it cannot be traced, there is no way of verifying its contents as cuttings from the same source as the British Museum books, but this seems very likely.

In the case of a second lost scrapbook, there is little doubt that the cuttings actually did come from the same manuscript. This book was sold in 1857 with the remainder of Mr Hanrott's library after his death. It was described in the Sales Catalogue[1] as follows:

'Alphabets and letters illuminated and painted in gold and different colours, on vellum, with curious small miniature figures and devices in many of them, cut from an early Missal and neatly arranged on blank paper, splendidly bound in brown morocco, super extra, gilt edges, with morocco linings and fly leaves tooled in the Grolier style, in a morocco case.'

The description of the binding sounds very similar to that of Add. 29704-29705, and the 'curious small miniatures' suggest the small, pen-drawn initials with scenes and heads and ornament found in great numbers in these volumes.

But there is even better evidence that the fragments in this scrapbook were from the same original manuscript as those in the British Museum. In the last plate of Henry Shaw's *Alphabets Numerals and Devices of the Middle Ages,* published in 1845, is an alphabet of engraved ornamental initial letters labelled as having been copied 'from a MS. in the possession of Philip Hanrott Esqre. Date about 1480.' The forms of these initial letters and also their designs (allowing for some variations in the engraver's copy) correspond so closely to those of the smallest fragments in the British Museum scrapbooks that there can be no doubt that the originals of the engravings came from the same manuscript, the date 1480 notwithstanding! Their arrangement as an alphabet strongly suggests that Mr Shaw was copying them from a scrapbook—perhaps the one sold in 1857, since his publication is dated later than the sale of the two big books and the unidentified small one sold at the same time in 1833.[2]

Until September, 1936, it appeared that four scrapbooks filled with cuttings from the destroyed Missal were all there were. Then a fifth volume was brought into the British Museum one day by two sisters, members of the Hanrott family who had learned from Mr Eric Hanrott, their nephew, about the reconstruction of the manuscript from which the cuttings came. One glance at the fragments in this album was sufficient to establish their identity as further remains of the same original manuscript. Moreover, inside the front cover was the name, 'Ellen A. Hanrott' spelled with the same kind of initial letters (gold, on blue and tan ground) which were used for the names and initials in the British Museum volumes (see Pl. XXXIX). On the green morocco cover are stamped in gold the letters: 'E.A.H.' Ellen Hanrott was the younger daughter of Philip Augustus, between May and Philip junior. From the more mutilated condition of many of the fragments in Ellen's book, it would appear that she got the leavings of the cut-up pages, after what was wanted

---

[1] S.C. 28 Jan., 1857, Lot 14.

[2] Since these statements were written, the scrapbook from which Mr Shaw engraved his alphabet was discovered by Mr Neil Ker in Glasgow University Library (MS. BD. 19–h.9. No. 1875—Euing Collection). Not only does the scrapbook fit the description and verify the deductions about it as given above, but it contains on a flyleaf an inscription in Mr Hanrott's handwriting, which reads, in part, as follows: 'This Collection of various small Alphabets and Letters in different colours . . . was selected and made by my dear relative Esther Cory from a large folio *imperfect*' (Hanrott's underscoring) 'Missal which I purchased at a Sale for £7.7'.

for the larger books had been chosen. The make-up of the pages in this scrapbook is not uniform. Many of the fragments were apparently mounted on sheets of variously tinted note paper, with the mark of Dobbs, London, impressed into the upper left corner of each sheet. These sheets are mounted, two to a page, on many leaves of the scrapbook. Other leaves have fragments arranged 'artistically' or in alphabetical series. The paper used in making the scrapbook is watermarked 1828, slightly later than the British Museum volumes. Ellen's scrapbook was acquired by the Museum and numbered Add. MS. 44892.

This is all that is known about the history of the cuttings. The history of the original manuscript before it came into Mr Hanrott's possession remains a complete blank. Some hints as to the circumstances which might have accounted for its being cut up have emerged during the process of reconstruction. It was only half of a Missal, the first, or winter, portion of the *Temporale* was missing. Its enormous size would have made it difficult to house in a private library. Some, at least, of the leaves had suffered from use or exposure and were brown and stained at the edges, and had been ruthlessly trimmed. These facts, together with the exceptionally high quality of the illumination (which we must give Mr Hanrott credit for appreciating) and the excellent preservation of much of the decoration within the pages, might well have suggested that not only would they make beautiful scrapbooks, but that they could be better preserved in a more manageable form.

But for the student and connoisseur, the cuttings meant little aside from their individual beauty. It was inevitable that an attempt should be made to reconstruct the original manuscript in order to determine, if possible, its format, its date, its provenance, its textual contents, and most important of all, its stylistic relation to other manuscripts of the period. The steps in the development of this fascinating project have been discussed elsewhere.[1] The processes by which the reconstruction has been accomplished have seemed to be of sufficient interest to be recorded, and these, together with the evidence on which the successive stages of the reconstruction rest, have been included in Appendix A of this book.

[1] *Speculum*, XVI, No. 1 (January, 1941), pp. 92–102.

I

The Format and Textual Contents of the Reconstructed Manuscript

A revised description of Additional Manuscript 29704–29705 in the British Museum would now read as follows: 'English Carmelite Missal, probably written at Whitefriars, London, before 1391, and illuminated before 1398 by several hands. Latin. Gothic script. 212 paper leaves 78·7 cm. × 56 cm. on which are mounted 1588 vellum fragments consisting of historiated and decorative initials, fragmentary borders and text. 3 volumes, bound separately, with continuous foliation, and contents as follows:

'Vol. I. Fols. 1–69: the summer portion of the *Temporale*, beginning with Easter Saturday and continuing through the last Sunday before Advent.

'Vol. II. Fols. 70–135: Prefaces and Canon of the Mass; Calendar; first six gatherings of the *Sanctorale*.

'Vol. III. Fols. 136–212: remainder of the *Sanctorale*; *Commune Sanctorum*.'

Each of the 212 leaves represents a leaf of the original Missal, laid out with margins ruled to correspond to those estimated as correct for the original manuscript page. No leaf is completely filled, but a number have all or nearly all of the larger initials introducing the different parts of the mass, that is, introit, collect, epistle, gospel, secret, and post-communion, together with text fragments on the reverse side (cf. Pls. XXXIV–XXXVIII). The fragments have been inlaid on the paper sheets in such a way that both recto and verso are visible and no textual evidence for placing the fragment has been covered up.

It is certain that the fragments as they now appear do not show the full margins of the original leaves, since there are many on which the border decoration has been considerably trimmed. In a number of these, the edges of the fragments are stained and soiled as though a considerable time had elapsed after the trimming and before the manuscript was cut up.

The measurements of the paper leaves and of the vellum leaves as reconstructed on them, are as follows:

	PAPER MOUNT	ORIGINAL VELLUM LEAF	EVIDENCE
Length: text space	51·0 cm.	51·0 cm.	fols. 176, 106vo.
margins, top	10·4 cm.	5·8 cm.	fol. 30vo.
bottom	17·3 cm.	7·1 cm.	fol. 196

	PAPER MOUNT	ORIGINAL VELLUM LEAF	EVIDENCE
Width: text space (two columns, each)	13·0 cm.	13·0 cm.	fol. 130
margins: centre	4·0 cm.	4·0 cm.	fol. 130
inner	13·0 cm.	5·0 cm.	fol. 196
outer	13·0 cm.	7·5 cm.	fol. 92vo.
Total length:	78·7 cm.	63·9 cm. (25¼ in.)	
Total width:	56·0 cm.	42·5 cm. (16¾ in.)	

The marginal rulings of the vellum fragments are in ink, varying from pale to dark brown, sometimes almost black. The corresponding ruling of the paper mounts has been done in pencil, on most pages only the margins being indicated. On a few pages, however, where a number of the smallest (one-line or less) fragments have been mounted (*e.g.* fol. 78, Pls. xxxiv and xxxv), the corresponding text lines have been ruled in so that the fragments might be more accurately placed.

The text is written in two columns with 29 lines to a column, each of *ca.* 1·75 cm., except in the Prefaces and Canon where the script is slightly larger and there are 27 lines to a column, each measuring 1·8 to 2·0 cm., or averaging 1·9 cm. This number of lines for the Preface and Canon pages is confirmed by the fact that a single line of music (as, for example, on fol. 76) requires three lines of space: two for the four-line staff with notes, and one for the words. The number of lines on a page having music, therefore, must be divisible by three; hence 27, which multiplied by 1·9 (the average width of a line) gives 51·3 cm. for the total length of the text column, thus approximating that of other parts of the Missal.

The lines are very often subdivided, not only for the music staff (where they are ruled in red) in Canon and Prefaces and in some of the masses of the *Temporale* and the *Sanctorale*, but for text written in half-size and smaller letters in many places throughout the Missal (cf. Pl. xxxvi). Half-size letters are frequently used: (1) for epistle and gospel passages which are written in large letters elsewhere in the Missal, as the epistle for Anna (fol. 123vo), which is also used and given in full for the mass of Mary Magdalen on a previous page (fol. 121); (2) for prose given in full, as 'Gaudeat ecclesia' for All Saints' Day (fol. 153) and for the psalms for the Commemoration of the Dead (fols. 154vo ff.); (3) for collects or whole masses for English feasts, and even for certain Carmelite ones such as that of the Three Maries and the Solemn Commemoration of the B.V.M. (fol. 120).[1] Still smaller letters varying in size, some being so small as to be barely legible without a magnifying glass, are used for such parts of the mass as the 'Gloria' of the introit (Pl. xxvi), the 'Gloria tibi domine' preceding the gospel, and the 'Credo' following it, and the dismissal, 'Benedicamus' or 'Ite missa est' (Pl. xxxvi). Usually these parts are not written out completely for each mass, but their use is designated by rubrics. It is puzzling to know why in this Missal they are given in such minute detail unless for the sake of absolute completeness. Certainly it would hardly be possible, even if necessary, for the celebrant to read

---

[1] In the case of some of the feasts latest in date, as the Solemn Commemoration of the Virgin, it might appear that they were introduced after the Missal was begun (see below, p. 39). Other feasts written in small letters, however, are much older than this manuscript.

these tiny letters in so huge a book standing before him on the altar. It might appear that the new Missal was intended rather as a magnificent show book than for use in the ordinary celebration of the mass.

The text of the *Temporale, Sanctorale,* and *Commune Sanctorum* is written in a good liturgical Gothic hand with well-formed, uniform letters, becoming toward the end of the manuscript somewhat stiffer and showing an increased tendency to attach flourishes to the letters. In the *Temporale* and early *Sanctorale* the letters are slightly smaller and more slender, and their curves are softer than in the middle and later parts of the *Sanctorale* and in the *Commune* (cf. Pls. III and XXXVII); the ink also in the *Temporale* and early *Sanctorale* is lighter in colour than in the later part of the manuscript. It is possible that the first two quires were written by a different scribe from the remainder, although the fragmentary condition of the text makes it impossible to determine conclusively. In the case of the Prefaces and Canon of the Mass (Pls. XXXIV–XXXV), however, there is no doubt that the hand is different: though of the same type, this hand is larger and heavier, with the feet of the letters more thorny. The ink is very dark (black?) and there is a stiff uniformity in the formation of the letters in this part of the book. Two sizes of script are used also in this part: full-sized for all the principal part of the text; half-sized for the long prayer for the Holy Land, beginning 'Deus venerunt gentes', which probably followed the Canon (see below, p. 37). Rubrics in the Canon and Prefaces seem usually but not always to have been written in large red letters; headings of masses and of parts of masses throughout the Missal are also in red or blue, and first words of introits of important masses are in decorative red and blue letters (Pl. III).

The collation shows that the original manuscript was in quaternions. The best evidence of this comes from the illumination in the *Sanctorale*: (1) the first eight leaves of this part have two-line gold initials on pinkish tan and blue backgrounds similar in style to those in the later part of the *Temporale* but utterly different in tones of colouring and in details of design, from the initials of the same size in the following leaves: (2) the next eight leaves contain initials similar in style to those of the leaves which follow, but differing so markedly in colour and in the use of shading on the motifs that it was possible during the process of the reconstruction to distinguish at a glance which of the initials belonged in this second quaternion (see Appendix A); (3) the last seven leaves of the *Sanctorale* have two-line gold initials on blue and yellowish tan background, with designs which are different in respect to motifs and colouring from all that precede, except the *KL* monograms of the Calendar. All these differences in the types of small initials clearly indicate that several illuminators were at work at the same time, and the fact that the reconstructed manuscript shows the differences in style to be confined to groups of eight leaves points to the practice (which would not be unusual) of parcelling out the quires, as they were written, to different illuminators for decoration. Finally, in the first quire of the *Sanctorale* there is further evidence of the make-up of the quire as a quaternion in the form of a misplaced leaf: fols. 88 and 89 have the flesh and hair side of the vellum respectively for the recto of the leaf, but fol. 90 also shows hair side for the recto as does fol. 91 (correctly); similarly, fols. 92, 93 (the gemel of 90) and 94 have flesh side for the recto, and 95 (the gemel of 88) has hair side for the recto. It is evident that the third double leaf of the gathering (fols. 90 and 93) was placed with the wrong side uppermost.[1] If the *Sanctorale* begins a new quire (as is indicated by the position of the Canon and Prefaces between the *Temporale* and *Sanctorale*,[2] the evidence seems conclusive for the arrangement of the quires in eights.

The collation of the whole of the reconstructed Missal has been worked out as follows:

Temporale: Quires I[6] (the first two leaves, preceding the leaf containing the *Exultet* are missing); II[8]–VIII[8]; IX[7] (the last leaf missing).

Sanctorale: Quires X[8]–XVIII[8]; XIX[7]. The last leaf should contain the mass of Thomas the Apostle (December 21) at the end of the *Sanctorale* according to the Carmelite use, but no fragment of this mass has survived; possibly it was damaged or lost before the manuscript was cut up.

Commune Sanctorum: Quires XX[8], XXI[7] (fol. vii contained only gospel passages which would be introduced by the initial *I* of 'In illo tempore',—fragments which are difficult to place because of having almost no text on the backs. It is likely that this leaf was present in the manuscript when it was cut up); XXII[7] (fol. iv has no identifiable fragments surviving for the same reason as in the preceding instance); XXIII[8]–XXV[8] (the position of fols. iv and v in Quire XXV is not quite certain; see Contents below); XXVI[o] (prayers for the Dead for which cues are given in the Table on fol. 212, fol. viii of the quire, would certainly occupy a large part of this last gathering which, perhaps because the manuscript was in a dilapidated condition and unbound, was already lost before the Missal was cut up).

The Calendar occupied a separate quire of six leaves with one month filling one side of each leaf. Four leaves have been reconstructed. The remaining double leaf (fols. ii and v of the quire) contained feasts for March–April and September–October, of which no fragment remains.

The Prefaces and Canon of the mass, occupying together at least fourteen leaves, were almost certainly present without any gaps when the manuscript was cut up, but owing to the loss of most of the text, the order of the Prefaces and the collation of the quires cannot be worked out with any certainty.

The position of the *Temporale*, *Sanctorale*, and *Commune* in the order of the missal is certainly fixed. The supposed position of the Calendar in the new Missal does not correspond to the usual arrangement of service books, which places it at the beginning, before the *Temporale*. Since the first part of the *Temporale* is lost, however, the Calendar, if originally there, would have been lost also. Its survival seems to indicate that in this Missal it occupied some other position than at the beginning. The only possible explanations are two: (1) either the Missal was found to be too bulky to be bound in a single volume and even before it was finished, possibly, was divided into two volumes (the second one beginning with the Holy Saturday rites from which the first recognizable fragments among the cuttings come) and a second Calendar added at the beginning of this volume; or (2) if in one volume originally, the Calendar must have been placed between the *Temporale* and

---

[1] Vellum usually showed considerable difference in the surface of the hair and flesh sides, and it was the practice to place the leaves in the gathering so that the verso of one leaf and the recto of the following one would have the same side of the vellum uppermost. The evident purpose of this would be greater uniformity in consecutive pages, since the two sides would take differently the ink and what is more important, the paint of the decoration.

[2] See below.

the *Sanctorale* for more convenient use in connection with the *Sanctorale*.[1] Of these two possibilities, the first seems to receive some support from the division (in modern times, it is true) of the late fourteenth century missal made for Westminster Abbey.[2] In this case, the division is between the *Temporale* and the Canon of the Mass which follows it, and no second Calendar has been added, presumably because the Missal was no longer in use. The style of the illuminated initials in the Calendar of the new Missal corresponds so closely to that of the final quire of the *Sanctorale* as to appear to be the work of the same illuminator. Hence the Calendar must have been part of the original manuscript whether it was in one volume or two, and its place must, it seems, have been immediately preceding the *Sanctorale*.

The position of the Canon and Prefaces in the reconstructed Missal also was not the usual one, which is within the mass for Holy Saturday; certain evidence of this is the fact that the Holy Saturday Mass ends on the same page as the beginning of the Easter Mass (fol. 7vo). On fol. 7 (within the Holy Saturday Mass) are fragmentary rubrics for the Canon. The Canon and Prefaces presumably came between the *Temporale* and *Sanctorale*, as in the Westminster Missal and also in the later Sherborne Missal. They would thus form a separate section of the book which could be written conveniently and illuminated independently from the remainder of the Missal, as, indeed, the style shows to have been the case.

TEXTUAL CONTENTS

A synopsis of the liturgical contents of the reconstructed Missal, identified on the evidence furnished by the fragments,[3] appears as follows:

TEMPORALE	FOLIO
Sabbato in vigilia Paschae	
Blessing of the Pascal Candle, beginning with the *Exultet*, which is given in full with music	1
Prophecies, tracts, and collects	1vo
Litany	5
Mass	6vo
In die sancto Paschae	
Mass preceded by *Vidi Aquam*	7vo
Feria II–VI	8vo–13vo
Sabbato post Pascha	14
Dominica I post Pascha: Missa matutinalis: *Quasimodo*	15
Maior missa: *Resurrexi* (Commemoration of Resurrection, cues only)	16
Dominica II–V post Pascha	16vo–19

[1] This position for the Calendar is sometimes found in breviaries, as in the large and elaborate one made for Archbishop Chichele, now MS. 69 in Lambeth Palace Library.

[2] *Missale ad Usum Ecclesie Westmonasteriensis*, edited for the Henry Bradshaw Society by J. Wickham Legg, London, 3 vols., 1891–6, hereafter referred to as the Westminster Missal or the Lytlington Missal (see below, p. 76 and note 1). The manuscript is still in Westminster Abbey, in the library.

[3] A key to the identified text on all the fragments arranged in the order of their appearance on the successive pages of the Missal, has been prepared in typescript and is available for use with the reconstructed manuscript in the British Museum.

THE FORMAT AND TEXTUAL CONTENTS

[1] The Latin heading follows Sibert de Beka's Carmelite *Ordinale*, compiled *ca.* 1312; manuscript copy of *ca.* 1320 in Lambeth Palace Library, MS. 193, hereafter called Sibert. References in this book are to the printed edition by Fr Benedict Zimmerman, O.C.D.; *Ordinaire de l'ordre de Notre-Dame du Mont-Carmel* ('Bibliothèque Liturgique', Ulysse Chevalier, XIII), Paris, 1910

June 24	NATIUITAS SANCTI IOHANNIS BAPTISTE DUPLEX FESTUM IX LECCIONES—(gold)
August 15	ASSUMPCIO BEATE MARIE UIRGINIS TOTUM DUPLEX IX LECCIONES—(gold)
December 8	CONCEPCIO SANCTE MARIE UEL POCIUS UENERACIO SANCTIFICACIONIS SANCTE MARIE[1]. FESTUM DUPLEX IX LECCIONES —(gold)
December 29	[S]ANCTI THOME CANTUARIENSIS ARCH-IEPISCOPI ET MARTYRIS[2] TOTUM DUPLEX —(gold)

There are six colours used in the Calendar: gold, blue, two shades of red, purple ('PRIMUS ADUENTUS DOMINI') and black. The fragments that have survived have obviously done so because they were in gold letters.

SANCTORALE [*means that the feast is found in the fragmentary Calendar]	DATE	USE[3]	FOLIO
Rubrics: '[Quia supra in Temporali . . .] N [otandum autem hic in prin-cipio . . .]'			88
Maur	January 15		
Marcellus	16		
Anthony Abbot	17		
Prisca	18		88vo
Fabian and Sebastian	20		
Agnes	21		89
Vincent	22		89vo
Timothy Bishop and Martyr	24	C—(S)	
Conversion of Paul ⎫	25		90
Projectus ⎭			91
Julian	27		91vo
Agnes the second	28		
Mathias of Jerusalem, Bishop and Confessor	30	C—(S)	
Ignatius	February 1	C—(S)	92

[1] This title for the feast of the Conception (Sibert, 267) reflects the controversy over the interpretation of the Immaculate Conception of the Virgin, current in the fourteenth century, in which the Carmelites took a leading part.

[2] The mass for this day, according to the Carmelite use, would be included in the winter portion of this *Temporale*, now lost. See below, Appendix A, p. 125. The mass for the Translation of Thomas (July 7) is found on fol. 119vo.

[3] Feasts here designated as Carmelite (C) are from two sources: Sibert (marked S), and various Chapters of the Order (indicated by the date of their adoption); a question mark indicates that, according to the collation used here, the feast seems to be Carmelite but no specific source has been identified. See below, pp. 38f. Feasts marked E are English; and a question mark after the title signifies a questionable identification.

SANCTORALE [* means that the feast is found in the fragmentary calendar]	DATE	USE	FOLIO
Blessing of Candles (Procession) ⎫ Purification of the Virgin ⎬	February 2		93
Blaise	3		94vo
Agatha	5		
Vedast and Amandus*	6		95
Apollonia	9	C—(1321)	
Scholastica	10		95vo
Valentine	14		
Simeon of Jerusalem, Bishop and Martyr	18	C—(S)	
Saint Peter's Chair	22		96
Mathias Apostle	24		97
Perpetua and Felicitas	March 7		97vo
Forty Martyrs	11	C—(S)	98
Gregory	12		
Alexander of Jerusalem	18	C—(S)	98vo
Edward King and Martyr	19	E	
Cuthbert	20	E	
Benedict	21		
Annunciation	25		99
Octave of Annunciation (Rubrics)	April 1	C—(1362)	100
Richard of Chichester	3	E	
Ambrose	4		100vo
Sixtus I Pope and Martyr	6	C—(?)	
Tiburcius, Valerian, and Maximus	14		101
Alphege	19	E	
George	23		
Mellitus	24	E	101vo
Mark: Mass of saint ⎫ Litany (for Rogation days) ⎬	25		102
Cletus	26	C—(?)	103
Vitalis	28		
Erkenwald, Deposition (?)	30	E	103vo
Philip and James*	May 1		
Athanasius	2		104vo
Alexander, Eventius, and Theodore ⎫ Invention of the Cross ⎬	3		105
Quiriac of Jerusalem	4	C—(S)	106
John before the Latin Gate	6		106vo
Gordian and Epimachus	10		
Nereus and Achilleus	12		107
Dunstan	19	E	

SANCTORALE [* means that the feast is found in the fragmentary calendar]	DATE	USE	FOLIO
Urban } Three Maries }	May 25	C—(1342)	107vo
Augustine of Canterbury	26	E	108
Nicomed*	June 1		
Marcellinus and Peter	2		
Medard and Gildard	8		108vo
Translation of Edmund Archbishop*} Primus and Felician }	9	E (Sarum)	109
Barnabas	11		
Basilidis, Cirinus, Nabor etc.	12		109vo
Vitus, Modestus, and Crescentia	15		110
Translation of Richard of Chichester} Ciricus and Julitta }	16	E	
Botulph	17	E	110vo
Marcus and Marcellinus	18		
Gervase and Protase	19		
Paulinus	22	C—(S)	111
Alban		E	
Etheldreda } Vigil of the Nativity of the Baptist }	23	E	111vo
Nativity of the Baptist*} Morning Mass } High Mass }	24		112vo 113
John and Paul	26		114
Vigil of Apostles Peter and Paul} Leo }	28		114vo
Apostles Peter and Paul	29		115vo
Commemoration of Paul} Memoria of Peter }	30		116vo
Octave of Baptist	July 1		117vo
Processus and Martinian	2		118
Translation of Martin	4		
Octave of the Apostles	6		118vo
Translation of Thomas of Canterbury	7	E	119vo
Martial	8	C—(1339)	
Seven Brothers	10		120
Mildred	13	E	
Solemn Commemoration of the Virgin	?{16 {17	C—(1376—1387)[1]	

[1] The date of the institution of this feast, and even the day of the month on which it was celebrated in mediaeval times, are among the most controversial questions in Carmelite history. See below, p. 39.

SANCTORALE [* means that the feast is found in the fragmentary calendar]	DATE	USE	FOLIO
Margaret	July 20		120vo
Praxed	21		
Mary Magdalene	22		121
Apollinaris			
Vigil of James (Rubrics) }	23		122
James*			122vo
Cristofer and Cucufas }	25		123
Anna	26		
Martha	27	C—(S)	124
Felix, Simplicius, Faustinus, and Beatrix	29		
Abdon and Sennen	30		124vo
Germain	31		125
Saint Peter's Chains	August 1		125vo
Maccabees			
Stephen Pope and Martyr	2		126
Invention of Stephen	3		
Dominic	5	C—(S)	126vo
Sixtus, Felix, and Agapit }	6	C—(S)	127
Transfiguration			127vo
Donatus	7		128vo
Ciriac and Companions	8		129
Vigil of Lawrence	9		
Lawrence	10		130
Tiburcius	11		130vo
Hippolytus	13		131
Vigil of the Assumption of the B.V.M. }	14		
Eusebius			
Assumption of the B.V.M.*			
Procession }	15		132
Mass			132vo
Octave of Lawrence	17		133vo
Agapit	18		
Bernard	19	C—(S on 26th)	134
Octave of Assumption }	22		134vo
Timothy and Simphorian			
Zacheus	23	C—(S)	135
Bartholomew	24		
Louis King and Confessor*	25	C—(S)	135vo
Rufus	27		136
Hermes }	28		
Augustine of Hippo			

SANCTORALE [* means that the feast is found in the fragmentary calendar]	DATE	USE	FOLIO
Decollation of Baptist	August 29		136vo
Felix and Audactus	30		138
Giles	September 1		
Nativity of the B.V.M. } Morning Mass, Adrian } High Mass	8		138vo
Gorgonius	9		139vo
Proteus and Jacinth	10		140
Maurilius [of Angers]	13	C—(S)	
Exaltation of the Cross } Cornelius and Ciprian	14		141
Octave of Nativity of the B.V.M. } Nicomed	15		141vo
Euphemia	16		
Lambert	17		
Vigil of Matthew	20		142
Matthew	21		142vo
Maurice and Companions	22		143vo
Cleophas	25	C—(S)	
Cosmas and Damian	27		144
Michael Archangel	29		144vo
Jerome	30		145vo
Germain, Remigius, Vedast, etc.	October 1		146
Leger [of Autun]	2		
Francis	3	C—(S)	146vo
Patriarchs Abraham, Isaac, and Jacob	6	C—(S)	
Mark, Sergius, and Bacchus	7	C—(S)	148
Denis, Rusticus, and Eleutherius	9		
Ethelburga	11	E	148vo
Translation of Edward King and Confessor	13	E	
Calixtus	14		
Luke	18		
Eleven Thousand Virgins	21		149vo
Mark of Jerusalem	22	C—(S)	150
Crispin and Crispinian	25		
Vigil of Simon and Jude	27		150vo
Simon and Jude	28		151
Narcissus of Jerusalem	29	C—(S)	
Vigil of All Saints } Quintin	31		151vo \ 152vo
All Saints' Day*	November 1		

C

SANCTORALE [*means that the feast is found in the fragmentary calendar]	DATE	USE	FOLIO
Within the Octave of All Saints (cues)		C—(1342)	154
All Souls' Day*			
Commemoratio Animarum (in full)	November 2	C—(S)	
Mass			157
Leonard	6		158
Octave of All Saints?	8		
Four Crowned Martyrs*			
Theodore*	9		158vo
Martin Pope and Martyr	10	C—(S)	
Menna			
Translation of Martin of Tours, Bishop and Confessor	11		159
Brice	13		159vo
Translation of Erkenwald(?)	14	E	160
Edmund Archbishop	16	E	
Hugh (?)	17	E—(Sarum)	
Octave of Translation of Martin	18		
Edmund King and Martyr	20	E—(S)	160vo
Cecilia	22		
Clement	23		161
Chrysogonus	24		
Peter Bishop of Alexandria	25	C—(S)	161vo
Catherine*			
Linus	26	C—(S)	162
Saturninus*	29		
Vigil of Andrew			
Andrew*	30		163
Loy*	December 1	C—(S)	164
Barbara	4	C—(S)	
Sabba, Abbot [of Jerusalem]	5	C—(S)	164vo
Nicholas	6		
Octave of Andrew	7		165
Conception of the B.V.M.*	8		
Lucy	13		166
Lazarus	17	C—(S)	

COMMUNE SANCTORUM

Vigil of one or several Apostles			167
Day of one or several Apostles			168
An Evangelist (cues only)			170vo
A Martyr			

Musical notation was included in the Missal for many if not all of the principal masses. Because of meagre evidence, only a few of these fragments can be placed. Following is a list of those identified:

'Ite missa est'	10 fragments
'Gloria in excelsis'	18 fragments
'Credo'	4 fragments
'Benedicamus domino'	4 fragments

Antiphons for two processions, namely, Candlemas and the Assumption.
Requiem at the end of the Mass for All Souls' Day.

The reconstructed contents of the Missal as outlined in the preceding pages are based on the fragments which have been identified, in most cases with absolute certainty: all the evidence namely, the subject of a miniature, the verification of the text passages on both sides of the fragment, the appearance of the fragment as to vellum and script, style and colouring, is in agreement, and there seems no doubt, allowing perhaps for slight variations of a line or two where the fragment is not specifically placed by margin lines, that the position also is correct. There are a few instances, however, where the cutting has been placed when the textual evidence, though good, is not complete. Since the fragments showing incomplete evidence are all from masses of Carmelite or English saints, the failure to identify certain text passages (or the initials which begin them) seems to be explainable by the variation in form or wording which is known to exist even in missals of the same rite or use, or perhaps by the difference in date among them. Some of these instances will be noted in the discussion of Carmelite and English characteristics of the new Missal.

There is also the opposite situation, in which the text on a few fragments has been identified, but owing to total lack of evidence indicating their position in the Missal they cannot be placed. Two of these are important enough to describe in detail.

On the back of a three-line letter G (4/386)[1] is the following rubric written in half-sized letters (portions of text in square brackets are supplied):

'[. . . uel statim dicto *Dominus uobiscum* si *It*] e
[*missa est* dici non debe] at uertat se sacerdos ad al-
[tare . . . et s]uspiciens extensis manibus
[et statim reiunctis inclinando ante alta]re dicat *Placeat tibi etcetera*
[et hoc dicto erigat se et oscule]tur altare. Et statim post geni-
[bus flexis dicit antiphonam sequentem S]*alue regina* sine nota
[cum oracione *Oremus. Protege do*]mine etcetera Per christum dominum Simile *Fideli*—
[*um deus* . . .]'

The first part of the fragment through 'osculetur altare', is found in Rubric XLI in Sibert which describes the ceremony of the celebration of the mass; after 'altare' the rubric in Sibert continues as follows: 'et si consuetudo patriae fuerit det benedictionem, et non aliter . . .' From this it is evident that in the English Missal it was not customary to give the benediction at the end of conventual mass, but to follow mass with the *Salve Regina* as the text fragment shows.[2] Verification of the identification of the latter part of the text passage on the unplaced G was found in the (now destroyed) 1640 printed edition of the Carmelite Missal formerly in the British Museum. Although there is no question as to the part of the missal from which this initial comes, namely the *Ordo Missae*, which usually

---

[1] Numbers such as this are used throughout this book to designate individual fragments. The 4 means that the fragment comes from the scrapbook numbered Add. 29704; the other number is the one given to the fragment when it was still in the scrapbook. Similarly, fragments from Add. 29705 show a 5 before their number, and those from Add. 44892 show a 2. See also p. 116. The numbers often but not always may be seen on the plates.

[2] I am indebted to Father Norman Werling, O. Carm., Community of St Elias, Joliet, Illinois, U.S.A., for the following note: 'The first explicit law for the *Salve Regina* at the end of the conventual mass was the Provincial Chapter of Lombardy in 1328, in case one does not accept Fr Zimmerman's reasoning (Sibert, pp. xvi–xvii) that the General Chapters of 1321 and 1324 included conventual mass in the decree as equivalent to the canonical hours. Cf. *Analecta Carmelitana*, X, p. 378.' The *Salve Regina* is not found in Rubric XLI of the Lambeth manuscript of Sibert.

precedes the Canon of the Mass, and though the style of decoration, the vellum and the script would place the fragment with the Canon and Prefaces of this Missal, there is no indication of its position on the page, nor is there any other identifiable fragment which could join it or help to place it. This is most unfortunate in view of the importance of this scrap of liturgical evidence as to the English Carmelite use.

Similar difficulty occurs as to the placing of some other fragments identified as from the ceremony of supplication for the delivery of the Holy Land, beginning with the Psalm, '*Deus venerunt gentes*'. In Sibert, Rubric xliii specifies that it is to be said 'in feriis prostrationum immediate post *Pater Noster* in missa conventuali'. Its place in the new Missal (as also in the Venice 1504 printed edition)[1] was not there, but at the end of the Canon. Evidence is found in the new Missal in the occurrence of a tiny fragment of the '*Protege*' prayer on the back of one of the initials beginning the verses of the '*Deus venerunt gentes*'. Some other fragments with similar initials identified as probably from this same passage, and some not identified but in the style of the Canon, have blank ruled lines on the backs. It would appear from this evidence that the '*Deus venerunt gentes*' came last in the Preface-Canon portion of the Missal, and that part of the verso of the last leaf remained blank. This further supports the conclusion that the place of the Prefaces and Canon in the new Missal was between the *Temporale* and the *Sanctorale*.

The liturgical contents of the reconstructed Missal as a whole offer a good deal of interesting material for a complete study of the English Carmelite Missal of the late fourteenth century.[2] Such a study obviously lies outside the scope of the present book, though certain specific features seem worth noting as evidence of the use and date of the manuscript.

Evidence of the Carmelite rite identified in the text of the new Missal is mainly of three kinds: (1) distinctively Carmelite feasts[3] (2) special arrangement of the form of the mass or order of arrangement in the Carmelite missal; (3) Carmelite variants in the wording of text passages which are used also in other missals.

The *Temporale* contributes comparatively little evidence as to the Carmelite rite. The *alleluia* verses for the Sunday masses after Pentecost, which are a distinguishing feature of the different rites[4] rarely appear in the fragmentary text on the backs of the fragments in the *Temporale*, because of the fact that epistle and gospel passages (invariably written out in full in large script) occupy so much space that few initials occur on most of these pages. It is by the merest chance, therefore, that two fragments of *alleluia* verses have survived. These are (1) for Dominica VIII: 'Alleluia v. [Eripe me de inimicis] meis deus [meus . . .]', 5/918 on fol. 46vo; and (2) for Dominica XVII: '[Confitemini domino et inuocate nomen eius a] nnunciate [inter gentes opera eiu]s. . . .' 5/287 on fol. 54vo. (Words in paren-

---

[1] See Appendix A, p. 123, n. 1.

[2] An edition of this Missal was once contemplated by the Henry Bradshaw Society but in view of the many difficulties and uncertainties involved in dealing with so fragmentary a text, as well as the controversial points involved in the history of the Carmelite liturgy, the idea was abandoned. Some interest has been shown recently by the Carmelite Order in editing such a text, and it is hoped that eventually this will be done.

[3] By this is meant feasts which in the fourteenth century distinguish the Carmelite Missal from other missals of English usage. No attempt will be made here to deal with problems of the origins of these feasts.

[4] Cf. Abbé Victor Leroquais, *Les sacramentaires et les missels manuscrits des bibliothèques publiques de France*, Paris, 1924, pp. xxiv–xxvi. See also G. A. Gordon, *Manuscript Missals, The English Uses*; 'Sandars Lectures', Cambridge, 1936. Typescript copy in Brit. Mus., Add. MS. 44920.

theses are not found on fragments.) Both are found in Sibert and in the Manchester and 1504 Carmelite Missals,[1] but in no non-Carmelite sources.

The most important evidence of the Carmelite rite furnished by the *Temporale* text is the form of the heading and rubric for the Solemn Commemoration of the Resurrection which occurs on the last Sunday before Advent (fol. 67vo). On this and all the preceding Sundays beginning with the first after Easter, the high mass is the Commemoration of the Resurrection and the mass of the day is the *Missa Matutinalis* celebrated after Prime.[2] Parts of this heading are found on several fragments in the new Missal; the rubric and cues for the Commemoration of the Resurrection are given on the first Sunday after Easter in the new Missal (fol. 16, fragment 5/206).

Another characteristic, though not exclusively Carmelite, feature in the *Temporale* is the designation of the Sundays after Trinity as 'post festum sanctae Trinitatis' instead of after Pentecost,[3] as in the later Roman rite. Portions of the word 'Trinitatis' occur on some of the *Temporale* fragments (*e.g.* fol. 61, fragment 4/418) as evidence that this form was used in the new Missal.

In the *Sanctorale* there is much more evidence of the Carmelite rite: there are many special feasts peculiar, among English missals of the same date, to the Carmelites. The list of contents of the *Sanctorale* given on pp. 29–34 above, is undoubtedly not complete; some octaves (as of the Purification and of Michael Archangel) known to have been introduced into the Carmelite rite at General Chapters, were probably included, but no evidence of them has survived.

In order to distinguish English Carmelite use from general Carmelite use, on the one hand, and from other contemporary English, specifically London, uses on the other, the list of feasts for which there is evidence in the new Missal was checked first with the Ordinal of Sibert de Beka (adopted by the Order *ca.* 1312), and then with a Saint Paul's Cathedral Calendar included in the so-called *Statuta Majora*[4] (representing the London diocesan use, temp. Rich. II) and with the Westminster Abbey Missal (1383–4, representing the London monastic rite). One hundred forty out of one hundred ninety-nine feasts identified in the new Missal are common to Sibert and to one or both of the English uses; nineteen others are English feasts occurring in one or both of the two English sources; one only (Edmund King and Martyr) occurs in the English sources and also in Sibert. Of the thirty-seven Carmelite feasts found in the new Missal (not, of course, in Saint Paul's or Westminster) twenty-nine occur also in Sibert (marked C—S in the list) and therefore had been adopted before *ca.* 1320, the date of the Lambeth manuscript. Six Carmelite feasts were adopted at later General Chapters, the dates of which are given in the list.[5] Two

---

[1] Manchester, John Rylands Library, MS. 123, Italian, late fourteenth century. In the Kilcormic Missal (Dublin, Trin. Coll. MS. 82) the leaves containing this part of the *Temporale* have been eaten away by rats.

[2] Sibert, Rubric XXIII, pp. 37 ff.

[3] Sibert (p. 200) uses the designation, 'Post octavam Pentecostes'.

[4] W. Sparrow Simpson, *Documents Illustrating the History of S. Paul's Cathedral*, 'Camden Society Publications', London, N.S. XXVI, 1880, pp. 61 ff.

[5] The Acts of the General Chapters between 1327 and 1362 are published by Fr Benedict Zimmerman, O.C.D., under the title, *Monumenta Historica Carmelitana*, Paris, 1907. Two other series of the *Acts* have been edited by Fr G. Wessels, O. Carm.: *Acta Capitulorum Generalium*, I (1318–1593), Rome, 1912; II (1598–1902), Rome, 1934.

feasts (Sixtus I, Pope and Martyr, and Cletus, Pope and Martyr) do not occur in the English uses nor in Sibert, and no source of their introduction into the Carmelite rite has been found. Both are found also in the Oxford Breviary.[1] Two English feasts (Translation of Richard of Chichester[2] and the doubtfully identified feast of Saint Hugh) do not occur in either of the English sources. Both are high Sarum feasts. Many of the English masses are written in half-sized letters.

A similar manner of writing out in great detail but in half-size letters the mass for the Solemn Commemoration of the B.V.M. (July 16)[3] may have some bearing on the adoption of this feast in England. To clarify this point it will be necessary to review briefly the traditional history of its institution. Saint Simon Stock, a native of Kent, England, who interested himself very deeply in fostering the growth of the Carmelite Order in England, was praying one night to the Blessed Virgin Mary for the Order dedicated to her, when she appeared to him in a vision, bearing a scapular in her hand and saying: 'This is the privilege granted to thee and to all Carmelites; he who shall piously die wearing this habit shall be preserved from eternal flames . . .' This event took place, according to tradition, on July 16, 1251, at the Carmelite Convent at Cambridge. The scapular, which had been part of the Carmelite habit even before this, as a result of this vision, took on new meaning and greatly increased importance. It was subsequently adopted by pious persons outside the Order who wished to partake of the privilege granted by Our Lady. These persons made up the Confraternity of the Order, and it was fitting that their special feast should be that of the Solemn Commemoration of the Virgin, celebrating the vision of Saint Simon Stock. The institution of the Scapular Confraternity seems, however, not to have been officially recognized until after a second appearance of Our Lady to Pope John XXII supposedly described by him in a bull[4] dated 3 March, 1322, in which she told him to proclaim the privileges granted by her to those who wore the scapular.

The date of the introduction of this feast into England is controversial. The statement of Father Benedict Zimmerman, O.C.D.,[5] that it was between 1376 and 1387 seems to be lacking in proof. According to Father E. Magennis, O. Carm.,[6] the facts are that in 1376 at a general Chapter of the Order held at Doncaster, Father Bernard Olerius, Prior General, tried to introduce the feast of the Assumption as the principal feast of the Confraternity of the Order, but failed. This seems to suggest that the feast of the 17th July, first noted in the Calendar of Nicholas of Lynn[7] as 'festum confratrum', may already have been well-established in England. The question is of comparatively slight importance from the point of view of evidence *post quem* for dating the new Missal, since it could hardly on other grounds (iconography, costume, and style) be placed much earlier than 1387. However, the relative importance given to the Commemoration and the Assumption in the new

[1] *Breviary and Short Missal*, Oxford University College, MS. 9. Late fourteenth century.

[2] Richard of Chichester and Edmund King and Martyr are the only two English feasts added to the Calendar of the Manchester Missal.

[3] The date of this feast in the new Missal is questionable. In the calendar of the Oxford Breviary it is given on the 17th; in the Kilcormic Missal and also in the Calendar of Nicholas of Lynn (see below, n. 7) it is on the 17th. It is now celebrated on the 16th.

[4] *Mon. Hist. Carm.*, pp. 356 f.

[5] See *Analecta Ord. Carm.*, X, Fasc. VII, pp. 437–45. Fr Benedict's original statement was printed in *Mon. Hist. Carm.*, p. 335.

[6] *The Scapular and Some Critics*, Rome, 1914, p. 234.

[7] Brit. Mus. MS. Arundel 347. Compiled for John, Duke of Lancaster in 1386 (see fol. 3).

Missal, as indicated by the way in which each is written and decorated, might be interpreted as throwing some light on the incident of 1376 referred to above. The Mass of the Commemoration is written out in complete detail (even the hymn *Flos Carmeli*[1] is given in full) but in half-size lettering and with small decorative initials introducing the various parts (see Pl. xxxvi). It is very much crowded into a space too small for it, although it seems unlikely that it could have been introduced into the Missal as an afterthought. The Assumption of the Virgin, on the other hand, is also written out in full, even as to the procession which preceded it, with large, ornamental lettering, and it is introduced by a very large and elaborately historiated initial with full border containing medallions with incidents of a miracle of the Virgin (see below, p. 106) and with kneeling figures of a man and a woman who must certainly be 'donors', perhaps of this Missal. The overwhelming emphasis given to this mass, in the Missal, can hardly be accidental, but failing more specific evidence, any further historical interpretation would be purely hypothetical.[2]

One further characteristic of the Carmelite rite, already noted as having been employed in the reconstruction of the Missal (see Appendix A), is the fact that the *Sanctorale* begins with Saint Maur (January 15) and ends with Saint Thomas the Apostle (December 21).

Significant variations found in the wording of the fragmentary text are naturally not numerous. Two striking examples, however, may be cited. One is found in the collect for Saint Ambrose (fol. 100vo). The *D* beginning the cue given in Sibert, 'Deus qui populo tuo' (p. 219), was identified in the reconstructed Missal by a miniature of Ambrose teaching (Pl. xi*b*); but a fragment of text on the back of a similar historiated initial for Saint Richard of Chichester (immediately preceding the mass of Ambrose, on the recto of the same leaf), from its position would have to be part of this same collect, but did not agree with the text as found in either Sarum or Westminster, though these also begin 'Deus qui populo tuo'. The Manchester Missal, which in order of time was consulted before either the Oxford or Kilcormic Missals (see Appendix, p. 129), was found to have a still different form with the same beginning but yet not agreeing with the fragment. Later, when Oxford and Kilcormic became available, the Ambrose collect as indicated on the fragment was found to agree (with only a minor omission in Oxford) with both these manuscripts. Thus we have four variations in the body of a collect beginning with the same words; which one of these was intended in the cue given in Sibert cannot be ascertained, but the three Carmelite manuscripts agree on the following form (the words not in brackets are found on the fragment):

[1] Traditionally written by St Simon Stock (d. 1265), General of the Carmelite Order (1247), for the propagation of the adoption of the sacred scapular (see above, p. 39). The hymn, 'Flos Carmeli', is given in full in Herm. Adalbert Daniel, *Thesaurus Hymnologicus*, V (Supplement), Leipzig, 1856, p. 378, from which the fragment from the Carmelite Missal was completed as follows (words outside the brackets are given as spelled in the Missal):

> [Flos Carmeli, Vitis florigera, Spl]endor celi uirgo [puerpera
> Singularis Mater miti]s. Set uiri nesci[a Carmelitis
> Da Privilegia, Stella Maris.]

The hymn is still used in the mass of the Solemn Commemoration of the Virgin in the modern *Carmelite Missal*, Rome, 1935.

[2] Of the Calendar entries surviving from the Missal, the Assumption is one of three having the rank of *Totum duplex*. The others are: the Nativity, and Saint John the Evangelist. Might the importance given to the Assumption suggest that this was the feast of the confraternity at Whitefriars, and might the Missal have been given by them to the convent? No documentary evidence bearing on this point has been found.

'D[eus qui populo tuo sanctum ambrosium dedisti predicatorem concede quesumus ut tanti pontificis intercessione et tue pietatis defensio]ne ab omnibus li[beremur incommo]dis et tran[quilla prosperita] te in tua lau[de letemur].'

Another instance of a Carmelite variation in a passage of text, which is the more surprising because the fragment is so minute, is the single whole word found on the back of one of the smallest fragments of all. This one-line illuminated initial (4/597 on fol. 153) is one of a number which begin the verses of the passage (Rev. 7: 2–12) forming the Epistle for All Saints' Day; the text on the back is part of the prose used for that day beginning 'Gaudeat ecclesia'[1]. The particular word which constitutes the Carmelite variation is 'gracia', which in verse 6b ends the third of the four lines of the stanza instead of 'gloria', the ordinary form. Drèves[2] notes only one source which has 'gracia'—a Carmelite Gradual (Paris, Bibl. Mazarine, MS. 465). This is a precious bit of evidence for the Carmelite rite in the new Missal; it is a piece of sheer luck that this one special word should have happened to be preserved on this particular fragment.

The special Carmelite feasts were easier to identify than the English masses because these latter contain many variant collects for the same feasts, and some few in the new Missal, although believed to be identifiable on other grounds, could not be found to agree in wording with any English source, Carmelite or otherwise.

Since the Carmelite Missal was believed to have been made in London,[3] it would have been highly desirable to find another missal of the right date and of London use, other than the Westminster Missal, which being of a different monastic rite could not be expected to agree completely in text wording with the Carmelite book. A fifteenth century missal traditionally connected with Saint Paul's Cathedral (Brit. Mus. Harl. 2787) would have been of the utmost importance had it actually represented the ancient use of Saint Paul's before it was made to conform to the Sarum rite in 1414.[4] No other London missal of the right date has been found.

For the English saints not specifically connected with London, the Sarum Missal[5] formed the chief source for identifications, verified wherever possible by the English Carmelite use as represented by Oxford and Kilcormic.

Three English saints were more or less certainly celebrated with two feasts each in the new Missal, on the day of the deposition and on that of the translation:

1. Richard de Wyche, Bishop of Chichester and Confessor.

Day—April 3. Historiated initial introducing the collect; decorative initials for secret and postcommunion.

Collect: 'D[eus qui ecclesiam . . .]', and a fragment of text toward the end of the collect.

Secret: 'M[unera quesumus domine . . .]'

Postcommunion: 'P[resta quesumus omnipotens deus . . .]'

All three prayers are found in Kilcormic; the collect is found also in Oxford. The feast is

---

[1] Printed in full, Guido Maria Drèves, *Analecta Hymnica*, Leipzig, 1890, VIII, pp. 86 f.

[2] *Ibid.*, p. 87, footnote.

[3] Mainly on stylistic grounds. See Chapter III below.

[4] Simpson, *op. cit.*, p. xxvii. Cf. also W. Maskell, *The Ancient Liturgy of the Church of England*, 3rd ed., Oxford, 1882, pp. lxvi ff.

[5] Edited by F. H. Dickinson, *Missale ad Usum Sarum*, Burntisland, 1861–83.

found in Westminster with a different secret and postcommunion, and in Sarum with different collects taken from the Common of a Confessor.

Translation—June 16. Decorative initials and fragments of text:

Collect: 'D[eus qui nos . . .]'
Secret: 'O[fferimus ti]bi domine preces [. . .]'
Postcommunion: 'P[er hec sacramenta . . .]'

All have been identified for this day in Sarum. The collects for the Day in the new Missal are written in full-sized letters; those for the Translation are in half-sized script.

2. Edmund Rich, Archbishop of Canterbury.

Day—November 16. Historiated initial introducing the collect, and other decorative initials.

Collect: 'D[eus qui largiflue . . .]'
Secret: 'B[eati edmundi . . .]'
Postcommunion: 'M[entes nostras . . .]'

All are found in Sarum but in no Carmelite source except the new Missal.

Translation—June 9. Initials *O* and *H* for collect and secret.

Postcommunion: '[S]umpta domine [. . .] celestis misterii [. . .]'

None of the prayers indicated by these initials and the fragment of text has been found as yet; Westminster does not have the feast and Sarum uses different collects. The evidence that they belong to this mass is as follows: (1) the *O* and the *H* are definitely placed here by fragments of names, '(A)ugustini' and 'nichom(edis)' in the text on the backs, these masses preceding the one indicated by the unidentified initials in the correspondingly correct position (as described below, Appendix A, pp. 120 ff.); (2) no other mass has been found which would fit into this place. The mass of the Day of Edmund Archbishop is written in full-sized letters; that presumed to be for the translation in half-sized. The feast is one of the few entries surviving from the Calendar (see above, p. 28).

3. Erkenwald, Bishop of London and Confessor.

Deposition—April 30. Initials and text fragment.

Collect: 'D[. . .]'
Secret: 'M[. . .]'
Postcommunion: 'P[. . .]'

A text fragment with cues of epistle and grail, gospel and offertory written in half-sized letters.

Translation—November 14. Initials *H* and *S* probably for the secret and post-communion; text fragment, probably (judging from its position) partly of the collect and partly of the secret, but not as yet identified:

' [. . .] quesumus domine tibi sint ac-
   . . . is ad eterne beatitu-
   . . . a consequenda sint pi-
   . . . cia intercedente beato
   . . . atque pontifice per cu-
   . . . e ea tue offerimus
   . . . '

Only one set of collects for Erkenwald is known, those enjoined for use by churches in the London diocese on the two days of Saint Erkenwald by Bishop Braybrook in 1386.[1] These are not the collects used in the Carmelite Missal for the Deposition. 'Deus qui beatum erkenwaldum in primum pontificem et ydoneum ministrum elegisti . . .' is the collect in Oxford (fol. 315); 'Munera, domine tibi dicata . . .' is the secret used for the Common of a Bishop and Confessor in Kilcormic; or 'Munera quesumus domine . . .' as used there for Richard may be introduced by the *M* here.

The Translation initials *H* and *S* for secret and postcommunion in the Carmelite Missal could introduce the Saint Paul's collect: 'Haec sancta, domine, quae indignis manibus tractamus . . .' and 'Sacri corporis, domini nostri repleti libamus et precioso sanguine debriati . . .', or variants of these: the text fragment which appears (from its position) to belong partly to the collect and partly to the secret does not correspond, though there is a suggestion of similarity in the wording.

The fragments believed to form part of the Translation of Erkenwald have been mounted in the Missal, even though the text is unidentifiable, because the identification on the reverse side seems to be certain: the initial *H* contains part of the name of Cecilia, from the collect of her mass; the initial *S* has another fragment of the same collect on the back; the text fragment contains part of the sprays of the *M* introducing the postcommunion of Edmund Archbishop (November 16) and has on the back an historiated initial introducing the collect for Cecilia. The three fragments seem to be correctly placed, both in relation to each other and to Edmund and Cecilia. The text fragment believed to be from the Translation of Erkenwald is written in half-sized letters. Pending the actual identification of the text, however, the inference to be drawn from the inclusion of this mass in the new Missal as to its localization in London remains questionable.

The remaining sixteen English masses in the new Missal (like the three just described, marked E in the list of contents) have collects taken chiefly from three sources: (1) Carmelite, *i.e.* Oxford and Kilcormic; (2) Sarum, often but not invariably agreeing with the Carmelite source; (3) Westminster, as representing Benedictine London use, furnishing the unique source for the reconstruction of certain collects, as Mildred and Edward the Confessor, and for the collect of Ethelburga, and in agreement with certain collects in the Carmelite and Sarum sources. A few further observations as to source may be interesting. Often some or all of the collects used in the new Missal are taken from the appropriate common mass in a Carmelite source, as Botulph (a portion of whose name occurs in the secret) and Etheldreda, whose collect is verified by Westminster. Edward King and Martyr, and Cuthbert agree exactly in all three collects in Kilcormic and Sarum; those of Dunstan, Archbishop of Canterbury, agree in Oxford and Sarum. The collects used for Paulinus, Bishop and Confessor, in Oxford are found in the new Missal for both Paulinus and Mellitus, Bishop and Martyr (this latter, also, pointing to London.[2] The Translation of Thomas of Canterbury is given in full in Kilcormic as in the new Missal, and the collect agrees with Oxford.

---

[1] Simpson, *op. cit.*, p. 15. Reprinted from the bishop's *Register*; *ibid.* note 2. The same collects are used for the Deposition of Erkenwald in the Westminster Missal, col. 799.

[2] Mellitus was consecrated first Bishop of London by St Augustine and later (A.D. 619) succeeded Lawrence, Augustine's successor, as Archbishop of Canterbury.

THE FORMAT AND TEXTUAL CONTENTS

To sum up the evidence furnished by the textual contents of the Missal we find nothing positive for a date *post quem*. The date of the actual introduction of the Solemn Commemoration of the B.V.M. into the English Carmelite rite is too controversial to be reliable, and no other liturgical feature recognized in this text carries a specific date. On the other hand, there is excellent evidence for a date *ante quem*: three feasts which were introduced into the Carmelite rite in 1391,[1] and which are found in both Manchester and Kilcormic, have not been identified among the fragments of the new Missal, nor is there any space for them on the reconstructed pages where they should appear. These feasts are the Visitation (July 2), the Presentation of the Virgin (November 21), and Saint Mary of the Snows (July 28)—all very important for the cult of the Virgin. In view of the completeness of this text, it can thus be concluded that the writing of the Missal was finished in or before 1391.

[1] Sibert, p. xx. See also Leroquais, Victor, *Les bréviaires manuscrits des bibliothèques publiques de France*, Paris, 1934, I, p. cxi.

2

Iconography and Costume in the Miniatures of the Missal

The subjects of the fifty-two miniatures in the reconstructed Missal are described below (pp. 99–115). Some remarks on the general character of the iconography and some discussion of certain of its more unusual features, together with a brief survey of the costume and armour represented, may be of interest in relation to the date and source of the illumination in the Missal.

The general type of the illustrations is determined by the nature of the manuscript; it consists of a scene or a single figure within an initial letter, representing the subject of the mass which the initial introduces. In the *Temporale*, the five great feasts of the summer portion, and also the Dedication of the Church, have the largest sized initials—six-lines high—with pictures illustrating the feasts: the Resurrection, Ascension, Descent of the Holy Spirit, Trinity with a Baptism, Corpus Christi with the Last Supper and the Elevation of the Host in the ceremony of the Holy Sacrament, and the Procession around the church in the ceremony of its dedication. The remaining miniature in the *Temporale*, illustrating the Holy Saturday service, is in a smaller initial; this subject, so far as I know, is unique in missal illustration. In the *Sanctorale*, all the six-line historiated initials are used for the feasts of the B.V.M.: the Purification, the Annunciation, the Death and Assumption, the Birth of the Virgin, her Coronation among All Saints, and her Conception. This is not surprising in view of the great veneration of the Virgin as patroness of the Carmelite Order. What is not so easily explained is the omission of any illustrations of other special Carmelite feasts, as the Solemn Commemoration of the Virgin, the feast of the Three Maries, and that of the Patriarchs Abraham, Isaac, and Jacob. Neither is there any illustration of any of the special Carmelite saints as single figures, though three English saints are represented—Richard of Chichester, Edmund Archbishop, and Edmund King and Martyr. In the *Commune* two small miniatures illustrate the Virgins and the Matron, and one five-line historiated initial introduces the mass of the Votive Trinity.

Of foremost iconographic interest in the new Missal are the representations of the Trinity, of which there are three, one each in the *Temporale*, the *Sanctorale* and the *Commune Sanctorum*, all by different artists. They represent the two main types[1] most popular

[1] On the history of representations of the Trinity, see Didron, M., *Iconographie Chrétienne: Histoire de Dieu*, Paris, 1843, especially pp. 523–607. A more recent study of the subject by Dr Alfred Hackel, *Die Trinität in der Kunst*, Berlin, 1931, includes a good working bibliography on pp. 4 and 5. The earlier development of the forms used in the Carmelite Missal is much too complex to be dealt with fully here.

in the late fourteenth century, yet each is a variant of its type, and each has certain peculiar features, not all of which can be explained. They also are typical of the difference in approach to subject matter displayed by the three artists of the Missal.

The older of the two types is the partially anthropomorphic form in which God the Father and Christ the Son are seated side by side, with the Holy Ghost in the form of a dove, hovering between them.[1] This form is used in the miniature for the Votive Trinity (fol. 193vo, Pl. XXXIII). Here the figures are not identical: God the Father is an old, grey-haired man with a grey beard, and Christ the Son is much younger. This manner of representing the Trinity is described by Thomas Netter (Waldensis), a famous Carmelite of Whitefriars, London, in the late fourteenth and early fifteenth century, in his *De Sacramentalibus* presented to Pope Martin V in 1427.[2] The origin of the form seems to be connected with an interpretation of the opening words of Psalm 109 (110), beginning, 'Dixit dominus domino meo sedete a dextro meo', which it frequently illustrates, either with or without the dove. The idea of Christ seated at the right hand of God the Father is expressed in Christ's own words to His disciples before His death, and also in the Apostles' Creed. In the Carmelite miniature the Holy Ghost sends forth twelve rays which suggest the Holy Spirit of Pentecost.[3]

God the Father and Christ the Son in this Trinity miniature are seated, not on a throne as is more usual, but on a rainbow; and in the corners of the miniature are the Symbols of the Evangelists. These two features, together with the figure of the Virgin in a form suggesting the Apocalyptic Woman ('clothed with the sun and upon her head a crown of twelve stars', Rev. 12. 1) introduce the idea of the Judgement Christ,[4] and this is further shown in the fact that Christ, clad only in a mantle, displays the five wounds. This form of Trinity, though in general typical of the fourteenth century, seems rather pointedly dogmatic here, and this trend is further illustrated by the texts on the scrolls held by the four Beasts, which are taken from gospel lessons for four great feasts of Christ and the Virgin:

Matthew (winged man): 'Cum natus esset' (Matt. 2. 1), gospel for the Epiphany.
Mark (winged lion): 'Recumbentibus' (Mark 16. 14), gospel for Ascension Day.
Luke (winged ox): 'Missus est' (Luke 1. 26), gospel for the Annunciation.
John (eagle): 'In principio' (John 1. 1), gospel for the Nativity.

The curious feature of showing the feet of Christ with the bleeding wounds actually touching the nimbus of the Virgin, in contrast to the obscuring of the feet of God the Father in cloud, seems to be intentional and this physical closeness may be explained by the text which the Virgin holds in her right hand: 'Genui deum et hominem', a paraphrase of the *alleluia* versicle for the Annunciation Mass in Easter time, and also for the Votive Mass of the Virgin.[5] The text in her left hand, 'Elegit et preelegit me dominus', is a para-

[1] Dating back, says Hackel, to the eleventh century. *Op. cit.*, p. 67.
[2] Part III of his great work, *Doctrinale Fidei Ecclesiae Catholicae contra Wiclevistas et Hussitas*, Tit. XIX, cap. 155. The latest edition of this work is by Père Blanciotti, Venice, 1757. Netter became a Carmelite in London in 1395, and died in 1430–1.
[3] John 14, 15, and so forth.
[4] The lesson for the mass of Trinity Sunday is from Rev. 4, in which are mentioned the throne, the rainbow, and the beasts; the elders are not included in this representation.
[5] Sibert, 285. The versicle begins, 'Virga Jesse' and is used from the Purification to Easter and from Trinity to Adv nt.

B. Carmelite Missal, fol. 38: Initial C introducing the introit of the Mass for Corpus Christi

phrase of the versicle of the hymn, *O gloriosa domina* . . . 'elegit eam deus et preelegit eam', used as the antiphon at lauds of the Carmelite Saturday Commemoration of the Virgin between the Nativity and the Purification.[1]

The other texts in the miniature are taken (with some variations) from the Canon of the Mass or the Litany of Holy Saturday. 'O beata Trinitas' is from the third prayer after communion in the *Ordo missae*: ['Tibi laus, tibi gloria, tibi gratiarum actio] o beata [et benedicta et gloriosa] trinitas, Pater, et Filius et Spiritus Sanctus.' 'Speritus (*sic*) sanctus, unus deus' seems to be a paraphrase from the Litany of Holy Saturday: 'Spiritus sancte, [Deus, miserere nobis. Sancta Trinitas,] unus Deus, [miserere nobis.]' 'Pater de celis [Deus] miserere nobis', on the scroll held by the kneeling man, and 'Sancta Maria, ora pro nobis', held by the woman, are also from the Litany. '[Et] per ipsum et cum ipso et in ipso' is from the Canon of the Mass, immediately preceding the *Pater noster*; the biblical verse from which it is taken (Rom. 11. 36) is the last verse of the epistle for the Votive Trinity.

The tone of this miniature, as suggested above, seems strongly dogmatic: the Blessed Virgin, Patroness of the Carmelite Order, as intercessor between mankind and the Holy Trinity. The tendency to associate the Virgin with the Trinity, like the tendency to substitute the Trinity in the manifestations of Christ, was characteristic of the later fourteenth century.[2] We shall find this even more evident in another one of the Trinities in the Carmelite Missal.

The second type of Trinity represented in the Missal is the so-called *Gnadenstuhl* or Mercy Seat type. Characteristic of this form are God the Father enthroned holding with His two hands the ends of the cross on which hangs the crucified Christ; between the Father and the head of Christ is the Holy Spirit in the form of a dove, flying downward.[3] This type of Trinity seems to have appeared first in the twelfth century[4] and become very popular in all countries in the thirteenth and fourteenth centuries. In the Missal, the *Gnadenstuhl* is used in the miniature for the mass of Trinity Sunday (fol. 36vo, Pl. v), but there is a very important omission in the iconographic formula: the Dove of the Holy Spirit is missing, though the pattern formed by the beard of God the Father against His breast, at first glance would suggest (perhaps intentionally) the shape of the dove's wings. Strange as it may seem to omit the Third Person from the Trinity in an illustration of the mass for this feast, it is not infrequent in English art both of this period and earlier.[5]

However, in this case there may be another explanation of the omission of the dove. The lower part of the picture contains a baptism scene, and the significance of the Trinity here seems to be indicated by the words on the scrolls attached to the foot of the cross:

[1] *Ibid.*, 34. It is used similarly for the Conception, Nativity of the Virgin, Annunciation, and Assumption.

[2] Hackel, *op. cit.*, p. 2.   [3] *Ibid.*, pp. 122 ff.

[4] Various examples, all of the twelfth century, are cited as the earliest. Didron (*op. cit.*, p. 518) says a window in St Denis is the earliest; Clemen believes its earliest appearance to be in the Psalter of Landgraf Herman von Thuringen in Stuttgart. See Clemen Paul, *Die gotischen Monumentalmalereien der Rheinlande*, Düsseldorf, 1930, I, p. 162.

[5] Some late examples are: a Psalter written for one of the Bohun family, Brit. Mus. Egerton MS. 3277, fol. 112; an English missal of about 1400, Valencia, Cath. Libr.; and a book of religious treatises, Oxford, Bodl. Libr., MS. Eng. poet. a. 1, fol. 265.

'In nomine Patris, Filii et Spiritus Sancti', with which the act of baptism is performed. It is possible that the Third Person of the Trinity is represented here in the form of the water of baptism, as suggested in the Golden Legend[1]:'. . . spiritus sanctus vocatur aqua, quae habet vim regenerativam. Joh. vii: "flumina de ventre ejus fluent aquae vivae." Hoc autem dixit de spiritu sancto, quem accepturi credentes in eum.' A similar conception seems to be inherent in a representation of the Trinity in the early fourteenth century manuscript of Walter de Milemete[2]: on fol. 5 is a Trinity of the *Gnadenstuhl* type, with no dove, and below, the words: 'In nomine patris et filii et spiritus sancti amen.' The Trinity combined with the sacrament of Baptism as in the Carmelite Missal, is, so far as I know, unique in illustrating the great Trinity mass.

The most puzzling of all the Trinities in the Carmelite Missal is represented in an historiated initial not connected with a mass for the Trinity but introducing the feast of All Saints. The composition is again a complex one; the theme is the glorification of the Blessed Virgin Mary as the Virgin of Virgins, crowned and enthroned, surrounded by saints and angels (Pl. xx). The Coronation is one of the subjects most frequently represented in art; its origin goes back at least to the twelfth century[3] and its popularity steadily increased throughout the Middle Ages and the Renaissance. Its formula down to the mid-fourteenth century is simple and consistent: the Virgin seated at Christ's right hand shares His throne; He either crowns her, or blesses her while she is crowned by an angel or by Christ Himself, as in the Assumption miniature in this Missal (fol. 132vo). He usually holds in His left hand a book, an orb, or a sceptre. Angels with censers or musical instruments surround the throne and (especially in Italy) saints in increasing numbers witness the Virgin's glory.[4]

But the Coronation in the Missal is not by Christ, but by a *Gnadenstuhl* Trinity, and herein lies the puzzle. The idea of introducing the other Persons of the Trinity into the scene of the crowning appears, it is true, in representations as early as the mid-fourteenth century,[5] and is found fully developed in the latter part of the century, as in the Franco-Flemish drawing in the Louvre,[6] in which the Virgin kneels before God the Father who blesses her while Christ holds the crown over her head and the Dove flies down from above. Coronation by this form of Trinity (which is that of the Votive Trinity in the

[1] Jacobus da Voragine, *Legenda Aurea*, Graesse, 3rd ed. (1890), p. 330.

[2] Oxford, Christ Church College MS. E. 11. Reproduced by M. R. James, for the Roxburghe Club, Oxford, 1913, Pl. 9.

[3] The earliest example is said to be the mosaic in the apse of S. Maria in Trastevere, Rome. See C. Jocelyn Ffoulkes, 'Le Couronnement de la Ste Vierge', in *Revue de l'art chrétien*, Ser. IV, Tome IX (1898), p. 44. The first appearance of the theme in monumental sculpture in France is generally believed to be in the tympanum of the west portal of Senlis Cathedral, *ca.* 1185–90. It spread rapidly and is found in the sculpture of nearly all the French Gothic cathedrals, as well as commonly in Gothic ivories and manuscripts.

[4] The theme is the Virgin as Intercessor. Cf. *Leg. Aur.*, pp. 727 f.

[5] Clemen (*op. cit.*, p. 174) describes a fresco of *ca.* 1350 representing the subject at St Severin, Cologne: Christ and Mary are seated on a throne; Christ crowns Mary and hands her a sceptre; above them, the dove of the Holy Spirit and above that, the hand of God extended in blessing. Farcy, L. de, *La broderie du XIe siècle jusqu'à nos jours*, Suppl. I, Angers, 1900, Pl. 149, reproduces a chasuble cross and orphreys described as English and though undated, placed between Pls. 148 (first half of the fourteenth century) and 150 (end of the century). In a mandorla, the Virgin and Christ are seated. Christ holds the orb in His left hand, and blesses with His right. The Virgin is crowned. A downward flying dove radiating rays hovers overhead, and above, in a mandorla supported by angels, a bust of God the Father blessing.

[6] Reproduced, Fierens-Gevaert, Hippolyte, *Hist. de la peinture flamande*, Brussels, 1927, I, Pl. XIV.

Missal) became increasingly popular[1] in the fifteenth century, probably under the influence of the mystery plays.

But the Coronation by the *Gnadenstuhl* Trinity is another matter; its occurrence in the Missal seems to be unique, and its explanation is not clear. It is possible that the popularity of the *Gnadenstuhl* form itself may account for its substitution for Christ in this scene to show increased honour to the Virgin. It is also possible that the artistic composition influenced its adoption here.[2] A third possible source of influence on the invention of a *Gnadenstuhl* Coronation is an equally curious use of the *Gnadenstuhl* in the so-called *Vierges Ouvrantes*, which in the last decades of the fourteenth century made their appearance in various parts of Europe, though apparently originating in Germany.[3] Two appear in the inventory of 1380 of Charles v of France[4]; there was one in the Carmelite Convent in Paris[5] which was criticized severely as anti-dogmatic by Chancellor Jean Gerson in a sermon of about 1400. This image is dated *ca.* 1390 and could possibly have been seen by the Carmelite Missal artist. The form is an image of the Virgin which is made to open out like the doors of a shrine, showing inside a carved *Gnadenstuhl* Trinity. On the inside of the doors are painted votive figures kneeling under the outstretched arms of the Virgin who, therefore, is represented as a Madonna of Mercy. The idea of the *Gnadenstuhl* Trinity Incarnate might have been carried over into the form of Coronation Trinity as found in the Carmelite Missal. In any case, no prototype for it has appeared and no other examples of it are known to me.[6]

Next to the Trinities, probably the most iconographically interesting miniature in the Missal is that of Corpus Christi (Pl. vi), since it not only illustrates the ceremony of the Carmelite celebration of mass, but also introduces (in the four corners of the initial field) some extraordinarily vivid topical matter in the two figures of Carmelite friars and the two white dogs. If the pictorial evidence in this miniature is interpreted correctly, the Corpus Christi picture furnishes a direct reference to the violent controversy of 1382 waged between the orthodox Roman Catholic church headed by the Archbishop of Can-

---

[1] For a useful list of variants in the form of the Coronation by the Trinity, taken chiefly from Italian examples, see Ffoulkes, *op. cit.*, pp. 48 f. and 117 ff.

[2] The artist of this miniature was overwhelmingly interested in the problems of his art rather than in dogmatic exposition, as is made amply clear later on in this study. On the freedom of the mediaeval artist in dealing with subject matter, see an interesting article by Rudolf Berliner, 'The Freedom of Mediaeval Art', in *Gaz. des Beaux-Arts*, Ser. 6, New York, Vol. 28 (1945), pp. 263–88.

[3] See Walter Fries, 'Die Schreinmadonna', in *Anzeiger des Germanischen Museums*, Nürnberg, 1928–9, pp. 5–69.

[4] Labarte, Jules, *Inventaire du mobilier de Charles V*, Paris, 1889, pp. 263 (No. 2459) and 277 (No. 2586).

[5] Now in Cluny Museum, Paris. See Berliner, *op. cit.*, pp. 282 ff. Reproduced Fig. 11. Reproduction of outside and inside in Fries, *art. cit.*, Pls. 5 and 6. In England, Durham Cathedral may have had one before 1380. See Evans, *op. cit.*, p. 82.

[6] Another curious and perhaps unique use of the *Gnadenstuhl* Trinity (without the dove, apparently) is its combination with the Annunciation in an English alabaster of about 1375, formerly in the Kunstgewerbe Museum, Cologne. See Hildburgh, W. L., 'An Alabaster Table of the Annunciation', in *Archaeologia* LXXIV (1923–4), pp. 203–32, reproduced Pl. XLV. This representation also seems to involve the idea of the Trinity Incarnate (see p. 207) as in the Coronation of the Virgin in the Missal, and might be an earlier stage of the idea of the 'Vierge Ouvrante'. Neither instance, however, explains fully the *Gnadenstuhl* Coronation. It may be worth noting that an idea associated with the Trinity Incarnate, as in the Annunciation, is suggested in the Votive Trinity of the Carmelite Missal, in which the Virgin holds a scroll which reads, 'Genui deum et hominem' (Pl. XXXIII), though in this case the Trinity is not of the *Gnadenstuhl* type.

terbury and supported by the four orders of friars on the one hand, and Wyclif and his followers on the other, over the doctrine of transsubstantiation, one of the principal Wycliffite 'heresies'. The gist of the story, which is too long to be related completely here,[1] is as follows.

Peter Stokes or Stocks, a Carmelite of Hitchin, Doctor of Theology at Oxford before 1382,[2] was particularly active in refuting the Wycliffite teachings, and in consequence was deputed by the Archbishop of Canterbury (William Courtney) to publicize the twenty-four articles selected by a council at London as the most heretical or erroneous of Wyclif's doctrines. The time chosen for this proposed publicization was Corpus Christi Day, before the sermon by Philip Repyngdon, a close follower of Wyclif, who had been selected to preach at Saint Frideswide's Church, Oxford, on that day. Three of the twenty-four articles (the first three listed in Courtney's letter to Stokes[3]) concern the Holy Sacrament and the doctrine of literal transsubstantiation, which seems to be illustrated in the miniature by the introduction of the Last Supper and Christ's own words in instituting the Sacrament, which are written on the scrolls. Peter Stokes, because of his activities against Wyclif was referred to in a bitter reply by Wyclif by the name 'albi canis, ob pallium album Religionis'.[4] The name given in opprobrium seems to have been accepted by the Carmelites[5]: the two white dogs painted in vigilant attitudes in the Corpus Christi miniature represent, almost certainly, these 'albi canes'. They are watching the two Carmelites opposite, whose lolling attitudes and impious expressions seem to exemplify something of Wyclif's own vituperation against the friars. That the artist was not himself a Carmelite is suggested by the colour of the habit which he has painted brown, whereas that of the Carmelites in other miniatures, where they are introduced as kneeling votive figures, is black[6]: the white mantle, which is actually of very thick woollen material, in this miniature appears to be soft and semitransparent, so that the limbs show under it; and more important even than this inaccuracy, is the improper posture in which no friar would be likely to represent himself or his brothers. Moreover, in no other miniature by this artist are Carmelites introduced —a fact which further points up their presence here.

[1] Documents relative to the controversy in which Stokes played a leading part are given in *Fasciculi Zizaniorum*, ed. by the Rev. Walter Waddington Shirley, Rolls Series, London, 1858, pp. 275 ff. Though commonly ascribed to Thomas Netter Waldensis, the *Fasciculi* may have been written largely by Stephen Patryngton, Netter's predecessor as Carmelite Provincial. See *ibid.*, p. lxxvii.

[2] For an account of the facts of his life, see *Dictionary of National Biography*. He died in 1399.

[3] *Fasc. Ziz.*, pp. 277–82.

[4] See Villiers de St Étienne, *Bibliotheca Carmelitana*, Orleans, 1752, II, 601–2. The term, 'canis niger', was applied by Wyclif to a Benedictine monk. *Fasc. Ziz.*, p. 239.

[5] Whether or not there was any association in the minds either of Wyclif or of the Carmelites with the opening words of Archbishop Courtney's letter is problematical. The figure of speech used in this letter is of wolves in sheep's clothing who threaten the safety of the flock (*Fasc. Ziz.*, p. 275 and also 239). It may well be that the idea of being considered faithful dogs to guard the sheep pleased the Carmelites, particularly in view of the appellation, 'Domini canes', already applied to the Black Friars. Cf. the fresco representing the Triumph of the Church in the Spanish Chapel, of the Dominican church of S. M. Novella, Florence, in which they are represented as black and white dogs.

[6] This might have resulted from ignorance. But, on the other hand, it might have been intentional as indicating sympathy with the Constitutions of 1324 to 1369, ordering brown as the colour of the habit, whereas in the Vatican manuscript of the Constitutions of 1396, black is ordered (*Analecta Ord. Carm.*, III, p. 151). In 1473 Sixtus IV declared black for the Order but there was opposition till 1626 when brown was finally re-established. I am indebted to Fr Norman Werling, O. Carm., for bringing this information to my notice. The two colours are both clearly used in the Missal, in the miniatures by different artists. The two artists who reproduce votive Carmelites in their pictures invariably give them black habits.

Likewise somewhat unorthodox is this artist's manner of illustrating the Ascension (Pl. III). In the upper half of the picture is an incident preceding the Ascension (Christ at supper with the apostles at Emmaus), and in the lower half, the scene which follows the Ascension, namely, Christ seated at the right hand of God, while the two men in white point out the event to the disciples. The usual manner of representing the Ascension of Christ is to show either His whole figure lifted up into the clouds, or at least His feet or His footprints.[1]

The same avoidance of a literal representation of a miraculous event is seen again in the Resurrection miniature: in neither of the two scenes does Christ appear rising from the tomb, as was more usual from the late twelfth or early thirteenth century.[2] In the top scene, the women are arriving at the closed tomb, and below they are told that Christ has risen. If the omission of the risen Christ is following a tradition, it is very old-fashioned at this time.[3] The grotesque angel in the lower curve of the initial, like the monster in the upper one, and like the Carmelites in the Corpus Christi picture, suggests a levity hardly in keeping with the subject. The ostrich outside the initial could, perhaps, represent the badge of Anne of Bohemia; or it may be here as commonly, a symbol of the Resurrection.

Again in the Pentecost picture, the iconography is unusual and even incongruous: below, Christ promises to the disciples the coming of the Comforter in the form of the Holy Spirit; but in the upper part of the picture, the Spirit in the form of eleven rays is already descending upon the same group of disciples. Not only is the presence of Christ at this moment unorthodox, but so is the absence of the Virgin, traditionally and consistently present in the midst of the disciples when the Holy Ghost descended upon them.[4]

How can one account for the queer ideas of the artist of these five key miniatures in the *Temporale*? Elsewhere in this study it is suggested that his style echoes strongly Bohemian tradition or influence. Is it fantastic to imagine that he not only was not a Carmelite but that he had ideas somewhat unorthodox if not smacking of free thinking such as Wyclif himself held, or if he were Bohemian, could he be leaning toward pre-Hussite heresies?[5]

The artist of the Votive Trinity miniature also displays a characteristic attitude

---

[1] Cf. Giotto's picture in the Arena Chapel, Padua, one of the finest early representations showing the whole figure ascending. The type of Ascension shown in the Carmelite Missal does not correspond to any of those distinguished by Ernest T. Dewald, 'The Iconography of the Ascension', *American Journal of Archaeology*, 2 ser., XIX (1915), pp. 279–319; nor is it discussed by Hubert Schrade, 'Zur Ikonographie der Himmelfahrt Christi', in *Vorträge der Bibliothek Warburg*, 1928–9, pp. 66–190.

[2] Künstle, Karl, *Ikonographie der Christlichen Kunst*, Freiburg i/Br., 1928, I, 504 ff. On the controversy over the influence of the Easter mystery play, 'Quem-quaeritis', on representations in art, see *ibid.*, pp. 501 ff.

[3] Examples do persist, however, as in an English Psalter (Brit. Mus. Eg. 3277), and a missal of Lyons, Bibl. Municipale, MS. 1394 (1269) of the second half of the fourteenth century (reprod. Leroquais, *Les sacramentaires*, II, 357). It may be noted also that the Feast of the Three Maries introduced into the Carmelite Rite in 1342 'with the office in use in France' (Sibert, p. xx), might have had some influence on the form of resurrection as found here. Regarding the painting of the Three Maries at the tomb generally attributed to Hubert van Eyck, formerly in the Cook Collection, now in the van Benningen Collection, Rotterdam, Professor Erwin Panofsky says it 'betrays in a work of this period a certain attachment to a belated and basically Italo–Byzantine tradition'. *Art Bulletin*, XVII (1935), p. 472.

[4] Künstle, *op. cit.*, I, 518 f.

[5] The Bohemian reformer, Matthias Janovins (d. 1394) was confessor to the Emperor Charles IV, father of Anne of Bohemia. Among her Bohemian attendants there may well have been some with unorthodox leanings.

toward his other subject matter, particularly on two of the most elaborately illustrated pages, containing respectively the mass for Lawrence and that for the Assumption of the B.V.M. (fols. 130 and 132vo, Pls. XIII and XV). The details of these pictures have been described elsewhere (see below, p. 105); a few comments on their interpretation may be added here.

Of the eight scenes in the miniature and decorative border for the mass of Lawrence, the top five represent, literally, successive incidents in his life culminating in his martyrdom, which occupies the central position in the initial. The two lower scenes in the initial and a medallion outside, introduce the story of Lawrence's intercession on behalf of the Emperor Henry II and his wife, Cunigunda, which forms part of the Golden Legend version of the saint's life.[1] Thus the scenes form a continuous narrative in three phrases: before the saint's death; his martyrdom; and after his death. To make their meaning unmistakably clear, scrolls with explanatory texts are introduced where necessary. A significant literal touch is given in the representation of a Carmelite as the hermit who addresses the devil as he passes on his way to the deathbed of Henry; but a contradictory note as to the illuminator's grasp of all the details of the story is shown by his error in writing on the scroll 'herod' instead of 'henrici'.[2]

Evidence that the Carmelite hermit was not accidental, is the introduction of a kneeling Carmelite in the lower medallion of the border, corresponding to the top medallion with the first scene from the life of Lawrence. It is unfortunate and inexplicable in view of this artist's preoccupation with detail in his representations, that the scroll held by the Carmelite has been left blank; here was an admirable opportunity for the artist to introduce some legitimate publicity for himself or his convent.

So similar in character is the interpretation of the Assumption miniature that, even apart from the style, there could be no doubt of the identity of the artist. There are eight or nine separate scenes of which four or five (according to the way in which the figures inside and outside the space enclosed by the initial are combined) illustrate the apocryphal account of the death and assumption of the Virgin as commonly represented in later mediaeval art. The literalness of the artist's mind is shown in the manner in which the angel grasps the forelocks of two of the disciples to lead them to the bedside of the dying Mary. The miracle of the Jews who tried to profane the body of the Virgin is somewhat less commonly found than the death and assumption.[3] The legend of the Virgin's girdle is rarely represented outside Italy, Prato being the centre of its popularity owing to the fact

---

[1] The incident was represented by Riemenschneider on the Emperor's tomb in Bamberg Cathedral. It was also represented by Orcagna in a predella panel of his altarpiece in S.M. Novella, Florence.

[2] The director of the group of illuminators working on the Missal, whose business it would be to plan out the decoration for the whole book, would write in the margin or in the places where the historiated initials were to be, full directions for the illuminator to follow, including the very words to be written on the scrolls. It might be one of these director's words (perhaps written carelessly in crayon) that the illuminator misread and consequently wrote incorrectly on the scroll.

[3] The sculptured representation of the death of the Virgin on the west front of Senlis Cathedral seems to be the earliest example; this was followed shortly after at Chartres and Laon, and Notre Dame (Paris). In the reliefs of the exterior wall of the apsidal chapels of Notre Dame, probably by Pierre de Chelles, ca. 1315, a series of scenes representing the death, funeral cortège (with the impiety of the Jews) and the assumption is found. The miracle of the Jews is also illustrated in a painting in the Germanisches Museum, Nürnberg, of the late fourteenth century (reprod. Stange, Alfred, *Deutsche Malerei der Gotik*, Berlin, 1934, II, Fig. 222).

that the girdle was traditionally preserved there. Both of these incidents are, however, found in English manuscripts, wall painting and embroidery of the fourteenth century. A very complete cycle of murals at Chalgrove (Oxon)[1] includes them, and in fact, the whole series, and has the same literal, illustrative quality in relation to the Golden Legend, which is characteristic of the Missal miniature.

The miracle of the Virgin[2] in the four medallions of the border may be in some way related to the two kneeling figures, man and woman, as the Carmelite is to Saint Lawrence in the miniature described above. The two figures also recall the two very similar ones in the Votive Trinity. Since there is not in either case any specific evidence for identifying them, there is no way of knowing who they are or precisely why they are introduced in these two most important illuminated pages. It appears certain that they were connected with the convent, perhaps as benefactors or possibly even as donors of the Missal.

Of similar iconographic character is the third of the narrative miniatures by this same artist, the Decollation of John the Baptist (fol. 136vo, Pl. xvi*b*). The main part of the representation is divided into four scenes which, reading from upper left to lower right, illustrate the usual incidents in the story of Salome (the daughter of Herodias) and the death of the Baptist. An unusual feature is the death of Salome, who is pictured as a charming little fourteenth century lady in coif and kirtle in her unending punishment of drowning. The presence of the Carmelite here and in the miniature of the Nativity of the Baptist may be especially significant; the Baptist was held in particular esteem by the Carmelite order in view of the words of Luke 1. 17: 'And he shall go before him in the spirit and power of Elias . . .' The prophet Elijah is the traditional founder of the Carmelite Order.

Less inspired as to the handling of his subject, but equally literal-minded and also, apparently, a Carmelite, is the artist of less ability working in the same style who painted the Annunciation miniature (fol. 99, Pl. x) and the Nativity of the Baptist (fol. 113, Pl. xii*a*). The iconography is extremely simple, consisting of a single scene with a minimum of detail. Explanatory texts are used as in the other miniatures in the same style.

Finally, as to the characteristics of the iconography of the artist of the All Saints miniature. Although he also shows some interest in the continuous narrative type of representation, as in the Conception of the Virgin (Pl. xxx), his presentation is different in that the separate scenes are all placed within the same spatial setting, thus losing all sense of historical sequence. His interpretations here and in other miniatures by him are based rather on a conception of everyday surroundings, of ordinary people participating in familiar scenes, as in the picture for Holy Saturday (Pl. i), with the bell-ringer and the singing choir; in the Dedication of the Church (Pl. vii), with the procession of clerics and the group of laymen following at a distance; in the Birth of the Virgin (Pl. xviii), with the homely details of interior furnishings, and the group of women standing round the bed handling the swaddled child; in the Purification of the Virgin (Pl. ix), with two people

---

[1] Reproduced, Borenius, Tancred, and Tristram, E.W., *English Medieval Painting*, Paris, 1927, Pl. 53; dated *ca.* 1325.

[2] *Leg. Aur.* (Graesse, 3rd ed., 1890), pp. 513–4. The same miracle is represented in the Psalter of Queen Mary, Brit. Mus. Roy. MS. 2 B. VII (early fourteenth century), fols. 216vo and 217. See facsimile published by the British Musum, with introduction by Sir George War ner, London, 1912, Pls. 230d and 231a.

hurrying in the church door, as though late for the ceremony; and in the splendid panoply and marvellously differentiated types of knights in the Exaltation of the Cross (Pl. xixa). The artist of these miniatures was not instructed in dogma nor yet was he copying any iconographic formula. His interest in people as individuals is evident in certain extra-miniature figures, as the kneeling boy outside the Saint Nicholas picture (Pl. xxix) and the two men, of different types and ages, who are seated at the lower corners of the Dedication of the Church picture, holding up the initial. This artist is apparently somewhat fanciful (unless there is more meaning in these features than meets the eye): the column encircled by an acanthus scroll, its base resting on the back of an animal, its capital bearing a gilded nude figure (an idol?) armed with shield and spear in the Dedication picture (Pl. vii); a similarly encircled tree resting on the back of a fox-tailed animal in the margin of the Purification miniature (Pl. ix); and the two *bas-de-page* pictures, one a hunting scene accompanying the All Saints miniature (Pl. xx), and the other a fishing scene, appropriately accompanying the Calling of Peter and Andrew (fol. 162, Pl. xxvi).

Grotesques also appear in this artist's work: three of the 'centaur' type with human head and animal hind quarters (fol. 162), and two animal grotesques: the front part of a dog and the hind quarters of a very long-tailed lion, and a monkey with bear's legs. In both of these, as in the centaur, the juncture of the body and the head is concealed by a garment. One of the centaurs is fighting a devil-like creature with a dragon's head and long curly ears, one clawed and one cloven foot, and a forked tail. True animals which are identifiable are also introduced, perhaps with reference to the text, as in the Conception miniature (Pl. xxx; see below, p. 113 f.). There is an unconventional freedom in such features which places the pictures in a different category from either the persistent insinuation of unorthodox elements, as in the five *Temporale* miniatures (though this artist also introduced a few animal grotesques), or the earnest and literal dogmatism of the miniatures with votive Carmelites.

As a whole, then, the iconography of the subject matter in the Carmelite Missal presents a curious mixture of characteristics which can only be accounted for by the obvious fact that it was not following any fixed prototype or tradition, but resulted from collaboration of widely differing personalities.

Costume

Saints and lay figures in the Missal are usually distinguishable only by the nimbus of the former; but there are instances, notably in one group of miniatures all by the same artist, where no haloes are worn by Saints Richard and Ambrose (Pl. xi), Elizabeth (Pl. xiia), the Apostles (Pl. xiib), and Saint Augustine (Pl. xvia).

Both saints and lay people usually are dressed in such a way as to show their rank or position: kings are robed in ermine and wear crowns; bishops and archbishops are clothed in pontifical robes; Lawrence is dressed as a deacon; knights are clad in armour. In general, both men and women wear contemporary dress; but there is some variation in types of dress among the three artists.

The differences in armour show clearly in the representations of knights in two miniatures of different style, namely, the company of knights on horseback in the Exaltation of the Cross (fol. 140) and on foot in the Saint Maurice miniature (fol. 143vo, Pl. xix).

Saint Maurice is dressed in typical English armour of the type known as camail, which was worn throughout the second half of the fourteenth century. Over a hauberk or shirt of mail (visible only at the neck and at its bottom edge) is worn a jupon or tight-fitting sleeveless tunic, made of leather or some other stout material, tightly fitted in at the waist, scalloped at the bottom, and decorated all over with a coloured pattern, which ordinarily consisted of the owner's blazon. The arms are entirely encased in brassarts of plate, having *coudières* or elbow-pieces, and at the shoulders, *épaulières* consisting of several overlapping plates. Jointed gauntlets cover the hands. On the thighs are *cuisses*, apparently of the type consisting of pieces of leather studded with small metal roundels fastened by means of rivets. On the knees are plate *génouillières*. The girdle or sword belt is worn very low on the hips; attached to it in front is the misericord or short sword, somewhat larger than a dagger. The knight's pointed bascinet, to which is joined the camail or tippet of chain mail covering the neck and shoulders (which gives this type of armour its name) lies on the ground before Maurice. On his bare head, the saint wears a chaplet. Examples of this type of armour occur in English brasses from as early as about 1360.[1]

The knights represented on horseback in the miniature of the Exaltation of the Cross (on the same plate), wear many different kinds of armour but, so far as can be seen, there is little correspondence to that of Maurice except, indeed, some of the least pointed bascinets with attached camail. In some cases, however, the camail is replaced by a gorget, apparently of stitched leather. In one case, a hinged visor is attached to the bascinet, and in at least two other cases, an aventail is worn, a visor made of overlapping plates which could be drawn up to cover the face as far as the eyes. One soldier wears a *chapel de fer* over a chain mail bascinet or coif. Several knights at the back of the group wear pointed tilting helmets topped with a plume.

This artist represents many different kinds of knightly headgear, but I see no evidence of difference in their date, since all were worn, apparently, throughout most of the fourteenth century. One of the oldest forms is the *chapel de fer* which was worn as early as the mid thirteenth century over the cap of chain mail.[2] The feature latest in date seems to be the hinged visor attached to the bascinet, which could be raised or lowered at will. An even slightly later date (that is, early fifteenth century) is given by Planchè for the aventail of overlapping plates, known as the beaver ('bavière' from the source of its origin).[3] These two last-named features would date the armour very late in the fourteenth century.

The jupons worn by the knights in the Exaltation miniature differ markedly from the tunic worn by Maurice. In fact, these seem to be garments of an entirely different type, namely, the sleeved doublet or jacque (or jacquette) of leather or heavy fabric worn over a metal breast-plate. Below the tight-fitting waist is a kind of peplum, sometimes pleated sometimes fitted close to the hips. The sleeves are of the bag type, very full and gathered

[1] Cf. Boutell, Charles, *Monumental Brasses and Slabs*, London, 1847, pp. 48 ff. Also, by the same author, *Monumental Brasses of England*, London, 1849, reproductions of effigies dated 1360-8 (plates not numbered). The dates of decease incised on effigies are not necessarily applicable to the costume or armour, since sometimes the tomb is made during the person's life, sometimes after his death. In either case, often the effigy represents the person in a costume that long antedates the year of his death.

[2] Gay, Victor, *Glossaire archéologique du moyen âge et de la renaissance*, Paris, 1887-1928, I, p. 323.

[3] Planchè, James Robinson, *A Cyclopedia of Costume*, London, 1876-9, I, p. 8.

in at the wrist.[1] Gauntlets with jointed fingers and shallow flaring cuffs protect the hands. Only two of the knights show the leg armour, which seems to consist entirely of plates, with laminated sollerets having very long pointed toes. Spurs, which are not fastened to the sollerets, are, curiously enough, of the early prick form. The Emperor's horse wears an elaborate trapping and plate armour on its neck. The saddles are of the Spanish jousting type known as bastard, high in the seat and with protection and support for the legs, to prevent the rider from being easily unhorsed in the shock of combat. The tunics as shown here are also found in Spanish monuments of about the 1380's and 1390's; they were known as the *aljuba* and were used for fêtes and tournaments.[2]

The differences between the armour in the two pictures seem not to be so much a matter of date as of usage and style, especially as to the type of tunic (see below). In armour represented by the artist of the Exaltation in other miniatures in the Missal, as on the full length standing soldiers in the miniatures of the beheading of Chrysogonus (fol. 161, Pl. xxiv*b*), the martyrdom of Catherine (fol. 161vo, Pl. xxv), and Andrew before the Proconsul (fol. 163, Pl. xxvii*a*), out of seven soldiers whose armour can be seen clearly, four wear chain mail chausses; the other three wear plate armour and laminated sollerets as in the Exaltation picture. All wear the full-sleeved tunic or jacque probably over a breast-plate as in the Exaltation. One of the figures has a tunic with a full skirt reaching to the knees; he also wears a *chapel de fer* over his chain mail coif.

Chain mail is believed to have begun to give place to steel plates between the battles of Crecy (1346) and Poitiers (1356),[3] and to have gradually disappeared until by 1400 it is scarcely to be found except in the camail and the shirt of mail. Soon after 1400, taces appear, that is, a series of overlapping plates fitting the body closely from waist to hips. Two early English examples are found in a brass of Sir Thomas Braunstone (dated 1401) at Wisbech,[4] Cambs., and in one of Sir John Hawley (dated after 1403) at Dartmouth, Devonshire. In these figures the shirt of mail and camail both have survived. In a brass probably dating shortly after 1413, the making of which Sir Simon de Felbrigge[5] himself supervised after the death of his wife in that year, chain mail has entirely disappeared except for a fringe on the steel gorget and on the lowest tace. The absence of taces in the armour in the Missal, the survival of a considerable amount of chain mail and the scarcity of visors furnish contributory though not conclusive evidence of a date for the Missal before rather than after 1400.

Civilian dress, like the armour, shows some differences in apparently contemporary styles. The full-sleeved tunic or jacque is worn without armour by various male figures represented by the artist of the Exaltation. The style is best seen in the Martyrdom of Edmund (fol. 160vo, Pl. xxiii*a*), both in the knee-length and in the very short form. On one of the figures the quilting in a barred pattern is clearly shown, as are also the ends

[1] Without visible armour, they are worn also by two of the executioners in the martyrdom of Edmund (Pl. XXIIIa).

[2] See Valentin Carderera y Solano, *Iconografía Española*, Madrid, 1856–64, Pls. XXXV (1382), XXXIII (1384), XXV (1394). In an English manuscript (Brit. Mus. Cott. Nero D. VI, after 1386) the king of Spain is represented in such a tunic (fol. 56vo). The jacque, however, is thought to be of German origin.

[3] Macklin, H. W., *The Brasses of England*, London, 1907, p. 50.

[4] Boutell, *Monumental Brasses*, unnumbered plate.

[5] Felbrigg Church, Norfolk. *Ibid.*, unnumbered plate; Macklin, *op. cit.*, p. 153.

of the laces which fastened the tunic, and the fringe around the bottom, armholes, and neck. The sleeves are very full both at armhole and elbow, hanging in a baglike form, drawn in tightly at the wrist. The same form is found a little later in Dutch miniatures in a Bible written at Utrecht and finished in 1403.[1]

In miniatures by other artists in the Missal, several types of male costume are found, all of which are seen commonly in English brasses more or less closely dated in the last quarter of the fourteenth century.[2] These types are three in number: (1) the short, shaped tunic with long, tight sleeves, scalloped or furred round the bottom, and sometimes buttoned down the front; always worn with a low girdle, and often with a tippet and hood (Pls. XIII and XVIb); (2) plain hooded gowns of different lengths, sometimes with long sleeves, sometimes with sleeves cut off at the elbow and finished with points (Pls. XIIa and XIX c); (3) a long tunic belted and apparently opened down the front, over which was worn a voluminous hooded mantle, buttoned on the right shoulder and thrown back over the left arm, leaving the right arm free; it is usually lined with a contrasting colour and suggests a rich and luxurious garment such as would be worn by a franklin or rich merchant; (Pls. VI, XV, and XXXIII),[3] Only one example of a motley gown (popular in a slightly earlier period) is found in the Missal (Pl. V).[4]

Women's dress in all the miniatures seems to follow a fairly universal late fourteenth century style, with some variation in the matter of headdress and in the form of the outer mantle. The dress is a close-fitting kirtle with full, flaring skirt and long, tight sleeves. The neck is round, and the dress is buttoned down the front with many small or fewer large buttons; the sleeves likewise are buttoned from elbow or sometimes from shoulder to wrist (Pl. XVIb, Salome). Over this is worn one or more of the following: (1) a mantle fastened only at the throat with a clasp or a cord; (2) a sleeveless jacket, known as a *côte-hardi*, slit up the sides and edged with fur (Pl. XXXIIb); (3) a second gown worn over the kirtle with elbow sleeves from which long lappets hang to the ground (Pl. XVIb, Herodias); (4) a long overcoat buttoned up like a kirtle but hanging straight and full, with long tight sleeves usually a little shorter than those of the kirtle, which show below the overcoat sleeves at the wrist (Pls. XV and XXXIII). Headdresses are mostly of one type, though varying in details. The hair is plaited and gathered into a net which forms a frame for the face, the veil hanging over the back of the head. Sometimes little knots of hair are allowed to fall into the net on the shoulders (Pls. XV and XXXIII). The veil as distinguished from the net apparently is sometimes of dark stuff matching the cloak (Pl. XXXIII). Maidens may be bareheaded or wear only chaplets or jewelled bandeaux (Pl. XXXIIb), matrons wear the veil either as described or with a wimple (Pl. XXXIIa).[5]

[1] Brussels, Bibl. Roy. MS. 205, fol. 1. Signed by Henricus van Arnhem, scribe, and made at the monastery of Nieuwlicht, near Utrecht. Reproduced in Byvanck, A. W., and Hoogewerff, G. J., *La miniature hollandaise dans les manuscrits des 14e, 15e, and 16e siècles*, The Hague, 1925, Pl. 201. A miniature probably by the same artist in a manuscript in the Walters Art Gallery, Baltimore (MS. W.171), datable in 1404, shows precisely the same style. See Rickert, Margaret, 'The Illuminated MSS. of Meester Dirc van Delf's Tafel van den Kersten Ghelove', *Journal of the Walters Art Gallery*, XII (1949), Fig. 7.

[2] Macklin, *op. cit.*, pp. 58–60.   [3] Well illustrated, *ibid.*, p. 59, *ca.* 1380.

[4] Motley gowns occur in the Liber Regalis (see Pl. XLIV), painted in a style related to this artist's. See below, pp. 76 ff.

[5] One of the finest extant brasses, that of Eleanor de Bohun (d. 1399), widow of Thomas, duke of Gloucester, in Westminster Abbey, illustrates clearly the wimple. See Macklin, *op. cit.*, p. 57. In this representation she wears, apparently, both mantle and overcoat over her kirtle, since two sleeves can be seen at the wrist.

ICONOGRAPHY AND COSTUME IN THE MINIATURES

Considering the iconography and costume as a whole, we find very little evidence for a closer dating of the illumination in the Missal than has been suggested by the textual contents. The representation of the white dogs in the Corpus Christi miniature furnishes a date of 1382 *post quem*. The costume and armour cannot be more closely placed than within the last two decades of the fourteenth century, but neither do they seem to be later than 1400. Evidences of different temperaments and traditions are to be found in both iconography and costume, and in the latter, certain features as the jacque (which is represented by one artist only), seem to be of foreign rather than of English usage.

3

Styles of the Illumination in the Missal and their Sources

In its original completeness, the illumination of the Carmelite Missal was as rich, both in amount and in variety, as was consistent with the tasteful design and the superb quality of the work. The decoration is distributed throughout the whole of the manuscript; almost every mass begins with a large initial and has smaller illuminated letters introducing its various parts. The historiated initials are noticeably more numerous in some parts than in others, particularly in the latter part of the *Sanctorale* of which the last quire alone, though having only seven leaves, contains seventeen such initials—nearly one-third of the entire number in the Missal. (See fols. 162, Pl. XXVI, and 164, Pls. XXVIII and XXIX.)

The underlying principle of the illumination is the use of initial letters of sizes ranging from six lines ($4\frac{1}{2}''$) to half a line ($\frac{3}{8}''$) in height, either painted in colours on highly burnished gold ground, or of gold on coloured ground; the smallest are drawn with a pen and tinted with coloured ink or thin paint. The painted initials contain either pictures (historiated initials) or a filling of decorative leaf and branchwork (decorative initials). To both kinds are attached various types of foliate branches and/or sprays, which run along the left-hand, top and bottom, and centre margins. In the branches of the historiated initials and their marginal borders there are frequently human or animal figures or grotesques, and on two pages *bas de page* scenes are introduced (fols. 152vo, Pl. XX, and 162, Pl. XXVI).

The following table shows the distribution in the three main parts of the Missal of the larger painted initials:

PART OF MISSAL	TYPE OF INITIAL	SIZE	NUMBER	TOTAL
Temporale	Historiated	6-line	6	
		4-line	1	7
	Decorative	5-line	10	
		4-line	6	
		3-line	37	53
Sanctorale	Historiated	6-line	6	
		5-line	8	
		4-line	8	
		3-line	20	42

PART OF MISSAL	TYPE OF INITIAL	SIZE	NUMBER	TOTAL
	Decorative	5-line	14	
		4-line	20	
		3-line	42	76
Commune Sanctorum	Historiated	5-line	1	
		3-line	2	3
	Decorative	5-line	9	
		4-line	4	
		3-line	51	64
				———
				245

The variety of types and sizes of initials interspersed in the fine gothic script, and the richness of the border designs filled the enormous pages with a beauty and brilliance which can hardly have been surpassed in any other manuscript of its time, and which can be realized only now that the manuscript has been partially restored.

The Styles of the Historiated Initials

The historiated initials, though considerably less than one-third of the whole number of three to six-line letters, are unquestionably the crowning glory of the Missal. With few exceptions they are in perfect condition. Their colour is vibrantly rich, the pigments and gold being of the finest quality imaginable. The colour schemes and their use in the design vary among the different miniature styles, thus avoiding monotony; the colouring of the miniature always harmonizes with that of the decorative work on the same page. Technically, each style is consistently finished and competent, and many of the miniatures are masterpieces of their style.

In order to present more clearly the distinctions between the various miniature styles, as well as to avoid repetition of the same features as they occur in each style, let us look first at the general scheme governing the design of the historiated initials.

First, the position of the initial letter in relation to the text passage which it introduces is always fixed; hence the position of the picture on the page also is predetermined, and this means that if more than one historiated initial occurs on a page, the designs must be planned in relation both to each other and to the decoration of the whole page, instead of being individually treated and placed at will, as is possible with the detached picture. Second, since the historiated initial is part of the decoration, such planning can assure the harmony in colour and the unity in the general design of the page.

The fact that the picture is confined within the space of an initial letter, however, strongly affects the composition of the scene, not only as to limitations in size and shape, but as to the spatial relation of the picture to the letter. There are two principal ways of solving the problem of this relationship: the initial letter may be treated (1) as a picture frame, completely detached from the picture itself which would remain unchanged if the letter should be removed; or (2) as a decorative design combined in some manner with the picture it contains. These two different modes of dealing with the same problem constitute one basis for distinguishing styles in the miniatures.

Another general characteristic of the historiated initial with attached border is that it favours the introduction of figures in the decoration outside the picture, of which all the artists in the Missal took advantage, more or less, in order to enrich the decoration and to crowd in more subject matter than the initial space itself allowed.

Finally, the uniformly high quality of the pigments and other materials of the historiated initials, the consistent scheme of painting pictures upon burnished gold or coloured diapered or arabesque grounds, and the technical excellence displayed in all the work, furnish a further basis for judging the variations in individual styles.

In fact, the distinction of styles presents little difficulty. If, for example, we consider three historiated initial S's (fols. 118vo, 27vo, and 93, Pls. xIIb, IV, and IX) from the point of view of (1) treatment of the initial in relation to the picture, (2) treatment of the figure composition as to spatial and three-dimensional conceptions, (3) treatment of individual figures, especially in regard to draperies and facial types, we will notice unmistakable differences.

(1) The letter S (on fol. 118vo, Pl. xIIb) is treated as an inseparable part of the picture as well as of the decoration. The two scenes illustrating Peter walking on the water are enclosed in the two spaces formed by the closed letter S; they are entirely separate one from the other, yet the left half of the cross-bar of the letter is almost completely hidden by the figures of the lower scene; in other words, the letter passes behind these figures, although in the upper scene, on the right side, it obscures the feet of Christ. Moreover, in this upper half, the head of Christ is outside the upper curve of the letter S, even as the foliated end of this upper curve, passing behind the cross-bar, is drawn outside over the lower curved right side of the letter. In short, the terminal of the letter is treated in exactly the same manner as the figure of Christ in the upper picture, that is, as part of a flat interlacing pattern.

The closed letter S on fol. 27vo (Pl. IV) also divides the picture into two parts with Heaven and God the Father above, and earth with the disciples and Christ below. But the two parts form a single picture representing a single idea, and are united also in composition, since the rays of the Holy Spirit descend without interruption across the bar of the S from the Father to the Disciples. Apart from this one detail, the two portions of the picture may be thought of as behind the initial letter; except for this, the letter would serve as a fixed frame, which cuts off the feet of the figures and one of the haloes on the left side and the trees and the halo of Christ on the right. Actually, the rays cause a slight confusion of compositional idea in this initial letter: it must be in front of the picture as a frame (and hence separate from the picture) and yet behind the rays, the iconographic importance of which would be lost if they were made to pass behind the initial.

The initial S on fol. 93 (Pl. IX) furnishes a strong contrast to both the other examples of S's in the basic principle of its design. Here, as in the Pentecost picture, a single scene fills the whole of the space, not only representing one single idea but designed as one single composition regardless of the initial letter. In order to produce this composition, the artist had to choose between two possible treatments of the initial itself, particularly in respect to the crossbar: he could either place the picture behind the initial, the cross-bar of which would then pass in front of the picture obscuring part of it as on fol. 27vo; or he could place the picture in front of the cross-bar of the initial, as, in fact, he has done. The third possibility as used on fol. 118vo, namely of weaving the initial in and out of the figure composition, would not be feasible here, because of the unity of the scene. Unmistakably, the artist of the Purification scene is interested primarily in the pictorial composition, and is using the initial letter only as a decorative frame around the space in which the scene is composed. But not only that. The initial itself is formed in part by two elongated serrated leaf forms, seen in profile with the serrations of the two leaves facing each other, and shaded to suggest the plastic, softly curving form of just such a leaf as is seen, in its broader aspect, in the border. This thick though pliable form of initial letter is treated as though it could be bent not only from side to side but from front to back. In the upper right corner of the picture, it follows the curve of the roof and dome of the chapel and seems to cut slightly across the final of the pinnacled pier buttress at the extreme right. At the left of the picture, as already noted, the initial disappears behind the entrance of the chapel and reappears only at the extreme right side, thence curving downward, and on the right cutting across the lower corner of the same buttress which it cuts off above. The lower curve, passing toward the left, determines the foreground line of the picture (note the contrast between the flower-dotted grass and the decorative pattern of the corner of the square field on which the initial is placed); but at the extreme left it once more passes behind the entrance step of the chapel and closes the picture space. In other words, the initial is designed not flat against a flat surface, nor weaving in and out with other elements in a flat pattern, but as though it were placed at an angle, nearer to the spectator on the right side than on the left, since on the right it passes in front, and, on the left, in back of a solidly conceived building. Similarly, the building itself also is placed obliquely in relation to a flat picture plane: at the left, the building seems nearer to us than at the right, because at the left it is in front of the initial. Thus we have a kind of 'x' design conceived in spatial depth; and this is quite apart from the use of the initial as a frame for the picture. Furthermore, the oblique lines of the roof, both of the chapel and of the vestibule, indicate that the building itself is not set squarely with the plane of the picture, and there can be little doubt that the artist was intentionally using the initial to emphasize further this position and the resulting effect of solidity in the building. This conception is something very different from the decorative use of the initial as we have seen it in the other two examples examined.

(2) Moreover, the composition of the picture itself as to spatial conception shows marked differences in these three examples. In the initial on fol. 118vo a setting is suggested by the details of water and boat, but there is no real rendering of space; all is on a flat two-dimensional plane. Noticeable in this composition is the reversal of the setting and the corresponding figures in the upper and lower scenes, resulting also in an x-like design but in two dimensions, thus differing from that on fol. 93. As already noted, in the Peter scenes the pattern formed by initial and picture is flat, as the composition of the pictures is two-dimensional. The scrolls containing the words spoken in these scenes also emphasize the idea of the interlace, as does the design of the initial itself. This design is characterized by the typical linear pattern which persisted in England even in the late middle ages as a survival of the Anglo-Saxon and Celtic interlace.[1]

---

[1] This decorative form, together with other elements of Anglo-Saxon and Celtic style, was incorporated in Carolingian illumination, particularly in the Saint Gall and Franco-Saxon schools. It undoubtedly was reintroduced into England in the late tenth century under the influence of Continental work, and as a congenial form particularly suited to the initial decoration, it never wholly disappeared from English illumination.

C. Carmelite Missal, fol. 140: Initial N introducing the introit of the Mass for the Exaltation of the Cross

On fol. 27vo we have a similar summary treatment of the landscape setting, with no clear conception of space. The figures are arranged below (on the earth) in a shallow semicircle following the shape of the lower band of the initial, and above (in the heavens) God the Father, choirs of angels, and the sun and moon are all placed in the positions most effective decoratively in relation to the available surface space, which is the same decorative space as appears outside the initial letter. Here, also, a slightly diagonal axis for the composition is used, but the symbolic nature of the composition as well as the emphasis on the decorative scheme precludes any suggestion of real spatial depth.

On fol. 93 the situation is quite different. The chapel is conceived as a solid structure with an interior and exterior view, and a connection between the two is made by means of the figures entering the vestibule at the left. The exterior architecture shows a good deal of late Gothic decorative detail, such as tracery, crockets, and cusps; within, the dim space between vaulted ceiling and tiled floor and between the back and front walls permits the arrangement of the ten figures in front, at the side, and behind the altar which, like the building itself, is set diagonally in relation to the picture plane. The nearness of the building to the spectator at the left side is further emphasized by the two figures in the vestibule. Despite its faulty perspective, and the placing of the figures one above another, there can be no doubt about the spatial intention here.

(3) Finally, in figure types also, the three pictures we are comparing show marked differences. On fol. 118vo, the figures are small, with flat, doll-like faces, thin arms, and large hands; although there are a few variations in the features (some being bearded, some not) the expressions of all are identical. The technique of representing the features is linear, as is that of the draperies and details of the setting, On fol. 27vo, the figures are more carefully painted, both as to faces and as to draperies: there is a considerable amount of shading in colour and a definite painting technique of the flesh and of the eyes, for instance, which suggests that the artist was influenced by a different technique from that of fol. 118vo. However, in spite of the gracefully flowing draperies and softly tinted flesh, there is a uniformity about the faces and figures, as well as about the hair-pin curve of the draped mantles which indicates that the artist was following a formula, and that his real interest was not in the representational but in the decorative elements. This interest is further displayed in the exquisite delicacy of the colouring and the richness of the stippled gold backgrounds. Finally, the artist of fol. 93 again stands apart from the other two in his entirely different conception of figures and faces. The figures are short and rather broad, and appear even heavier bundled up in their thick draperies. The faces are highly modelled, with a dark underpainting, white for highlights and red for nostrils and lips. Hair is represented both with the fineness of individual hairs, and having the texture of the soft mass shaded underneath. Dress and features are varied, and most noticeable of all, expressions as well as positions of head and gestures of hands are markedly varied. As this artist was interested in problems of space, so he was also in living figures as solid forms individualized, if not in the sense of portraits, at least as clearly distinguished types.

From this comparison of the three miniatures, it is clear that we are dealing with three very different styles, two of which seem to have more characteristics in common than the third has with either.

This third style is recognizable in another fine historiated initial (4/51, fol. 165, Pl.

xxx). Although the composition here consists of five distinct scenes composed in a continuous space, instead of one scene only, as on fol. 93, in the relation of the initial to the picture (here the building at the top leans forward from the picture plane, the initial passing behind it), in the spatial conception, in the solidity of the figures, and in the vivid, fully modelled faces, it associates itself unmistakably with the artist of the Purification scene.

In the case of another historiated initial *G*, containing several scenes (4/58, fol. 132vo, Pl. xv), representing the Death and Assumption of the Virgin, the composition again is based on the flat, interlacing pattern. The initial in combination with the decorative terminals used to separate the death from the funeral in the lower half of the picture, suggests the weaving patterns found in a simpler form on fol. 118vo. The doll-like facial and figure types, also, and the thin arms and large hands, the simple delineation of features, and the sketchy draperies and landscape details correspond to those on fol. 118vo. Yet if the two pictures are compared closely, the faces in this initial *G* are seen to be more carefully indicated as to eyelids, eyebrows, noses—in short there is a kind of modelling technique here, using browns and strong whites, which attempts to give some degree of solidity to the forms which those on fol. 118vo lack. Moreover, there is an attention to detail in the matter of position and gesture as expressing emotion; and finally there is a brilliance and depth to the colouring which betray a more masterly handling of this style than on fol. 118vo. The artists of these miniatures may be distinguished as Hands 1 and 2 of this style. Similarly, the artist of the miniatures on fols. 93 and 165 may not have painted with his own hand all the other miniatures in this style, but two other artists may have assisted.[1] In all, six different miniaturists seem to have produced the fifty-two miniatures, which are distributed among them as shown in the following table, in the order in which they appear in the manuscript.

> Hand A[1]—the Holy Saturday picture (fol. 6vo) and the Dedication of the Church (68vo) in the *Temporale*; and many miniatures in the *Sanctorale*.
>
> Hand B—the Easter picture (fol. 7vo) and the four following it (fols. 21vo, 27vo, 36vo, 38) in the *Temporale*.
>
> Hand C[1]—The Annunciation (fol. 99) and six miniatures following it, the last of which is the Octave of the Apostles (fol. 118vo).
>
> Hand C[2]—The Saint Lawrence initial (fol. 130), and a number of others following it, including the Death and Assumption of the Virgin (fol. 132vo) and ending with 136vo; also three miniatures in the *Commune* (fols. 192, 193vo).
>
> Hand A[2]—Saint Louis (fol. 135vo), on the last leaf of a quire illustrated by Hand C[2].
>
> Hand A[3]—Saints Lucy and Lazarus (fol. 166) at the very end of the *Sanctorale*.

The distribution of these different miniature styles throughout the Missal further supports the distinctions of hands, and bears out very neatly the hypothesis that the quires when written were given out to various artists available for the decoration of the book.

The layout of the Missal in quires and the distribution of hands may be seen clearly in the following table:

---

[1] The importance of distinguishing the two assisting hands from that of the master will appear in the following chapter where the influence and spread of this style are discussed. See below, pp. 91 ff.

Temporale

Hand A¹. Fol. 6vo in Quire I: Holy Saturday (4/93). The missing first two leaves of the quire may have contained an unplaced fragment of border decoration with an angel (4/42); Cf. Quire XIX below)

Hand B. Fol. 7vo in Quire II: Easter (4/43)

Hand B. Fol. 21vo in Quire III: Ascension (4/44)

Hand B. Fol. 27vo in Quire IV: Pentecost (4/45)

Hand B. Fols. 36vo and 38 in Quire V: Trinity (4/61); Corpus Christi (4/40).

Quires VI–VIII, fols. 39–62, no miniatures

Hand A¹. Fol. 68vo in Quire IX: Dedication of the Church (4/89)

Sanctorale

Hand A¹. Fols. 90 and 93 in Quire X: Conversion of Paul (4/48); Purification of the Virgin (4/18)

Hand C¹. Fols. 99 and 100 in Quire XI: Annunciation (4/8); Richard (4/84); Ambrose and Sixtus (4/82, 2/101)

Quire XII, fols. 104–111, no miniatures

Hand C¹. Fols. 113 and 118 in Quire XIII: Nativity of Baptist (4/1); Translation of Martin (4/78); Octave of the Apostles (4/26)

Quire XIV, fols. 120–127, no miniatures

Hand C². Fols. 130, 131, 132, 133 in Quire XV: Lawrence (4/59); Hippolytus (4/86), Vigil of Assumption (4/92); Assumption (4/58), Octave of Lawrence (4/85)

Hand A². Fol. 135 in Quire XV: Louis (4/83)

Hand C². Fols. 136 and 143 in Quire XVI: Augustine (4/81) and Decollation of the Baptist (4/46); Maurice (4/60) and Cleophas (4/77)

Hand A¹. Fols. 138 and 140 in Quire XVI: Giles (4/50); Nativity of Virgin (4/13); Exaltation of the Cross (4/72)

Quire XVII, fols. 144–151, no miniatures

Hand A¹. Fols. 152 and 159 in Quire XVIII: All Saints (4/55); Martin (4/52); Brice (4/78)

Hand A¹. Fols. 160, 161, 162, 163, 164, 165 in Quire XIX: Edmund Archbishop (4/64); Edmund King and Martyr (4/74), Cecilia (4/79); Clement (4/70), Catherine (4/71), Chrysogonus (4/87); Linus (4/76), Saturninus (4/88), Vigil of Andrew (4/33); Andrew (4/73); Loy (4/69), Barbara (4/37), Nicholas (4/91); Octave of Andrew (4/54), Conception of Virgin (4/51). [Angel 4/42 may have belonged here]

Hand A³. Fol. 166 in Quire XIX: Lucy (4/67), Lazarus (4/39)

Commune Sanctorum

Quires XX–XXII, fols. 168–191, no miniatures

Hand C². Fols. 192 and 193 in Quire XXIII: Matron (4/80); Several Virgins (4/66); Votive Trinity (4/90)

Quires XXIV–XXVI, fols. 200-212, no miniatures

The above table shows not only the distribution of the fifty-two miniatures painted by the six different artists in successive parts of the Missal, but also the absence of miniatures in nearly half of the quires (twelve out of twenty-six). The actual amount of work done by each miniaturist, and the practice followed, with only a few exceptions, of having a single artist paint all the pictures in any one quire will, perhaps, appear more clearly in the following recapitulation of this distribution.

Recapitulation of the Distribution of the Different Miniature Hands in Quires

HANDS $A^{1,2,3}$	HAND B	HAND C^1	HAND C^2	NO MINIATURES
Quire I	Quires II–V			Quires VI–VIII
Quires IX, X		Quire XI		Quire XII
		Quire XIII		Quire XIV
Quire XV (fol. viii)			Quire XV (fols. iii, vi)	
Quire XVI (fols. iii, v)			Quire XVI (fols. i, viii)	Quire XVII
Quires XVIII, XIX				Quires XX–XXII
			Quire XXIII	Quires XXIV–XXVI

As the table shows, usually only one artist worked on a gathering. This is important in view of the fact that, as we shall see, there is little or no evidence that one style influenced another during the progress of their collaboration. There are two exceptions to this general practice: quires XV and XVI contain miniatures by two artists, but the two halves of a double leaf are painted by the same artist.

Two further details of the apportionment of the work among the various hands may be mentioned. Hand A^2 (who did the miniature of Louis on the last leaf of Quire XVIII which also contains miniatures by Hand C^2) appears to be formed on Hand A^1 but shows different characteristics of facial and drapery technique. This miniature may have been missed when the quire was being illuminated, and added by a different artist when the omission was discovered.

Likewise Hand A^3 who painted only the last two miniatures in the *Sanctorale* seems to have been learning from Hand A^1, since there is a marked difference in the quality of these miniatures.

THE STYLES OF THE DECORATIVE INITIALS AND BORDERS

In the *Temporale* and *Sanctorale* the general scheme for the use of the various sizes and kinds of initials is the following: (1) letters of from four to six lines introduce introits, or, less frequently, collects, as when cues only are given for the introit[1]; (2) if a large initial introduces the introit of a mass, the collect, epistle, gospel, secret and postcommunion are introduced by two-line letters; if the large initial introduces the collect, the secret and post-communion have two-line initials; (3) the grail, offertory, and communion begin with a one-line initial which is, apparently, most often a gold letter flourished in coloured or black ink. (Cf. Pl. XXXIXc and the *U*[enite] of the communion ('Cō') on fol. 164, Pl. XXVIII.)

In the *Commune Sanctorum* a different practice was followed in the use of the two-line capitals. In these masses a large number of alternate forms are regularly given for epistles,

---

[1] Both are illustrated on Pl. XXXVI, as are also two-line initials used as described here.

grails, gospels, offertories, and communions, and in such cases each begins with an illuminated two-line initial. Thus it often happens that the initials stand so close together in the column of text that the marginal decoration of one overlaps that of the one above or below. These pages are among the richest in the whole Missal (*e.g.* fol. 182, Pls. XXXVII and XXXVIII).

The pages of the Prefaces and Canon of the Mass are also very rich in decoration: each division of the text of the Canon (fol. 78, Pl. XXXIV) and each Preface begins with a large initial measuring three to five lines, and each saint's name in the invocations (fol. 78vo, Pl. XXXV), as well as other important words, begin with a small (one-line) blue, tan, and gold letter.

The great number of pen-drawn letters containing little scenes, often extremely interesting in subject and exquisite in design, must have been used chiefly to introduce the verses of epistle and gospel passages when these were given in full. Evidence for this conclusion is furnished by the fact that three sets of such initials so used have been placed in the reconstructed manuscript: two in the All Saints' mass (fol. 153vo) and one in the Easter mass (fol. 8, Pl. II). Portions of similar pen-drawn initials on the backs of certain fragments, introducing the first words of verses, first gave evidence of this practice. Some of the small initials were used also as the second letter of a word introduced by a larger initial (Pls. IV and C). Although all the figures and scenes represented in these small letters cannot be identified, enough of them have been recognized to give some idea of the kinds of subjects they illustrate. Besides a great number of representations of Christ (with cruciform nimbus) talking to the Apostles (recognizable by their haloes) or to other persons, evidently illustrating gospel or epistle passages, there are many representations of Carmelites, reading or officiating at mass, or having visions. These are among the most interesting of the series. Other scenes show details of the apocalyptic vision, or single figures of bishops and martyrs; and a considerable number of letters have heads drawn either in profile or in front view, mostly fantastic, but in a few cases possibly intended to represent individual persons.[1]

In addition to the initial letters, many whole words are written in decorative letters, either in gold or colours, this being usual for forms of the words *Jesus* (IHC), *Christus, Maria, Pater, Filius,* and others. The heading of an important mass (Pl. D) and sometimes the first few words of the introit text (Pl. III) are also frequently in decorative letters, and the headings of parts of the mass (*Oracio, Secretum, Epistola,* and others) are always in rubric often elaborately ornamented with skilfully drawn heads and other designs.

There were undoubtedly many decorative line-fillings throughout the Missal, such as the one illustrated in Pl. XXXIV. They occur also on Preface pages, and in the *Temporale.* Most of these were probably not considered worth cutting out of the manuscript, but a good many survive in the Glasgow scrapbook.

The larger decorative initials (measuring three to five lines) are all similar in design and colouring but differ noticeably in details and in workmanship; it is evident that more than one illuminator painted them. Before attempting to distinguish these hands,

---

[1] Although it has not been possible to incorporate most of these initials in the Missal, a study of them could be made and might prove interesting and profitable for both stylistic and iconographic reasons. A great many additional ones are contained in the Glasgow scrapbook.

however, it is necessary first to describe the features common to all of the large decorative initials.

The basic principle of the design is a letter painted upon a square of stippled gold ground; the empty space enclosed within the letter is filled with foliage arranged in a design appropriate to the shape of the letter. The letter itself may be ornamented in one of two ways: either it is painted in solid colour and decorated with simple linear patterns in white, suggesting (especially in the coarser work) a buttonholed edge; or it may be composed of narrow bands which interlace and form a trelliswork and then continue into the foliate design enclosed by the initial, thus forming a very beautifully organized pattern.

The finest of these trelliswork initials is the *T* of the '*Te igitur*' beginning the Canon of the Mass (Pl. XXXIV); the solid initial type is illustrated on Pl. XXXVI. Many of the motifs used both in the initial design and in the attached sprays in these two examples are very similar in form and in technique, thus indicating that they are probably the work of the same group of illuminators. These motifs are very simple in form and few in number: they consist chiefly of (1) elongated, oval leaf forms, slightly pointed and irregular in shape, sometimes with a single lobe on one side, as though seen in profile, bending gracefully on their hair-line stems, sometimes flat and sometimes shaded to look hollow ('spoon leaves', Pl. XXXVIII); (2) curled or folded leaves, shaded to represent their rounded forms; (3) thimble-shaped forms; (4) wide open flowers of four or five petals with the tips of the petals curling over (used mainly for initial filling); (5) flat, kite or wafer-shaped motifs (used on sprays only). The colours are a soft, yellowish tan and a very beautiful dull blue (not ultramarine, but perhaps cobalt) and a little rich terra-cotta red. The brilliantly burnished gold ground, stippled in conventional patterns, is visible in the interstices of the filling and of the initial shaft, if that is of the trellis form. The coloured motifs used on the sprays are interspersed with small burnished gold balls and hair-line pen-flourishes.

The chief difference in style between the two types of larger initials is in quality, which, in the inferior style, is manifest in the stiffness of the design, as fol. 120, the harsher colouring, the poorer quality of the gold, and the flatness and conventionality of the motifs. In addition to the motifs used by the superior hand (Pl. XXXIV) which undergo some variations in the work of the poorer hand (Pl. XXXVI), some new ones are introduced: trefoils, hearts, and elongated leaves with two sharp points on each side and one at the tip suggesting holly leaves. It is probable that this second and inferior illuminator was either an apprentice or an assistant to the better one, and that the two divided the work between them throughout the Missal. It seems certain that the better of the two was responsible for that whole portion of the Missal containing the Prefaces and Canon of the mass, as well as for some of the more important large initials of the *Temporale* and of the *Sanctorale* (James, 4/113, fol. 122vo, John before the Latin Gate, 4/229, fol. 106vo, and the Patriarchs, fol. 146vo); the second, less skilled and less artistic decorator apparently painted the *KL* letters of the Calendar, a great many of the large initials of the *Commune Sanctorum*, and the two-line letters of the last quire of the *Sanctorale*. Further distinction between the two hands is not important since their style is essentially the same.

The other element of page decoration in the Missal is the border, which is invariably attached to both painted decorative and historiated initials. The border consists of a coloured bar on a gold ground which, like the square field on which the initial is painted, varies in outline, sometimes showing points, sometimes serrations, which give it an irregular contour and lend variety to the design. This gold ground under the border is also stippled in simple patterns. Sometimes the border runs nearly the whole length of the page, sometimes it divides into two parts and runs across the top or the bottom margin, and sometimes it extends only a short distance beyond the initial. In the better work (as distinguished above, in the description of the decorative initials) the bar is gradually attenuated into a point from which issues a hair-line spray containing the motifs described in the preceding paragraphs: in the work of poorer quality, the bar often is cut off squarely at the ends, and the spray is made to shoot out from one or both corners of the truncated end. This latter style, needless to say, is much less graceful and pleasing.

On the first leaf of the last quire of the *Commune Sanctorum* a very interesting innovation occurs in the sprays of the large initials. The pen-flourishes suggesting curling tendrils on a stem, which have up to this point in the manuscript always been drawn in black ink, begin to be touched at the tip with a small spot of bluish green.[1] The use of these green dots in the Missal is probably the earliest occurrence in English illumination of a feature which becomes characteristic of the style of the first quarter of the fifteenth century.[2] Its introduction into the last quire of the Missal (accompanied by a change of tones in the other colours used) may be due either to a new illuminator, or to one of the earlier illuminators who had picked up or invented the new idea.

The historiated initial borders vary greatly since they appear to have been painted at least in part by the miniaturists themselves. For this reason, they will be discussed under the various miniature styles.

The only feature of the decoration still to be described is the many hundreds of two-line initials. The general form of these is a stippled gold letter placed on a square ground painted in two colours (pink, tan or red, and blue) and decorated in white or light grey (perhaps oxydized white) with conventional lines or dotted patterns. Attached to the outer corners of the ground (to three corners if the initial happens to stand at the top or bottom of a column as on fol. 21vo (Pl. III) are hair-line sprays, similar to those ornamenting the large initials and their border framework, containing (1) coloured motifs of various kinds, (2) small gold balls, (3) hair-line pen-drawn flourishes suggesting tendrils on the stems. The number of these motifs varies from two to seven according to the length and position of the spray. The gold balls also vary in number and alternate with the same types of coloured motifs as in the large initial borders and sprays. Markings of these motifs, however, and in some cases, even the shapes of the motifs, differ in the small initial sprays to such an extent that they are not always recognizable as the same forms.

The two-line initials were evidently painted by at least four illuminators; the different hands may be distinguished as follows: (1) gold initials stippled in delicate scroll or arabesque patterns, placed on squares, half pale blue and half pinkish tan; motifs in sprays are of only a few types, kites, spoons, and trefoils, holly leaves and wafers (fol. 21vo, Pl. III),

---

[1] Reproduced in Brit. Mus., *Schools of Illumination*, Part IV, 1922, Pl. 3.

[2] For a study of the development of fifteenth century English border decoration, see Chapter on Illuminations in *The Text of the Canterbury Tales* by J. M. Manly and Edith Rickert, Univ. of Chicago Press, 1939, Vol. I, pp. 561–83.

usually slightly shaded to suggest roundness of forms; (2) gold initials stippled in circles and lines of dots, placed on squares painted half in a brighter blue than the preceding, and half in a yellowish tan; the motifs correspond closely in form and markings to those in the inferior large initials; (3) gold initials stippled in patterns like the preceding, placed on squares of very deep, rich crimson and deep blue (ultramarine); the motifs both within the initial and in the sprays strongly shaded to indicate form; (4) gold initials stippled as in the two preceding styles, placed on squares of lighter red and bright blue, strongly marked with white or grey patterns, giving a very brilliant effect to the colour; the motifs also brightly coloured with much use of orange-red and painted in flat colour without shading (fol. 182, Pls. XXXVII and XXXVIII).

From these distinctions it seems clear that the styles are too different to have been painted by a single illuminator; and this conclusion is supported by their localization in different parts of the Missal, and by the shift from one style to another at the quire divisions.[1] Thus (1) is found in the whole of the *Temporale* and continues through the first quire of the *Sanctorale*; (2) is found in the last quire of the *Sanctorale* only; (3) is found in the second quire of the *Sanctorale* only; (4) continues through the remainder of the *Sanctorale* (except the last quire) and the whole of the *Commune Sanctorum*.

To assume, however, that there were four illuminators working on the small initials, and an additional two doing the large initials, besides the miniaturists who apparently painted the border decoration of their own miniatures, and still other artists doing the penwork in the small initials, would imply a total of some dozen or more different persons engaged on the decoration of this manuscript. This may have been the case if the work was being rushed; for either these artists could have been brought together in a scriptorium (although there is no record of one at Whitefriars) or, what is more likely, the Missal, as it was written, may have been parcelled out in quires to different decorators, who did the work at home or in their own shops. However, it seems possible to attribute tentatively the illumination of at least some of the small initials to other hands working on the Missal, thus reducing the number of artists presumed to be engaged on it. For example, number 2 is so similar in character to the illuminator of the inferior large initials and the *KL* monograms in the Calendar that there seems little question of the same hand in both types of letters; number 3 likewise shows some of the same strong colouring and the tendency to shade forms which is found in one of the miniature styles (C[1]; see below). It is also possible that both the very beautiful small initials in the *Temporale* and the best of the large ones (such as the *T* of the '*Te igitur*' in the Canon) are by the same hand, and that hand conceivably may be that of the miniaturist of the five great feast pictures in the *Temporale* (Hand B; see below). These two latter attributions will be considered further in the following sections on the sources of the styles.

THE SOURCES OF THE MINIATURE STYLES

From the detailed analysis presented earlier in this chapter, of the methods of handling composition and figures in certain miniatures in the Missal, and from the differences of iconographic approach noted in the preceding chapter, it is evident that several distinct

---

[1] The usefulness of being able at an early stage to distinguish the styles of the two-line initials is apparent in the description of the processes of reconstruction. See Appendix A, p. 131.

stylistic traditions are represented in the illumination of this manuscript. Having isolated these traditions, here designated as Hands A (1, 2 and 3), B, and C (1 and 2), it is our next task to identify them in other contemporary illumination and to try to explain their origins.

The English Tradition: Style C

Hands C^1 and C^2, though not the first to appear in the order of the Missal, nevertheless will be examined first, since they represent the style most commonly found in late fourteenth century English illumination.

The most outstanding characteristic of this style is the lively narrative interest shown in the multiplicity of scenes in a single initial, in the expressiveness of pose and gesture of the figures, in the attention to details, particularly as to contemporary costume, and even in suggestions of dialogue in the form of text scrolls which contain words spoken by the participants in the story. Settings are very simple and, though some architecture is introduced into the scenes, backgrounds are invariably of stippled gold or decorated with diaper and other patterns. Clouds, water, and ground (when represented) are conventionalized; trees, which are shown in only one miniature (the Assumption, Pl. xv) have solid masses of pale green foliage with large leaves indicated by dark outlines.

The technique of modelling the faces and the resulting facial types are very interesting. The basic flesh colour is brownish yellow, on which white patches and lines are painted to indicate the highlights on forehead, upper eyelid, nose and chin. Eyebrows are dark brown arched lines which continue down each side of the nose. Moustaches and beards are brown except on old men, where they are touched with white, as are also the eyebrows. The edges of the upper eyelids, the eye-balls, nostrils, and mouth are outlined in black. Irises seem to be attached to the upper eyelid and are usually placed in one corner of the eye socket; mouths tend to droop at the corners and are often crooked, and moustaches emphasize this downward curve; ears, which only occasionally show, are badly drawn and wrongly placed (see the Carmelite in the Annunciation, Pl. x). The facial types resulting from this method of modelling are (*a*) beardless, round-chinned faces used for clerics, very similar to the type used for women; (*b*) heads with beards, single or double-pointed, brown or white, used for most other men. There is, however, more variety among the faces than would seem possible from the small number of types; this is largely because of the liveliness of expression which the artist more or less correctly gives to the eyes. He even distinguishes dead faces from living ones, as in the Decollation of the Baptist (Pl. xvi*b*). Only twice does this artist attempt a full-face view: in the picture of St Augustine (Pl. xvi*a*) and in a God head in the Annunciation—both representations of a somewhat hieratic character.

The principal colours used in the miniatures of Style C (Pl. D) are two shades of blue and two of red. The blues are a fine dark ultramarine and a lighter cobalt, the two often used in combination, one as shading for the other. The reds are a dull soft red, probably a poor quality of vermilion with a yellowish tint becoming almost orange in the lighter tones, and a crimson or lake; a rose pink is used with these. The two reds and the pink are often found juxtaposed in the painting of garments, with an unharmonious, crude effect. A richer, brighter red is used sparingly in background patterns, and a dull yellow, like raw sienna, is used for hair, for the ground colour of tiles and woodwork, and, mixed with the yellowish red, in leaf motifs of the border decoration. The better red is used for shading and for patterns on the gold ground with a jewel-like effect which is brilliant and often very beautiful. Green is not used in the border decoration and only sparingly in the miniatures; an example is the swamp in which Salome is sinking in the Decollation of the Baptist. It is bluish in hue, probably the verdigris as used in the earlier part of the four-teenth century. Black is used for indicating facial features, for outlining, and for details, as the iron grills in buildings, and for shoes. White is used for highlights on faces, for the Carmelite cloaks, for veils, and for other details of costume. No attempt is made in this style to distinguish the texture of materials. There is some small evidence of shading and modelling with colour, especially in drapery folds, the method employed generally being that of darker tones on lighter of the same colour. Occasionally black or a different red or blue is added to deepen the tone.

The backgrounds of the miniatures in Style C are (a) gold stippled with groups of four dots (4/90, Pl. D) or with a running pattern (4/80, Pl. xxxiia); (b) gold and colour, diapered in geometrical designs (4/1, Pl. xiia); (c) solid colour decorated with a running vine pattern in gilt paint (4/26, Pl. xiib); (d) solid colour with a diaper or running vine pattern in a deeper shade (4/84, Pl. xia). By far the greater number of miniatures in Style C have backgrounds of type a; patterns consisting of groups of four dots frequently ornament garments, as in 4/59 (Pl. xiii).

The border decoration of Style C is painted chiefly in reds, pink, and blue—all rather strong shades. The motifs are, in general, those of the small initials in styles 2 and 3 (see above, pp. 69 f.); the 'kite' is used particularly freely. There is much strapwork and interlace, both in initial shafts and in the framework of the border. Some of the motifs are in a shaded technique, but most of them are painted in flat colour ornamented with conventional patterns in white. Both design and colour seem to indicate that the two C hands painted some of their own borders themselves, and that C¹, in addition, illuminated part of the small initials in the *Sanctorale* and *Commune Sanctorum*, in other parts than those containing his own miniatures.

For the comparison of the miniatures of Style C with certain other English manuscripts similar in style, the question of two separate illuminators working in the C style is of special importance. Although the outstanding characteristics of the style as described above are present in all the C miniatures, even to the facial types, yet their difference in quality is so great that it is difficult to believe that the same artist (even allowing for his good and bad days) could have produced such unequal work as, for example, the Annuncia-tion (4/8, Pl. x) and the Votive Trinity (4/90, Pl. xxxiii). The greatest difference in the degree of artistic skill displayed in these two initials is in the colouring: in the Annunciation the reds and blue are strong and harsh and they are unharmoniously combined, while in the Trinity they are clear and brilliant yet soft, and the extraordinarily deep, rich ultra-marine and the rose pink, with the small amount of vermilion, produce a colour harmony against the brilliantly burnished, tooled gold ground. The designs of the Annunciation artist, moreover, are less good than those of the Trinity painter; and there is uncertainty both in the drawing of the figure and in the painting of the faces, as well as lack of taste in the scheme of colouring. Another initial showing the same feeble workmanship of Hand C¹ is the Octave of the Apostles (4/26, Pl. xiib).

The explanation of these two artists' work in the Missal is difficult in view of the fact that the poorer one appears first; he may have been a Carmelite, since figures of Carmelite friars appear in most of the miniatures by his hand. Among possible explanations two are, perhaps, most plausible; the first hand of style C may have improved during the course of the work (but if so, the improvement seems to have taken place suddenly at one certain point); or, he was an imitator of a better style and, after having been tried out on the decoration of the Missal, his work may have proved unsatisfactory as compared with that of the artists of the *Temporale*, and he may have been replaced by another, more expert English miniaturist, Hand C[2], who painted the Saint Lawrence, the Assumption, and the Trinity. The first English miniaturist (*i.e.* Hand C[1]) may then have been set to doing the small decorative initials and perhaps painting some of the borders, since certain pages show the same hot colours, unharmoniously combined, as are found, for example in the Annunciation miniature. It is noteworthy that Hand C[1] uses decorative motifs in his border sprays which are more varied in form and more suggestive of East Anglian motifs than does Hand C[2]. Hand C[2] uses the kite on hair-line sprays almost exclusively, as in the latter part of Vienna 1826* (*q.v.* below).

The two manuscripts which are closest in style of decoration to the miniatures in Style C are a beautiful psalter in Edinburgh[1] made for Eleanor de Bohun, Duchess of Gloucester (*d.* 1399, Pl. XLII), and the first four quires of another psalter, in the British Museum[2] (Pl. XLIb). The facial types represented in these manuscripts are so closely related to those of Style C in the Missal as almost to suggest that the same individuals are pictured in the three manuscripts: the modelling of the features is identical; the hands are another striking point of identity among the three—large but expressive and with the thumb long and curving toward the fingers. Other features which we have noted in Style C are also present in the two other manuscripts: the consistent use of contemporary costume and even the same types of dress, as the woman's tight-fitting dress and mantle, the man's short, hooded tunic with elbow sleeves edged with points (as Zachariah in the Birth of the Baptist, Pl. XIIa). The Trinity in the Bohun Psalter (Pl. XLII) is very similar in type to that in the Missal (Pl. XXXIII). The method of shading drapery in darker tones of the same colour occurs in all three manuscripts, as well as such details as the 'turned down' angels' wings, the cruciform nimbus with projecting points (cf. Pls. XLIb, XLII, and XXXIII), the patterns in the floor tiles, the manner of representing trees, and the fondness for scrolls bearing inscriptions.

The colours used in the three manuscripts are very similar, although the shades vary slightly; but the manner of combining the colours, especially in the costume, is identical. The backgrounds in the Bohun Psalter are all gold leaf decorated with the groups of four dots; in the British Museum Psalter the first few miniatures have gold backgrounds decorated with circles of dots or running vine patterns, but the majority have plain burnished gold grounds. Some of the border designs in the Edinburgh Psalter are very similar to those in the Missal.

Two interesting points must be noted in the British Museum Psalter: one is the fact that the miniatures use a different colour scheme from that found in the border decorations, the motifs of which, moreover, are different from those in the Eleanor Bohun Psalter and

[1] Edinburgh, Nat. Libr. of Scotland, MS. Adv. 18.6.5.   [2] Add. MS. 16968.

in Style C of the Missal; the blue particularly, is entirely different from the good ultra-marine found in the Bohun and in the Missal, being much lighter, and slightly greenish in colour. Clearly the miniatures and the borders in Additional 16968 are by different hands, a conclusion which is supported by the complete detachment of the former from the other decoration. Moreover, the miniaturist several times put his pictures into miniatures instead of into initials, although the initial letters are necessary for the completion of the first word of the text passages which they introduce. In many cases small initial letters have actually been added later in a corner of the miniature, in the same colours as in the border. The other point to be noted in this manuscript is the occurrence in three of the miniatures of what is perhaps a signature of the miniaturist since it is in each case put in with the same kind of black as is used in the picture. It consists of the two letters *bu* or *bn* and is found on folios 10, 19 and 24 (not reproduced). No explanation of these letters has yet been found but they might be a clue to an identification of the miniaturist of this manuscript and there-fore to one of the English Missal hands. Which of the C artists it might be is difficult to say, for the British Museum Psalter seems to combine characteristics of both C¹ and C². Since the psalter appears to be slightly later than the Missal, the combination style in the psalter might be taken as evidence that Hand C¹ did develop into Hand C² as suggested above. But there is no way of proving this. At any rate the close similarity between the two psalters and the C style miniatures of the Missal is unmistakable.

The source of Style C may be traced back through the Edinburgh Bohun Psalter, which is one of the latest of a series of Psalters and Hours made for mem-bers of the Bohun family.[1] These show a most interesting development from the surviving East Anglian tradition, through Italian and other influences, to the English style of the late fourteenth century as represented in Style C of the Missal. The main steps in this development leading up to the style of the Edinburgh Bohun Psalter may now be traced briefly in order to establish beyond a doubt the English character of this tradition.

1. A psalter of the Bohun group in Vienna[2] is decorated in two distinct styles. In the early part, illustrated by fol. 15vo (Pl. XLa) the historiated initials and their decorative borders are painted in a debased version of the East Anglian style.[3] The technique is linear; figures and faces are cramped and lifeless and their composition is bad. The borders show a survival of East Anglian motifs, such as oak leaves and scroll work; the grotesque figure climbing in the foliage is a feeble reminder of the lively and inexhaustible humour found in the best East Anglian manuscripts of the early part of the fourteenth century. The grounds for both initial and border are of gold. The initial itself is formed of long-necked monsters, which remotely echo the Anglo-Celtic lacertine types.

In the latter part of the manuscript from fol. 50 onward (but probably not later in

---

[1] See M. R. James and Eric G. Millar, *The Bohun Manuscripts, a Group of Five Manuscripts Executed in England about 1370 for Members of the Bohun Family*, Roxburghe Club, Oxford, 1936. A sixth manu-script has since been added to the group and is now Egerton MS. 3277 in the British Museum.

[2] Nazionalbibl., MS. 1826*. Dated before 1372, since Humphrey de Bohun (d. 1372–3) was men-tioned in the prayers (the name now erased).

[3] For a discussion of the East Anglian style, see Sir Sydney Cockerell, *The Gorleston Psalter, . . . Described in Relation to Other East Anglian Books of the Period*, London, 1907. See also Eric Millar, *English Illuminated Manuscripts of the Fourteenth and Fifteenth Centuries*, Paris, 1928, pp. 1–10.

date, since there is a continuity in the decorative motifs of the borders), illustrated by fol. 153 (Pl. xl*b*) there is clear evidence of strong North Italian influence[1] on the earlier style. The figures have become larger and bolder, and the faces are of a new type, with rounded cheeks and bulging eyes whose heavy lids are emphasized by means of white highlights, as are also eyebrows, noses and mouths. Beards and hair are softly shaded, usually black; draperies also are shaded deeply and with a feeling for the play of light and shade among the folds of the soft material. The hands are large and conspicuous. Gold backgrounds are patterned with bolder designs, in square or diamond shapes. The decorative initial also is of different form; the motifs are larger and are shaded with white spots on colour.

2. A manuscript of Lancelot du Lac[2] written in French in the early part of the fourteenth century, has two miniatures painted over an earlier French style, and some coats of arms added in the later part of the century in a style closely corresponding to that which is found first, apparently, in the Vienna Bohun Psalter. Folio 102vo (Pl. xlc) of this manuscript illustrates the figure types with black beady eyes and soft black hair and beards. The coats of arms are those of Bohun combined with the royal arms of England; they may date therefore from not earlier than 1380 when Mary, the younger daughter of Humphrey de Bohun (for whom the Vienna manuscript was made) married Henry of Lancaster, later King Henry IV of England. The costumes and general style of the figures as well as the type of decoration carried out in the shaded technique which we saw in the Vienna manuscript, correspond closely to this and to certain other members[3] of the so-called Bohun group.

3. Bodleian MS. Laud. misc. 188 combines the Bohun style (the first five quires, of which fol. 1 is reproduced in Pl. xl1a) with a different and better East Anglian style in later parts, containing decoration similar to that which is found in 4 below.

4. The style thus formulated, apparently as a result of direct Italian influence on the remnants of the East Anglian tradition, becomes established as the characteristic English style, of which the most elaborate and magnificent example is the Lytlington Missal, made at Westminster Abbey in 1383–4. In this manuscript, however, there is perhaps additional Italian influence from a different source, namely, the mixture of French and Italian styles

---

[1] Political relations between Lombardy and England were particularly close in the third quarter of the fourteenth century. In 1366 power was given to Humphrey de Bohun, Earl of Hereford, and Sir Nicholas de Tamworth to treat for a marriage between Lionel Duke of Clarence and Violanta, daughter of Galeazzo Visconti, Lord of Milan, and Blanche of Savoy, or, alternatively, between Edmund Earl of Cambridge and Violanta (Rymer, *Foedera*, Westm. R. iii, p. ii, 797; O. vi, 509; H. iii, p. ii, 114). The marriage of Lionel and Violanta was solemnized at Milan in 1368 and brought a large number of Englishmen to Italy. See warrant for a payment of expenses of passage from Dover to Calais of the Duke of Clarence going to Milan with 457 men and 1280 horses in his retinue. (*Ibid*, Westm. R. iii, 845; O. vi, 590; H. iii, p. ii, 145). One of these was Sir Edward le Despenser (*ibid.*, Westm. R. iii, 843) who has been identified as the courtier in white wearing the English Garter, in the fresco of the Church Triumphant in the Spanish Chapel of S.M. Novella, Florence. (See Sister Mary Aquinas Devlin, 'An English Knight of the Garter in the Spanish Chapel in Florence', *Speculum*, IV (1929), pp. 270–81.) A Book of Hours in Munich (Staatsbibl., Cod. Lat. 23215) illuminated for Blanche of Savoy (d. 1387) by Giovanni da Como (see inscription at the beginning of the manuscript) probably about 1378, combines with North Italian miniatures, borders containing both Italian acanthus leaves and English kite motifs. This would seem to indicate the presence of English illuminators or manuscripts in Italy, and it would not be unreasonable to expect an exchange of influences between English and Italian styles.

[2] Brit. Mus. Roy. MS. 20 D. IV.

[3] Notably Brit. Mus. Egerton MS. 3277, also containing the arms of Bohun and of England.

as found in the school of Avignon: the figures in the fine Crucifixion,[1] though Italian in type, are very linear in style.

5. A manuscript of English statutes, dating after 1386,[2] represents the English figure style in a form approximating that which we find in Hand C in the Missal. The figures are still done in outline technique but the faces are modelled in brown and white and elaborate care is shown in the details of costume. The initial is filled with shaded patterns and the background is patterned in lozenges, varied with circles. The style is not beautiful but has a certain richness of colouring and often considerable interest in subject matter, as in the miniature here reproduced, which represents King Edward III and his son Edward, the Black Prince, both clad in armour blazoned with the royal arms (Pl. XLd).

6. A copy of William of Nottingham's Commentary on the Four Gospels[3] given, according to an inscription on fol. 13, by Archbishop Thomas Arundel to Canterbury in 1397, has on fol. 5 a miniature of him enthroned among clerics, one of whom is offering him the book (Pl. XLIII). The miniature is painted in the C Style and the decoration has the same hot colour and heavy shading as in Hand C[1] of the Missal (e.g. the Annunciation, Pl. X).

These and other manuscripts of about the same time and in the same general style, would suggest a London shop, with a number of different illuminators working together for king and court and also for Westminster Abbey. Two of these illuminators may have been engaged on the Carmelite Missal also; or if one or both of the Hands C were Carmelite, he may have learned his craft under the influence of the current London style.

The English tradition is at its best in such illustrative compositions as we have seen in the Missal, for instance, those representing scenes from the life of Lawrence, where the love of detail in costume and gesture gives the picture a varied and lively interest, and where the intricate patterning and fine colour of the borders make a richly decorated page.

The Bohemian Tradition: Style B

The chief *Temporale* artist, Hand B, was primarily a magnificent decorator. All his compositions are planned in such a way as to fill the space with a well-balanced design which at the same time is adapted to the shape of the initial; we may note, for example, how the line of the heads of Christ and the Disciples in the Last Supper scene (fol. 38, Pl. VI) follows the curve of the initial; similarly, the row of Disciples in the Pentecost picture

---

[1] Reproduced in Millar, *op. cit.*, Pl. 71. In the abbot's treasurer's roll of 1383–4 is a payment to Fr W. Warfeld for board and lodging of Thomas Preston while he was writing the Missal; and in the same accounts are payments for materials, illumination, and other items including binding of the Missal; for painting the Crucifixion ten shillings were paid. See Robinson, J. A., and James, M. R., *The Manuscripts of Westminster Abbey*, London, 1909, p. 8. Thomas Rolf who is mentioned in other documents as illuminating another missal for the Abbey, appears twice in the London records as 'lumynour': *Calendar of Select Plea and Memoranda Rolls*, 1381–1412, ed. A. H. Thomas (1892), p. 52, May 5, 1385; *Calendar of Close Rolls*, 13 Rich. II, p. 151, Feb. 25, 1390. The figure style in the Lytlington Missal Crucifixion and in some of the other miniatures, seems to suggest Sienese influence rather than North Italian. This may have resulted from contacts with Avignon through Cardinal Simon Langham, former Abbot of Westminster, who died at Avignon in 1376, leaving his books to the Abbey. Among those listed (see Robinson and James, *op. cit.*) there is no record of illuminations, but there may well have been some.

[2] Brit. Mus. Cott. MS. Nero D. VI. Dated by the textual contents. Another manuscript in the same style is Oxford, Bodl. MS. 581, made for Richard II and dated on internal evidence after 1391.

[3] Bodl. MS. Laud. misc. 165.

(fol. 27vo, Pl. IV) corresponds in its curve to the contour of the letter *S*. The designs are linear and flat, not three-dimensional.

The figures are rather tall and unsubstantial and are enveloped in draperies with voluminous folds which swirl about their feet. There is a good deal of uniformity in the figure types and drapery folds, but this very repetition of lines (which, owing to the colour, is less disturbing in the original than in a reproduction) gives a suave and harmonious rhythm to the design.

The faces in Style B are lightly modelled in a technique entirely different from that used by other artists in the Missal. The flesh colour is pale, the shadows are slightly green; there is a characteristic pink spot between the eyes and a half-circle of white is placed uniformly round the iris of the eye intended, presumably, to give the eye liveliness of expression. A number of lines in white are used also on the faces to indicate expression, particularly horizontal lines on the forehead, as in the face of God the Father in the Trinity picture (Pl. v). The modelling of the faces seems to follow a formula as, indeed, the facial types do also; they are very broad across the top of the head and narrow in the lower part of the face, and short from forehead to chin. Other characteristic features of the faces are the high, arched eyebrows and the heavy, drooping mouths.

The colouring is extraordinarily beautiful (Pl. B). Paler than Style C, the colours have an almost opalesque quality owing to the use of much white, both mixed with colours and superimposed on them. The pinks are particularly soft and lovely; the ultramarine is of the finest quality; the green is pale and bluish; and the red is true vermilion. Especially remarkable is the use of white for diaphanous materials, as the veil of the lady in the Baptismal scene (Pl. v) and the graveclothes in the Easter picture (Pl. 11).

The border ornament of Hand B is somewhat different in design as well as in colouring from that of Style C. There is a distinctly symmetrical, balanced arrangement of the foliate motifs, as in Italian early fourteenth century borders.[1] Moreover, the long serrated, curling leaf (the so-called acanthus) common in Italian manuscripts and found also in another form in Hand A, is occasionally used in place of the framework bar (fol. 21vo, Pl. III). The motifs used in the border sprays are the same as in the large decorative initials, especially those of the better illuminator: kites, thimbles, and spoons; variations of certain simple flower forms are also used. There is a good deal of variety in the motifs; this and the very beautiful luminous colouring against the exquisite, highly burnished, stippled gold ground make the borders and the historiated initials harmonize especially well, both in design and in colouring. In every detail of the work done by this miniaturist, his excellence as a designer and decorator is outstanding.

An analysis of the style of Hand B shows it to be full of puzzles and therefore much more difficult to explain than the English Style C, whose antecedents are clearly recognizable. Hand B seems to follow no single, clear-cut tradition, either English or foreign, but uses elements of both. The facial and figure types, the handling of the drapery folds, and the colouring in Hand B are closest to the style of the Liber Regalis,[2] written perhaps for or soon after the coronation of Anne of Bohemia at the time of her marriage to Richard

---

[1] Similar border designs are found also in Bohemian manuscripts of the Johann von Neumarkt group. See below, p. 78, n. 1.
[2] In the Library of Westminster Abbey.

II in 1382. It contains four large miniatures representing the crowning of a king, the crowning of a king and a queen (see Pl. XLIV), the crowning of a queen, and the burial of a king. These miniatures are surrounded by narrow border bands in colour containing simple, conventional, white line patterns. The border sprays are like those in the Lytlington Missal made at Westminster slightly earlier.

The backgrounds of the miniatures in the Liber Regalis are of very fine burnished gold, decorated with elaborate stippled scroll patterns resembling those in miniatures by Hand B. The most remarkable feature of these miniatures is the magnificent colouring: deep, rich ultramarine, soft shaded pink, and brilliant vermilion such as are used by Hand B in the Missal. It is the figures, however, that show the most striking similarity to those of Hand B, especially the types of faces with long noses, foreheads highlighted with white, drooping mouths, and a sly expression in the eyes, caused by the crowding of the iris into the extreme corner of the eye socket and emphasizing the white of the eye. Hands and feet are also very similar to those of Hand B, especially the hands, which are very wide across the knuckles and have long, tapering fingers usually held close together at the tips, thus forming a point, yet with wide spaces between them—most unnatural-looking hands, and generally very conspicuously placed; these hands are more exaggerated in the Liber Regalis than in the miniatures by Hand B, but the type is the same. The modelling of the faces in the Liber Regalis is soft, consisting chiefly of patches of pink or red, and white lines on greenish-grey flesh tone. In Hand B, the faces are somewhat rounder and the expressions are more childlike and less sly than in the Liber Regalis; nevertheless, there is an unmistakable similarity in the general types of the figures in the two manuscripts. The draperies, also, which swirl about the figures, and the interest in the representation of texture and materials are characteristic of the miniatures in both manuscripts.

The problem of establishing the source of the Liber Regalis style does not lie within the scope of the present study. It may help to accentuate the stylistic characteristics of Hand B, however, at least to suggest what appears to be the most likely explanation of this curious style. Many characteristic features of the peculiar figure types in the Liber Regalis are found in Bohemian manuscripts: the awkward positions of the seated figures and of the feet of the standing ones, the voluminous, clinging drapery with many superfluous folds, and most of all, the strangely-shaped hands and fingers. The feeble, superficial modelling, moreover, suggests similarities between the Bohemian style of painting and that of the Liber Regalis, while the colours, fine in quality and heavily overlaid with white in some of the Bohemian miniatures, also are very like those used in the Liber Regalis. Close parallels to the Liber Regalis figures, however, I do not find in either the earlier group of manuscripts made for Johann von Neumarkt[1] or in the later ones made for Wenzel,[2] but rather the style seems to fall between the two. In general, Hand B's colouring and exquisite decorative sense suggest the earlier style of the gospel book, Vienna 1182, illuminated in 1368, rather than that of the later *Wenzelsbibel* and related manuscripts.

[1] E.g., Vienna, Nazionalbibl. MS. 1182, signed and dated 1368 on fol. 91. Reproduced in colour by Max Jaffè, Vienna, 1948. See also Max Dvořak, 'Die Illuminatoren des Johann von Neumarkt', *Jahrbuch der Kuntshistorischen Sammlungen des allerhöchsten Kaiserhauses*, XXII (1901), pp. 35–126.

[2] Vienna, Nazionalbibl. Cod. 2759–64 (Ambras. 17). 6 vols. See Dr. Julius von Schlosser, 'Die Bilderhandschriften Königs Wenzel I,' *ibid.*, XIV (1893), pp. 214–319.

The sinuous draperies clinging to the figure yet flowing round it in soft, supple folds (as in the Carmelites of fol. 38, Pl. VI), the variety of shaded motifs in the rich border decoration, and especially the symmetry of the designs and the combination of interlace and softly curling acanthus leaves, suggest Hand B's familiarity with the Bohemian ornamental style.

Two other manuscripts, with decoration in pure English style, have miniatures displaying in different ways close affinities with those of the Liber Regalis; they are (1) a missal in Trinity College, Oxford, MS. 8, dating from before 1388[1] and (2) a book of Statutes in Saint John's College, Cambridge (MS. A.7) dated by its contents after 1387. These manuscripts may be transitional between the Liber Regalis and the Carmelite Missal and thus they may represent the influence of the Bohemian artist on the English style.

The Trinity College Missal contains historiated initials and beautiful decorative letters and partial borders on a very small scale but of very fine quality. The decorative work is so close in design and colour to that of the Canon and Prefaces in the Carmelite Missal (Pl. XLVa), as to suggest the same hand. The historiated initials show a variation in style as the work progresses. The first two (fols. 9 and 12) contain figures painted in a lightly modelled style which suggests an un-Italianate English tradition, but of much better quality and later date than, for example, the early part of the Vienna Bohun manuscript. On fol. 44vo an historiated initial containing an Adoration of the Magi has modelling in pinkish flesh colour with white highlights and the features indicated with lines in darker flesh pink. The drawing, though on a minute scale, is very precise, and the colour is rich, with a great deal of fine green used in the garments. On fols. 131vo and pages following to the end of the Missal, the modelling is in a still different technique which is extremely close both to that of the Liber Regalis and to Hand B. The miniature which is closest to Hand B is the Trinity (fol. 157vo, Pl. XLVa) of the *Gnadenstuhl* type as in the Trinity initial by Hand B in the Carmelite Missal (Pl. V).

It is difficult to know how to place this style in chronological relation to the Liber Regalis and the Carmelite Missal, if the hand is the same. The decoration of Hand B's pages is very different from that of the Trinity College Missal which, however, as noted above, is almost identical with the decoration on the Canon and Preface pages of the Carmelite book. There are two possible alternative explanations: if the hand of the miniatures in the two manuscripts is the same, the Trinity College manuscript might represent a slightly earlier stage of an English artist's style which had been influenced by the Liber Regalis but not directly by Bohemian decorative style; or (and perhaps this is more likely) if the Liber Regalis artist (and Hand B) were Bohemian, he painted only the pictures in the latter part of the Trinity College Missal and the English illuminator who had begun the decoration of the book continued to paint the decorative initials and sprays throughout. In this connection it will be remembered that the decorative initials and sprays in the *Temporale* of the Carmelite Missal also are in a different style from the decoration attached to Hand B's historiated initials. In any case, the miniatures in the latter part of the Trinity College Missal are the closest I have found to Hand B's style.

[1] On fol. 4vo (Calendar page for April) is recorded the birth in 1388 of Eleanor, first daughter of William Beauchamp, brother of the Earl of Warwick. Similar entries for later births (1397 and 1403) are recorded on other Calendar pages.

The second manuscript which shows in a different way the influence of the Liber Regalis, the Saint John's College Statutes, is also decorated in a thoroughly English initial and border style, much more elaborate as to amount and richness than the Trinity Missal. The Saint John's Statutes were made for Richard II and contain the portraits of successive English kings from Henry III (Pl. xlv*b*) to Richard. The portraits are obviously copied from the king-type in the Liber Regalis, and all are very much alike in detail as well as in the painting technique. Like the faces of Hand B, these, too, are modelled with strong white lines and spots, but the flesh tone is brownish rather than greenish-grey, and modelling is done mainly in white after the manner of the Bohun manuscripts. The intricate patterning of the draperies, the curious shape of the hands, and the adherence to a single type in representing the kings (the only important difference between them being the colour of the hair) suggest an artist who is consciously copying a model, with consequent exaggeration of certain features, rather than one who is working in an understood technique. The Statutes seem to be the result of the influence of the Liber Regalis style directly on the Italianate English tradition as developed in the Bohun manuscripts, rather than the work of either Hand B or the Liber Regalis artist himself.

The further activity of Hand B after his participation in the Carmelite Missal is unknown. The extraordinary, unorthodox spirit of his Corpus Christi miniature (see above, pp. 50 f.) might suggest that this was the last picture he was allowed to do in the Missal. But on the other hand, he may have died or ceased working for some other reason; or it is possible, though not likely, that he came under some other strong influence, such as that of Hand A, his collaborator in the *Temporale*, and that his style was in consequence transformed so as to be unrecognizable. He is an extremely interesting personality and a fine illuminator, and it would be highly desirable to find more of his work in England or on the Continent.[1]

The Dutch Tradition: Style A

The outstanding characteristics of Style A thus far noted are the composition of figures arranged in three-dimensional space, the substantiality of these figures, and above all, the expressiveness of their highly modelled faces, particularly their lively eyes and the naturalness and appropriateness of their gestures. It is clearly a painter's technique, for the composition, instead of remaining suitably enclosed within the flat space of the initial ground, pushes out over the boundaries formed by the initial letter and sometimes includes this in the three-dimensional space by placing it partly behind the architectural features as in 4/18 (fol. 93, Pl. ix) and 4/51 (fol. 165, Pl. xxx); sometimes on the other hand, the initial letter is treated as if it were a frame through which the spectator looks in upon the scene (as in 4/55, Pl. xx). The figures both inside and outside the space enclosed by the initial, are included in the design, as, for instance, in the Dedication of the Church (4/89, Pl. vii) where two seated figures in the lower corners of the gold field are supporting the initial letter as though it were a hoop. In another initial containing the Exaltation of the Cross (fol. 140, Pl. xix*a*) the horse in the foreground steps out over the initial shaft while another horse has his head thrust out beyond the framework. One of the most remarkable

---

[1] Dr Otto Paecht informs me that he has seen a manuscript in the library at Valenciennes which he believes to be by Hand B. I have not seen this manuscript.

examples of this type of composition is the Conception of the Virgin (4/51, Pl. xxx) in which a figure in the upper right corner holds in his two hands the twisted cords which form the initial letter; these cords issue from behind the building in the temple scene. In this same picture, the angels in the shaft of the initial play an important part in the scene, the one on the right speaking to Joachim, that on the left addressing Anna.

Usually only one scene is represented in any one initial, but when there is more than one, as in the pictures of Andrew (4/73, fol. 163, Pl. xxviia), Catherine (4/71, fol. 161vo, Pl. xxv), Martin (4/52, fol. 159, Pl. xxi), and the Conception of the Virgin (4/51, fol. 165, Pl. xxx) they are closely united into a single composition rather than represented as separate incidents occurring in a chronological sequence. There are three different schemes used in combining these scenes within the initial. First, dividing the space horizontally into an upper and a lower stage, each having depth from front to back, the boundary between the two forming the extreme foreground of the upper stage and also cutting off the far background of the lower stage. This arrangement is found in the miniatures of Martin and Catherine. Second, the obvious use of the natural divisions of the initial as the *M* in the Andrew picture to represent two scenes having separate spatial settings. Third, including several scenes in a continuous setting, thus representing the same persons more than once in the same spatial composition. The only example of this latter method is the Conception of the Virgin initial with scenes from the story of Joachim and Anna. Here the temple and the Golden Gate are situated in the same wooded setting in which Joachim is seen tending his flocks. The remarkable thing about Hand A's treatment of this very old-fashioned type of continuous narrative composition is the way in which he has given it a real spatial unity.

The figures are usually short and rather heavy-set, but occasionally are very tall and slender as Edmund (4/74, fol. 160vo Pl. xxiiia). In general, they are well drawn both in form and pose. Hand A's chief interest in drapery is its potential value for indicating the bulkiness of the figure underneath rather than in making a linear surface pattern out of the folds, as is characteristic of French gothic drapery. Folds are usually summarily indicated by irregular painted lines rather than by light and shade; the colours used most commonly to indicate shading are mauve or blue on white, brown on vermilion, crimson on pink, and white on blue.

Faces are invariably modelled with paint, though the colours show considerable variety in tone. Usually the underpainting of flesh is dark greyish-green or brown, and the modelling is done by means of highlighted areas in white chiefly on forehead, nose, cheek-bone, upper lip, and chin. Pink is used on the cheeks, often adjoining the white and thus intensifying it; red is used on nostrils and lips, and on the chin to indicate the hollow under the lower lip. Eyebrows are usually short and dark, seldom arched, but tilted up or down to give expression. Eyes are made lively by the use of a strong white spot contrasting with the dark iris; this is placed in different positions in the eye socket to indicate the focus and expression of the eyes. Dark shadows are used at the inner corner of the eyes, under the chin and on the neck. The modelling of the far side of the face is accentuated either by placing a dark background behind the head for strong contrast, or by a heavy brown contour line, if the background is light. There are indications that the artist observed and attempted to represent the foreshortening of the far side of the face, by lowering the far eye in relation to the near one. Sometimes the result is very successful, as in 4/89 (fol. 68vo, Pl. VII). Often, however, the far eye is thrown out of focus thus giving a slightly wall-eyed expression to the face, as in the Christ head of the same miniature (4/38). There is an amazing variety in facial types and a striking differentiation in age and in expression. If we compare, for instance, any one type of head, as the bearded men in the miniature just referred to (4/89), the Conversion of Paul (4/48, fol. 90, Pl. VIII), the Purification of the Virgin (4/18, fol. 93, Pl. IX), and the Conception of the Virgin (4/51, fol. 165, Pl. XXX), we find an individuality in each of these figures; the same is true, though in a lesser degree, of the female types. On the other hand, the representations of the same person in different pictures are carefully duplicated, as Andrew (fols. 162, 163 and 165, Pls. XXVI and XXVII).

The pigments used by Hand A are painter's colours (cf. Pls. A and C): pure ultramarine of excellent quality; rich vermilion; soft lake pink shaded with lake or madder red; dull yellow shaded lightly with vermilion; and very dull, dark green which, in many instances, is more blue than green and looks like a mixed colour. This is used invariably for the ground and trees in landscape settings. In addition to these colours, black and browns, greys, and terracotta in various tones are used, chiefly for architecture. The strong, rich colours are incredibly beautiful in combination with the gleaming burnished and stippled gold of the backgrounds.

One of the most characteristic and convincing uses of shading in colour is in the serrated scrolls or the folded leaves forming, in many instances, the shaft of the initial. A fine example is the Holy Saturday initial (4/93, fol. 6 vo, Pl. I) where the leafy scroll twists round and round most realistically with (seemingly) space between the folds. The colour here is grey touched with white for the high lights and with black for the shadows. Similar leaf scrolls coloured blue and shaded with white and black are seen in the Conversion of Paul (4/48, fol. 90, Pl. VIII), and in the Martyrdom of Edmund (4/74, fol. 160vo, Pl. XXIIIa) there are pink ones. When not composed of serrated leaves the initial shafts in Hand A's work are either filled with monochrome angels in blue, pink, or light red (All Saints miniature, 4/55, fol. 152vo, Pl. XX) or, rarely, formed by flat interlaced designs as in the Saint Loy initial (4/69, fol. 164, Pl. XXVIII).

To sum up the pictorial style of Hand A, it is plastically conceived throughout: scenes, figures, and initial decoration are all thought of as having substance and potential movement in three directions. It is an amazing early manifestation of that type of realism which formed the basis of Northern Renaissance painting in the early part of the fifteenth century.

The borders which join the historiated initials in Style A also show new elements: a long serrated leaf turning over and over, changing colour at each turn, which issues from the tip of the initial itself and continues a little way into the margin, and delicate hair-line sprays containing tiny gold motifs, chiefly trefoils, which issue from the points of the gold ground on which the acanthus scroll is placed, and extend out into the margin combining in a most pleasing manner with the heavier acanthus leaf scroll. Another use of the hair-line sprays and gold motifs is in combination with a heavier coloured branch bearing ivy leaf motifs and other lobed leaves in gold or heavy colours (Pl. XVIIb). These two elements, the acanthus scroll and the hair-line spray with tiny gold motifs, are found only with Hand A miniatures; but it is true that other historiated initials by this artist have borders in a heavily shaded version of the typical English style found in the decorative initials and on pages illuminated by Hands C (Pl. xxv). Sometimes this heavy-stem style is combined with serrated scroll forms and motifs suggesting the more formal border of Hand B (Pl. 1). This variation in border styles on Hand A pages may mean that the illuminators (as distinct from the miniaturists) were influenced by one another to a greater degree than were the miniaturists. It may also mean that only in certain instances Hands A painted their own border decorations.

As to the origin of Hand A's style, comparison of a single typical head with one by Hand C will demonstrate that it is not English. A comparison of the same head with one by Hand B will show less striking differences, but the solidity of modelling and the liveliness of expression in a Hand A head are lacking in Hand B. It is obvious that the source of this modelled style must be sought elsewhere than in the English or even in the Bohemian tradition, as found in the Missal.

The closest parallels to Hand A's figures thus far found are in the so-called Gelder *Wapengedichten en Wapenboek* (Brussels, Bibl. Roy. MS. 15652–56).[1] Three pages (fols. 15vo, 26 and 122) in this collection of heraldry and heraldic poems are painted in a style which is very different in character from the precise drawing and flat colour of most of the heraldic painting. Two of these pages are not in the text itself: fol. 26 with the Emperor and Electors miniature (Pl. XLVII) is inserted as a separate leaf, cut down and obviously originally designed for a different manuscript, suggesting, in fact, a picture for the head of a rotulus or a document (perhaps a copy of the Golden Bull)[2] not in codex form. The line drawn under the picture (now partly visible on the right margin of the page) may have separated the picture from the text beneath it. The other full page miniature (fol. 122, Pl. XLVIII) with the picture of a herald wearing a mantle blazoned with the arms of the Duke of Gelder, now forms one of the fly leaves at the end of the volume. The third leaf in this style in the *Wapenboek* (fol. 15vo, Pl. XLVIa), however, is a part of the original manuscript. It is, in fact, only on the verso of this leaf that the modelled style appears. The coat of arms in the left column is that of the count of Holland; the same coat appears again on another folio,[3] in the flat 'armorial' style, and a comparison of the two shows clearly the difference in technique: the helm, the mantling, the crown and even the peacock eyes on

---

[1] Published in facsimile by Victor Bouton, *Wapenboek ou Armorial de 1334 à 1372 . . . précédé de poésies héraldiques par Gelre, héraut d'armes*, Paris, 1881–86. The date of the *Wapenboek* and the identification of Gelre herald have been the subject of much disagreement. For a bibliography, see Ulysse Chevalier, *Biobibliographie*, I, Paris, 1905, col. 1687 (under Gelre). The most recent historical study of the manuscript is by W. A. Beelaerts van Blokland, *Beyeren quondam Gelre, Armorum Rex de Ruyris*, published by the Koninklijk Nederlandsch Genootschap voor Geslacht en Wapenkunde, The Hague, 1933. See also Gaspar, Camille, and Lyna, Frédéric, *Les principaux manuscrits à peintures de la Bibliothèque Royale de Belgique*, (Soc. franc. de reprod. des manuscrits à peintures), Paris, 1937, I, pp. 372–7.

[2] There is some difference of opinion as to the interpretation of this miniature. It is usually thought (cf. Beelaerts, *op. cit.*, pp. 24 f.) to represent the Emperor Charles IV (d. 1378) and the seven electors, as named in the Golden Bull issued by Charles in 1356. It has also been suggested, however, that the seven figures represent the Estates of Germany, namely, the Clergy, the Nobility, the Bourgeoisie, and the Peasantry. The seventh figure (at the extreme right) could perhaps be the herald Gelder. (Cf. Gaspar and Lyna, *op. cit.*, p. 375.) The interpretation of the miniature as the Emperor and his Electors seems most likely, although there is no resemblance between the Emperor and other portraits of Charles IV. If intended to represent him, it is an idealized portrait. M. Lyna dates the two miniatures 1370–80, and says of the artist, 'The herald Gelre who was the artist was gifted with an extremely sure and sensitive hand.' *Ibid.*, p. 376.

[3] Beelaerts, *op. cit.*, opp. p. 44.

the crest are shaded to suggest roundness of form. The arms of Rudolf of Nydou (*d.* 1375) in the right column, containing a charming girl's head as a crest, is modelled in a manner similar to that of the girl's head in the flower of the border in the Holy Saturday miniature (4/93, fol. 6vo, Pl. I) and of the head of Saint Anne in the Nativity of the Virgin (4/13, fol. 138vo, Pl. XVIII). The contour of these three heads is identical: the high, rounded forehead, the curve of the cheek, the small, fat chin. The features, too, are very similar: the wide-open eyes, the prominent nose, the long upper lip, and the full, red mouth drooping slightly at the near corner. Even more striking is the technique in which the heads in the two manuscripts are modelled. In the Brussels head we find again the high lights painted with white on forehead, cheek-bone, nose, upper lip, and chin, as in the Missal. Red is used on the far side of the nose, on the nostril (the opening is touched with brown to give depth), on the full lips (a white spot on the lower lip represents the light shining on the moist surface). The eyebrows are short and straight and there is modelling in brown both above and below the eye. In all three heads the contour of the far side of the face is sharpened either by contrasting with it a dark background (as the head in the flower on fol. 6vo) or by a firm, brown line as in the Brussels head and that of Saint Anne (fol. 138vo). In fact, the resemblance between these two latter heads is so striking in their technical handling as to leave little room for doubt that they are the work of the same master; the only real difference between the two heads is in the ages of the two women: the young girl with a fatter, rounder face and a more petulant expression; Saint Anne with a more mature face and a serious, contemplative expression.

The Empire picture on fol. 26 (Pl. XLVII) does not as a whole resemble any one miniature in the Missal so closely as does the head of the girl. Nevertheless, some of the different types represented in it can be paralleled in the Missal, as can also the position of the figures, their hands and feet, their draperies, and above all the modelling, which is suggested even though the technique is line drawing.

The type of head of the Emperor, with its broad forehead, prominent brows, pointed nose, long, full beard parted in the centre, with long moustache ends mingling with it, is found also in the heads of Paul (4/48, fol. 90, Pl. VIII) and Giles (4/50, fol. 138, Pl. XVII*b*). The finer pen technique lightly washed with thin colour has given the Brussels head a greater delicacy in the representation of the hair as well as in the modelling of the contours of the face; the identity of the type in the three pictures, however, is unmistakable. In both manuscripts, also, the method of shading the mass of the hair close to the face is the same. The other heads in the Brussels Empire picture can be matched in the Missal in quality though not so closely in exact type as the Emperor: the three prelates suggest at once the single figures of bishops and archbishops in the Missal and, even more, perhaps, the two bishops in the miniature of the consecration of Saint Martin (4/52, fol. 159, Pl. XXI). The man in the pointed hat in the Empire picture resembles in face as well as in headgear one of the companions of Paul in the Conversion (fol. 90). The amazing variety in types of faces and in expressions in the Brussels miniature is one of the outstanding characteristics of Hand A in the Missal.

The shape of the hands in the two manuscripts, usually with long first and middle fingers, is very similar in spite of the differences in the technique of rendering them with pen and paint. The Saint Nicholas miniature (4/91, fol. 164vo, Pl. XXIX) shows the bishop with this kind of hand, and also the kneeling youth drawn with brown ink outside in the margin. The fingers in these hands are separated widely and there is a tendency to bring the tips together in a manner which is not possible in actual life unless the fingers are either crooked or are pressed very tightly together. In both manuscripts the positions of the hands show a great deal of variety.

The herald picture in the *Wapenboek* (Pl. XLVIII) can best be compared with figures of the archers in the Martyrdom of Edmund in the Missal (4/74, Pl. XXIIIa) in the modelling of the feet and legs, the proportions of the figure and the delineation of the features of the herald (insofar as they can be seen through the oxydization of the pigments used in the modelling of the face). The herald seems to combine the two techniques of the Empire miniature and the Missal artist: the tunic with belt and dagger, and the hands and arms are done in tinted outline shaded with pen strokes; the rest of the figure and apparently even the face is painted with heavy pigments. It is a remarkable figure, full of vigour and strongly suggesting a portrait, of the Gelre herald who perhaps wrote[1] some of the poems in the *Wapenboek*: he wears the blazon of William Duke of Gelder[2] before he became also Duke of Juliers at the death of his father in 1393. The portrait element is also present in the work of Hand A in the Missal, as, for instance, in the lay figures who participate in the Dedication of the Church (4/89, Pl. VII), and the two figures outside this miniature, supporting the initial letter. The kneeling youth outside the Saint Nicholas miniature is a figure similar to the herald. From all these similarities there would seem to be little doubt that Hand A of the Missal and the artist of the three miniatures in the *Wapenboek* were the same person.

The *Wapenboek* has been variously dated from 1334 (this date appearing on the first page, in the first of the three hands who wrote the poems) to the end of the century. The poem about Rudolf of Nydou (*d.* 1375), with his arms containing the finely modelled girl's head, is in the second hand, presumed to be that of the son of the first Gelre herald who began the poems and who is supposed to have disappeared after the battle of Bastweiler, at which his master, Duke Edward of Gelder, was killed. In 1372 there was contention over the succession in Gelder, and, through the instrumentality of Emperor Charles IV, William, son of the Duke of Juliers, was designated to succeed as Duke of Gelder when he came of age in 1379. It would seem reasonable that the continuation of the poems in the *Wapenboek* might have dated from this time; at any rate, the herald portrait on fol. 122 dates from before 1393. The Emperor picture can perhaps be dated before the death of Charles in 1378. Thus the three pictures attributed to Hand A of the Missal fall within a time which is possible for earlier work than the illumination of the Carmelite Missal.

Some further documentary evidence lends weight to the possible early association of

---

[1] In a eulogy on the Duke of Juliers (d. 1393), father of William of Gelder, occur the following lines:

'mi dunct ic heb di gesien wel elre	('I think I have seen you elsewhere
en bistu niet geheiten gelre	and aren't you called Gelder?
du pleechst te dichten ente scriven'	you are wont to compose verses and to write')

Whether this Gelre herald, thought to be self-described as a poet in the foregoing lines, was the painter of this and the other two miniatures in this remarkable modelled style is, to my mind, highly questionable. The lines quoted are on fol. 19 of the *Wapenboek*.

[2] Cf. P. N. Doorninck and J. S. Van Veen, *De Graven en Hertogen van Gelre*, Arnhem, 1904, with ducal seals. See also the Gelder arms on fol. 88vo of the Brussels *Wapenboek*.

Hand A with Gelder. This is concerned with the close political connections between the Duke and Richard II of England and especially with the visit of the Duke accompanied by a large retinue to England in 1390. The visit is recorded in Froissart,[1] who speaks of the lavish entertainment provided by the English relatives of William of Gelder. Moreover, in the household accounts of William[2] for the years 1389–90, two heralds, 'Herman die Coningk' and 'Gelre' are given new clothes for the English journey. The public appearances and festivities which took place during the visit of the Duke undoubtedly required, in addition to the services of the heralds, artists to paint the heraldic devices. One of these, perhaps the one who collaborated in the painting of the Gelder *Wapenboek*, may have been Hand A, who was then invited to do some of the work on the Carmelite Missal (cf. Appendix B).

There is no one recognizable source for the style of the three miniatures in the *Wapenboek*. They do not seem to be either Italian or French, though the linear technique might suggest this latter influence somewhere in the background of their origin. The girl's head in the Rudolf of Nydou arms recalls in some general aspects the many heads of similar type on one of the fine pages in Johann von Troppau's Gospel book of 1368[3] but these are entirely different in proportions, expression, and above all, in technique. The *Wapenboek* head is more solid, and less mannered than the Bohemian heads. In fact, the miniatures in the *Wapenboek* seem not so much to derive from any style as to be the outgrowth of an individual interest and a natural skill in delineating types of persons, especially faces.

This individual skill apparently underwent some technical changes under the influence of a painting style, perhaps a phase of Bohemian style later [4] than that of the Johann von Troppau manuscript, and similar to that of another Vienna manuscript (Nazionalbibl. MS. 2765), a German translation of Durandus' *Rationale*. As the style of painting on fol. 1 (Pl. XLIX) is unique in the manuscript, and as fol. 1vo obviously was begun by the same hand and finished by another who, apparently, continued the decoration into succeeding parts of the manuscript, it seems probable that fol. 1 was painted shortly after the text of the Preface to the translation was written in 1384, by an artist who then departed, leaving the continuation of the decoration to other hands. The style of this second artist, though clearly based on that of fol. 1, is different and has no direct relation to Hand A's style.

The enlivening and individualizing of the faces on fol. 1 of Cod. 2765 is due to the variation in the positions of the heads, to the colour and texture of the hair and beards, and most of all to the eyes, which look naturally in one direction or another, even straight ahead in full-face views, and have a lively sparkle owing to the use of a tiny spot of white, setting off a dark pupil. Eyebrows, too, are no longer uniformly arched as in the earlier

---

[1] *Chroniques*, ed. Kervyn de Lettenhove, Brussels, 1871, XIII, p. 33. The date, however, seems to be confused with that of the earlier visit (1387) of the Duke's envoys who went to England to arrange an alliance between William and Richard. For a documented account of both visits, see Ernsing, Rudolf, 'William III von Julich', *Münsterische Beiträge zur Geschichtsforschung*, Heft 8, 1885.

[2] *Rekeningen van den landrentmeestergeneral van Gelre* fol. 72, in the Rijksarchief in Gelderland, at Arnhem (unpublished). Some further items from these accounts are included and discussed in Appendix B below.

[3] See p. 78, note 1 above.

[4] But not the phase found in the *Wenzelbibel* and other related manuscripts. Cf. p. 78, note 2 above.

Gospel book, but are often straight lines, slanting upward or downward toward the outer corners, or remaining horizontal, thus forming 'level brows'. This feature, together with a slight modelling in the eye-sockets themselves and on nose, lips, and chin, and the representation of hair with a soft, rough surface giving, especially in the bushy white beards, an extraordinary effect of actual hair, makes the faces strikingly lifelike. Flesh is modelled in a strong grey-green ground tone upon which high lights have been placed in white or pale pink, on forehead, nose, and cheek-bone, and the cheeks and lips have been coloured pink or red. The individualization of the faces is chiefly in types, though not all the white-bearded old men, nor all the younger ones with red, yellow, or brown hair look exactly alike. Archduke Albert, in a red mantle, is recognizable as the person represented three times on the same page. This enlivening and individualizing of the faces gives the figures on this page an extraordinary interest which is lacking in similar compositions by a different hand on the verso of the page.

There are many points of similarity between fol. 1 of the Vienna Durandus and Hand A's style in the Missal: the natural position and focus of the eyes, the short, accented eyebrows slanting up or down; and the roughened texture of the hair. Moreover, the heavier pigments and the stronger modelling of the flesh are characteristic also of Hand A's figures, as are the more convincing positions and the solidity of the body under the draperies. Examples are found in 4/64 (fol. 160. Pl. xxii*b*), 4/71 (fol. 161vo, Pl. xxv), and the kneeling youth in 4/91 (fol. 164vo, Pl. xxix).

Similarly, the impression of space in the three scenes in architectural interiors of the Durandus, resulting from gradations of light and shade which deepens from the front to the rear of the composition, is found in Hand A of the Missal, as in the Nativity of the Virgin, fol. 138vo (Pl. xviii). In both cases the roundness of the figures within this definitely conceived space is intensified by contrasting, wherever possible, dark surfaces with light ones, or vice versa; or, if this contrast of surfaces is not feasible, dark contour lines are used to accentuate the solidity of the face or figure.

Another similarity between the style of the Durandus artist and that of the Missal artist is the design of the centre border with the stems crossing and framing medallions in which are the angels and other figures in the branches of the decoration. (*Cf.* the girl's head on fol. 6vo, Pl. i, and angels in 4/55 and 4/52, Pls. xx and xxi). The acanthus leaves with their softly-curling tips, shaded in self-colour, and changing colour with each turn, are found also in the decoration of Hand A's miniatures. The colours of the decoration of the Durandus are: a fine, clear vermilion shaded with yellow or white for high lights, and a deeper red, touched with crimson or brown for shadows; a strong, ultramarine blue, shaded with white or a lighter tone; a dull, pale pink shaded with a deeper self-tone of lake or madder; green shaded with pale yellow and a deeper tone sometimes nearly black; yellow shaded with red; brown and grey, for architecture; and mauve, both pinkish and bluish, for draperies. These colours, corresponding in tone and quality, are found in Hand A of the Missal, with one exception: the dull, deep, bluish green used consistently for ground and trees, by Hand A, is lacking on fol. 1 of the Durandus, being replaced by a lighter, yellower green. On fol. 1vo, however, some of this dull green is found in the border; it is perhaps formed by shading or mixing the lighter green with dull blue. The depth and brilliance of the colours, with their strong contrasts between bright and dull tones, against the highly burnished gold are strikingly like Hand A's colouring in the Carmelite Missal.

The similarities between the *Wapenboek* and Hand A's miniatures on the one hand and between Durandus fol. 1 and Hand A characteristic modelling and colour on the other, pose the problem of whether one and the same artist might have worked on all three manuscripts, and if so, what might have been their chronological sequence. The Durandus style undoubtedly comes out of the earlier Bohemian style, but it seems to have acquired a greater vigour than is seen in, for example, the Johann von Troppau figures. A manuscript in the Pierpont Morgan Library (MS. 769), a copy of the *Christ-Herre Chronik* dated *ca.* 1375–80 and probably made in eastern Bavaria,[1] may suggest the source of this more vigorous figure style. The same kind of heavily modelled, rather crude figure types is found, moreover, in another Dutch manuscript (see below) which also is closely related to Hand A's style. This common source affecting the Bohemian tradition in the Vienna Durandus and the developing style of Hand A in the Low Countries may be the explanation of the striking similarities between the Durandus fol. 1 and Hand A's style.

The second Dutch manuscript which I believe can be attributed in part to Hand A is a copy of Jacob van Maerlant's *Rijmbijbel* (Amsterdam, Koninklijke Akademie van Wetenschapen, MS. XVIII, now deposited in the Royal Library at the Hague). This manuscript is variously dated between 1375 and 1400.[2] It contains ten miniatures in at least two styles, of which the first is found on fols. 1–3, and the second on fols. 101 and 130. The first style does not concern us here;[3] but the second is, I believe, work by Hand A in an earlier phase of development than the Missal, and under the influence of the heavily modelled technique such as is found in the Vienna Durandus and the Morgan MS. 769.

The miniature on fol. 101 (Pl. XLVI*b*) represents Christ standing, holding in His hands the Book and surrounded by the symbols of the four Evangelists—a curious type of Majesty, introducing the New Testament. The figure of Christ is broad and heavy, with drapery folds deeply shaded and highlighted to indicate the position of the bent knee. The gown is mauve. The face is modelled on a greenish flesh tone with highlights in white, slightly tinged with pink toward the far side of the face, becoming red at the contour line of the cheek. White lines are used on forehead, down the nose, on the cheek bone and on the lips and chin; red is used on the nostril and lips, the lower one showing the highlighted spot of white as in the head of the girl in the *Wapenboek*. There are white lines on the fingers. The eyes and the shadows around them are brown, and the hair is reddish yellow with single hairs done in very dark brown. The effect of the modelling and of the colour in general is very rich against the highly burnished gold background. The foreground is dull green touched with yellow. The Evangelist symbols are placed against roundels

---

[1] Folio 259 is reproduced in the catalogue of an exhibition in honour of Belle Da Costa Greene: *The First Quarter Century of the Pierpont Morgan Library*, New York, 1949, Pl. 19. Even better examples occur in the manuscript on fols. 282–4.

[2] Cf. Byvanck and Hoogewerff, *op. cit.*, I, p. 3 (in which the manuscript is dated *ca.* 1375), and II, Pls. 102–3 (in which it is dated *ca.* 1400). A date of *ca.* 1380 is given by Hoogewerff in *De Noordnederlandsche Schilderkunst*, The Hague, 1936, I, p. 82. Byvanck, in *La Miniature dans les Pays-Bas Septentrionaux*, Paris, 1937, p. 22, assigns it to the 'first years of the fifteenth century'.

[3] For a description of this style and its relation to another group of Dutch illuminators, see Rickert, 'The illuminated Manuscripts of Meester Dirc van Delf's Tafel van den Kersten Ghelove', *Walters Art Journal*, XII, (1949) pp. 79. ff.

(haloes?) of crimson or scarlet. The border is blue and dull pink, and the ornaments are gold. The whole effect is rich and dark, and obviously a painter's style rather than an illuminator's.

Even more unusual in the richness and depth of the colour and modelling is the miniature on fol. 130 (Pl. XLVIc) representing the destruction of Jerusalem. The Emperor in armour, wearing a crown and carrying a shield with the blazon of the two-headed eagle, and a sword, stands in the centre of a close-packed group of three against a background of elaborate architecture representing the city. The colours of the drapery are blue, mauve and scarlet, the architecture is red and grey with blue tiled roofs; the ground is dull green shaded with yellow. The modelling is in the same technique as that on fol. 101, but the faces are more individualized and firmer in the building up of the flesh as well as in the drawing, and the eyes have a bright and lively expression. The awkward composition of the figure group suggests inexperience in handling them; but it is noteworthy that the two figures behind the Emperor are not placed higher than he is, but their heads are almost on a level with his, and there is definite foreshortening in the far side of the face which suggests roundness of the head. Also, the group of figures and the buildings have some sort of spatial relation to the ground and one feels the artist's interests in these things rather than in the decorative arrangement of the various features on a flat surface.

Many of the characteristics pointed out in the two miniatures in Amsterdam XVIII can be found in Hand A's miniatures in the Carmelite Missal; the vividness of the faces and their differentiation one from the other, together with the rich colouring and the interest in the spatial composition are outstanding similarities. The Emperor in figure and in face recalls the Emperor of the *Wapenboek* miniature as well as similar figures in the Missal, for instance in the Saint Andrew picture (fol. 163, Pl. XXVIIa). It seems that the Amsterdam *Rijmbijbel* may represent an intermediate stage of Hand A's work between the *Wapenboek* and the Missal.

However, some elements of Hand A's style in the Missal still remain to be explained, which cannot be traced to any of the manuscripts to which it has thus far been related. Most of these are decorative elements: the hair-line spray bearing tiny gold oval motifs, often in groups of three (4/48 and 4/18, fols. 90 and 93) and combined with these, ivy leaves in gold or colour on thick stems (4/89, fol. 68vo, Pl. A.) originate, apparently, from French border decoration of the first half of the fourteenth century. Gold tooled backgrounds in elaborate arabesque patterns seem to occur more often in Bohemian illumination of the early period, as in the Johann von Neumarkt group; but the coloured grounds with diapered patterns and gilt arabesques (Pl. VIII) are found in French manuscripts of the second half of the century. Strikingly suggestive of the French school are the two *bas de page* scenes on fols. 152vo and 162 (Pls. XX and XXVI), as are also the grotesques on fol. 162. Gothic architectural detail occurs in some of the miniatures (4/18, fol. 93); the representation of the inside and outside of a building, as in French manuscripts affected by Italian influence, is found in many miniatures.[1] The type of architectural setting for the Purification (4/18), for example, is reminiscent of similar scenes in

[1] Cf. miniatures dated *ca.* 1380 by the so-called Master of the Narbonne Altarfrontal, in the *Très Belles Heures* of the Rothschild Collection, Paris. Durrieu, Cte Paul, *Les Très Belles Heures de Notre-Dame*, Paris, 1922.

Franco-Flemish miniatures by Jacquemart d'Hesdin[1] and even of the altarpiece of Melchior Broederlam ordered by the Duke of Burgundy in 1393 for the Chartreuse de Champmol at Dijon.[2] Italian also is the composition of the All Saints miniature, which is reminiscent of such paintings as the great *Majestas* by Lippo Memmi in the Palazzo Pubblico in Siena. These International Style[3] features suggest the strong probability that Hand A, before painting his miniatures in the Carmelite Missal, had some first-hand contacts with the busy ateliers of the French court and that in the process, some of the crudeness of his earlier work was eliminated under the influence of this more elegant style, while nevertheless retaining the fundamental vigour of its painter's technique. This new emphasis on the modelling of the figures, especially the faces, together with the new three-dimensional composition and the variation in decorative motifs, as the hair-line spray of gold motifs and the richly shaded acanthus scroll, form the basis of the New Style of illumination which appeared in England directly under the influence of the Carmelite Missal.

[1] For example, the *Très Belles Heures*, made for the duc de Berry before 1402, now in the Royal Library at Brussels, MS. 11060–1.

[2] Now in the Museum at Dijon. See also below, Chapter IV and Appendix B.

In the Purification miniature in the Missal (Pl. IX), there is something odd about the gold-robed figure in the foreground: the unbroken vertical of the back contour carried up by the line of the Virgin's mantle suggests the possibility that an architectural feature, such as a slender column or perhaps even more than one, may have been intended originally to support the roof, as in the panel of this same subject by Broederlam. If one or more columns had been intended in Hand A's miniature as designed, they would have had to pass in front of the two principal figures, the Virgin and Child. The modified arrangement, with the correspondence of tabernacle pendants and floor projections, is much more effective because less obvious: imaginary lines drawn between the two centre pendants and the floor, set apart the two central figures from the others without partially obscuring them. It may be noted that similar omission of columns occurs in some but not all of Jacquemart's miniatures in the *Très Belles Heures* in Brussels. A column is used by Hand A in the miniature on fol. 6vo (Pl. I).

Another feature of Hand A's miniatures which relates them to Broederlam's panels is the patterning of the tiled floors. The checkerboard design (as in Broederlam's Annunciation) and variations of it (as in his Presentation) are used with foreshortening to suggest space in Hand A's Purification, Nativity, and other miniatures. The meander (also in Broederlam's Annunciation) is used by Hand A in the Saint Brice miniature (Pl. XXIIa). An unusual pattern, combining checkerboard and meander, is found in the Saint Martin (Pl. XXI). It is possible that Hand A saw the Broederlam panels; but in view of his variations on both the architecture and the tile patterns, it seems more likely that the two artists got their ideas independently from the same source, which was perhaps North Italian painting, as Altichiero's frescoes in Saint George's Chapel at Padua (*ca.* 1380).

[3] On the International Style in general, see Marle, Raimond van, *The Development of the Italian Schools of Painting*, VII, The Hague, 1926, pp. 1–63.

4

The Influence of the Missal on the New English Style ca. 1400

The circumstances in which the Carmelite Missal was written and illuminated can only be conjectured, but two other similarly elaborate monastic missals, one earlier and one later, give us a clue. The Lytlington Missal was written and illuminated in 1383–4 at the Benedictine Monastery of Westminster by lay craftsmen who were paid for their work and their living while engaged there.[1] The Sherborne Missal was written by the Benedictine monk John Was and illuminated by the Dominican friar John Siferwas (as repeatedly recorded on many pages of the book), probably at Sherborne Abbey between 1396 and 1407.[2] In like manner, the Carmelite Missal, if the deductions from this study are correct, may have been made at Whitefriars Convent in London by craftsmen and artists introduced there for the purpose. Evidently neither Westminster nor Sherborne Abbey had its own illuminators at this time; and so it was, apparently, with Whitefriars. Yet it is reasonable to suppose that so important and costly a manuscript, whose liturgical accuracy was essential, would not be entrusted to a London shop, but would be made, or at any rate written as at Westminster and Sherborne Abbeys, at the Convent under the supervision of the Carmelite Friars. The frequent occurrence of Carmelites in the Style C miniatures strongly suggests, as already pointed out, that one or two of the six artists may have been Carmelite.

Under such circumstances it might be expected that the decoration of the manuscript would be uniform in style, as, in fact, is true of both the Lytlington and the Sherborne Missals, where variations in quality and in detail are indications merely that individual hands were working in the same style. The explanation of the three distinct styles in the Carmelite Missal may lie in the fact that, as each of the three main artists was a fully formed master of exceptional ability, it was in the capacity of being the best artists available that they were brought together to produce by their combined skills this magnificent manuscript.[3]

Hands A, B, and C seem to have influenced each other very little in the course of their collaboration. In their miniatures, Hands A and B in the *Temporale* and A and C in the

---

[1] See p. 76, note 1.

[2] In the Library of the Duke of Northumberland, Alnwick Castle. See J. A. Herbert, *The Sherborne Missal*, Roxburghe Club, 1920.

[3] Professor Charles L. Kuhn, in an important study entitled, 'Hermann Scheerre and English Illumi-

remainder of the Missal followed their own individual styles. In the decoration attached to the historiated initials, Hands A and B show some affinity which may be due partly to their association with each other, but more probably springs from the familiarity of both with Continental, especially Bohemian, illumination, as shown above (Chapter III). Hands C use the English idiom in ornament, and this also was apparently adopted with modifications in some of Hand A's decoration. In general, the decorative initials throughout the manuscript were done independently of the miniatures, though here and there some influence of the decoration attached to the historiated initials within the same page or area is evident.

Hand B disappeared from the Missal after painting the five *Temporale* miniatures, and his peculiar style did not appear to affect other manuscripts of the period.

Style C, on the contrary, is found, as we have seen, in a number of other late fourteenth century English manuscripts and probably represents the English style current in one or more of the London shops in this period. Three additional examples, similar to those already discussed are: (1) Cambridge, Trinity Hall, MS. 17 (Dymok, *Contra Haereses Lollardorum*), ca. 1390, made for Richard II and containing his portrait and arms, including the white hart badge[1]; (2) *Liber Necromanciae* (Bodl. MS. 581), also made for Richard after 1391,[2] containing miniatures very close in style to the Lytlington Missal, and decoration like that of the Liber Regalis; and (3) a particularly fine example of the style, the illuminated initial *R* (Ricardus) of the Charter given by Richard to Croyland Abbey in 1393 (Oxford, Ashmole MS. 1381). Although these manuscripts must be contemporary with the Carmelite Missal, Hands C do not seem to be identifiable in any of them. The English style gives way about 1400 to the new style in illumination, except in a few provincial manuscripts probably made in Norwich.[3]

What replaced the typical late fourteenth century English style comes directly out of Style A in the Carmelite Missal, though, strangely enough, no other work in England can be attributed to the best A hand. It has been noted in describing Style A that three of the miniatures seem to have been done by two different artists under Hand A's supervision, perhaps learning from him. In order to trace his influence on the new style it is necessary now to examine in greater detail Hands A[2] and A[3].

Hand A[2]. Folio 135vo in the Carmelite Missal contains a miniature (4/83, Pl. XVIIa) with Saint Louis which, if compared with the king in the Saint Loy miniature (4/69, fol.

nation of the Early Fifteenth Century', (*Art Bulletin*, XXII, 1940, p. 153) assumes that the miniatures by Hands B and A were done some twenty years later than those by Hand C, apparently because he wishes to relate the Missal more closely to the Bible (Royal MS. 1 E.IX), which he thinks (quite correctly, it seems to me) is not earlier than *ca.* 1410. Recently Professor Erwin Panofsky has expressed to me in a letter his concurrence with Kuhn's assumption. I can find no evidence of this chronological disparity in the styles of the Missal miniatures, either on grounds of their distribution in the Missal as reconstructed, or on iconographic or stylistic grounds. In view of the dating (1398) of the Lapworth Missal and of the dependence of its Crucifixion miniature on the style of Hand A in the Missal (see p. 93 below), Professor Kuhn's hypothesis seems to be founded on mere wishful thinking.

[1] First used, according to the monk of Evesham, at the Tournament of Smithfield in October, 1390. See M. V. Clarke, 'The Wilton Diptych', *Burl. Mag.*, LVIII (1931), pp. 284 f.

[2] I am indebted to Dr Otto Paecht for calling my attention to this and several other manuscripts of related style in the Bodleian Library.

[3] Brit. Mus., Cott. MS. Claud. E. VIII, Add. MS. 34114, Arundel MS. 74, made for Henry Spenser, Bishop of Norwich (died 1406). Other examples are Bodl. MS. Hatton 1, and Lambeth Palace MS. 330.

D. Carmelite Missal, fol. 193vo: Initial B introducing the introit of the Votive Mass for the Holy Trinity

164, Pl. xxviii), shows striking differences, though the pose of the figure is so nearly identical as to suggest copying: Saint Louis is broader in proportion to his height but less sturdy and he seems to be supported only by the heavy folds of drapery. The stance is badly balanced, with the body thrust forward and the head backward. The face is very lightly modelled, with thin red wash and white spots (now oxydized); the hair is pushed back over the ear. The hands have very long, curved fingers and the wide sleeves fall with a swinging curve. There is a somewhat mannered elegance in both drapery and pose in the Saint Louis which contrasts with the great simplicity and sparkling vividness of the Saint Loy miniature.

Closest to the Saint Louis figure in pose and modelling are some figures in a manuscript containing sermons of Saint Gregory in French (Brit. Mus. Roy. MS. 20 D. V.). The first page of this manuscript (fol. 3) is illuminated in French style of the late fourteenth century, with presentation miniature and ivy leaf border. From fol. 3vo onward, the miniatures resemble and often copy Hand A's figures and compositions in the Missal. Fol. 98 (Pl. liva) illustrates well the characteristics pointed out in the Saint Louis miniature. We shall meet this hand again in manuscripts in the New Style.

Hand A³. The Lucy and Lazarus miniatures in the Missal (4/67 and 4/39 on fol. 166, Pl. xxxi) show equally clear but different variations from Hand A¹. Lucy, like Louis, seems to be copied (almost traced) from the beautiful figure of Cecilia (4/79, fol. 160vo, Pl. xxiiib) obviously by Hand A¹; but the difference in delicacy and vividness of modelling is evident. The somewhat pop-eyed Lucy, with hair plastered over her forehead, uncertain in pose and with broad, stubby hands, is closer in feeling to Hand A¹ than is the Saint Louis, yet again it lacks the genius of Hand A¹ for infusing a sense of life into the figures. The 'Noah's Ark' oxen, probably inspired by the fine horses in Hand A's Exaltation of the Cross (4/72, fol. 140, Pl. xixa) do not suggest any potential movement. The figures in the Lazarus miniature come out rather better especially as to the faces, and it may be that Hand A did a little touching up on them. The mixture of patterns in the background and the feebleness of the drapery rendering, especially in the two women, look like the Lucy style, as does the face of Mary at the left side of the picture.

Hand A³ also is recognizable, I believe, in Royal MS. 20 D.V. Fol. 41vo (Pl. liiia) is a good example, which again, perhaps, was touched up as to the faces by Hand A¹. The inconsequent richness of the draperies, the hands in helpless gestures, the faces brighter in expression than the Lucy yet uncertain in the modelling, in spite of the sparkle in the eye resulting from the white spot in the corner, are not characteristic of the best Hand A. Still, in the Royal manuscript Hand A³ has greatly improved on his Lucy.

He seems to have found his form in a fine full-page Crucifixion, the only miniature in a missal (Oxford, Corpus Christi College, MS. 394, Pl. l) given to Lapworth Parish Church, Warwickshire, and dated 1398.[1] The facial technique and even the colouring echoes Hand A¹'s, but the meaningless gestures and helpless hands, the rich but curiously uncertain drapery patterns with conspicuous edges running in intricately curved lines, are not in the best A style of the Carmelite Missal. The Christ on the Cross has gone wrong in its

---

[1] Date from an erased inscription on fol. 257: '.. anno domini M⁰CCC nonogesimo octavo istud missale erat plenarie et integre perscriptum'. The inscription was first read under ultra-violet ray by Eric G. Millar, to whom I am indebted for the information.

proportions; perhaps the drawing was better, as in the small, delicately drawn figure at the bottom of the page, which reminds one strongly of a similar figure by Hand A[1] in the All Saints miniature in the Missal (4/55, on fol. 152vo, Pl. xx). Hand A[1] could perhaps have drawn this figure. The border decoration on the Crucifixion page is purely English and has the fine quality of the decorative initials and borders in the Canon and Prefaces of the Carmelite Missal. It could be imagined that this miniature was copied from a similar page by Hand A[1] in the Carmelite Missal, now lost. The ox of the Evangelist Luke in the lower right corner is as awkward as are the oxen in the Lucy miniature.

The date 1398 is very valuable evidence for a certain date *ante quem* for the Carmelite Missal illumination: the Crucifixion page is inconceivable earlier than Hand A. So is the Gregory manuscript, in which compositions of Hand A in the Carmelite manuscript are copied: the Calling of Peter and Andrew (fol. 136vo in Roy. 20 D.V. and 4/33 on fol. 162 in the Missal) is one of several examples.

The two variants of Hand A's style identifiable in Roy. 20 D.V. and Corpus Christi College 394 are the first steps in the spread of the New Style introduced into English illumination by Hand A. This style reached its flowering in a great Bible of the early years of the fifteenth century (Roy. MS. 1 E. IX in the British Museum), the size and magnificence of which emulate but do not equal that of the Missal.[1] In this manuscript, if anywhere, Hand A's own work should be found if he were still working in England. But the supervision of this illumination seems to have been in other hands, namely, those of a second outstanding artistic personality who developed apart from Hand A though influenced later by his style. This is Hermann Scheerre, whose full name appears with the words 'me fecit' on one of the small miniatures (fol. 37) of a modest manuscript of Offices and Prayers (Brit. Mus. Add. MS. 16998).[2] The decoration is a very simple form of the English type of bar and branch, and it would seem to date from close to 1400. The touches of green paint on the curleycews of the border occur, it will be remembered, in the very last pages of the Carmelite Missal.

The source of Hermann's style is a puzzle. The modelling of the faces in Add. 16998 is very different from that of Style A in the Missal, the features being indicated with great delicacy in brown on a thick white flesh paint. The drapery is richer and softer, and the folds fall in sweeping gothic curves. There is no interest in spatial setting, but backgrounds and floor are patterned flatly. The pictures are miniatures, in frames, not historiated initials. There is an extraordinary delicacy and softness in the figures and great sensitiveness in the faces and gestures. These qualities are seen at their very best in an exquisite full-page miniature inserted in a Book of Hours (Brit. Mus. Roy. MS. 2 A. XVIII, fol. 23vo, Pl. LI) representing an Annunciation with donors who have been identified as John Beaufort, Earl and Marquess of Somerset, and Margaret Holland his wife.[3] On the *prie dieu* is a green

[1] This is presumed to be a royal manuscript, but because of its stylistic dependence on the Missal, it could hardly be early enough to have been made for Richard (1377–99); if made for an English king, it must have been Henry IV (1399–1413). The untenable chronology of the Missal in relation to the Bible, which is offered by Kuhn, (*loc. cit.*, pp. 152–3), has apparently been accepted by Miss Joan Evans (*English Art, 1307–1461*, p. 98), who further confuses the situation by finding a stylistic connection between this Bible and the Lytlington Missal.

[2] See *Burl. Mag.*, LXI, 1935, pp. 39 f. Cf. also Kuhn, *loc. cit.*, Fig. 12.

[3] The Royal Catalogue gives the date as before 1399 when John Beaufort was married to Margaret Holland. Since the *Memoria* of Saint John of Bridlington is included in the manuscript, however, the book

and gold cover with bands of lettering which read: 'omnia leuia sunt amanti; si quis amat non laborat. de daer (m?,' on the line below). In spite of the cryptic 'de daer . . .?' following the mottoes which are used also in other manuscripts signed by Hermann (see below), it has been assumed that Hermann painted the miniature, but the quality of the painting is so fine that it is difficult to believe it could have been done by him unless at a much later date than Add. 16998 and the big Bible. That it is earlier than the Additional manuscript and also than the Chichele Breviary (Lambeth Palace Library, MS. 69, before 1416[1]) is evident from the copying of the Annunciation on fol. 17 of 16998 by Hermann and on fol. 4vo of the Chichele Breviary[2] by the hand we have identified as Hand A[3]. Also earlier than the Chichele Breviary is another manuscript much closer to Add. 16998, Oxford, Bodl. MS. Lat. lit. f. 2, datable 1405–13.[3] Though some of these miniatures, notably fols. 2vo, 10 (Pl. LIIa) and 19vo, show evidence of direct influence if not of copying from the Annunciation in Royal MS. 2 A. XVIII, they lack the exquisite enamel-like finish of the facial modelling in the Beaufort Annunciation. I am convinced, therefore, that the Beaufort miniature was done not by Hermann, but by someone else, who knew at first hand Broederlam's altarpiece wings (1393–99) at Dijon. There is no doubt that Hermann owed much to this unknown artist.[4]

Neither in the Beaufort Annunciation nor in Add. 16998 nor in Bodl. Lat. lit. f. 2 nor in still another small book of hours by Hermann, not signed (MS. Stowe 16 in the British Museum[5]) is there evidence of Hand A's influence on the figure style or the iconography. The miniatures in Royal 1 E. IX, however, are unthinkable without the Carmelite Missal. Hermann's hand is recognizable, I find, in the first miniature (fol. 2) representing a kneeling figure presenting a book to Saint Jerome (Pl. LIIb). The exquisitely sensitive modelling of the pale faces and the gothic rhythm of the drapery are close to Add. 16998 (fol. 68) and Bodl. Lat. lit. f. 2 (fol. 10, Pl. LIIa), but the architecture with its carefully disposed interior and exterior, while reminiscent of Royal MS. 2 A. XVIII, is more detailed and

was probably made between 1401 (when this saint was canonized) and 1410, the date of Somerset's death. See J. A. Herbert, *Schools of Illumination*, IV, 1922, p. 7 and Millar, *op. cit.*, Pl. 85. There is no external evidence that the kneeling donors are actually as identified, or that the manuscript was made for them, since the miniature with the Annunciation is on an inserted leaf and the miniatures that precede it are by a different artist, the so-called Master of the Beaufort Saints. See Kuhn, *loc. cit.*, Figs. 5 and 7.

[1] The evidence for the date is given in the *New Pal. Soc.*, Ser. II, Pl. 131. It is based on the absence of offices for SS David, Chad, Winifred, and John of Beverley, all four of which were ordered by Archbishop Chichele himself in 1416.

[2] Reproduced Kuhn, *loc. cit.*, Fig. 16.

[3] The office of Richard le Scrope, Archbishop of York (beheaded 1405), is illustrated with a miniature (fol. 146vo), the last in the manuscript. This office was in use only till the death of Henry IV in 1413. See *ibid.*, p. 141, and Fig. 1.

[4] Compare, for example, the virgin on fol. 10 (Pl. LIIa) with the virgin in 2 A. XVIII, and John with Gabriel; also, the donors in the miniature on fol. 2 with the donors in 2 A. XVIII. The attribution of the Beaufort Annunciation like that of the Wilton Diptych in the National Gallery, London, has long been a subject of controversy. This is not the place to enter into a full discussion of these two superb examples which, oddly enough, have certain characteristics in common, namely, the enamel-like, very delicate modelling of the faces, the supple gothic draperies, and their exquisite colouring and rich patterning. Since the Beaufort Annunciation had great influence on the development of the new style in English illumination, its origins are particularly important. Some source material bearing on this question has therefore been included in Appendix B of this volume, pending a complete study of the Continental background suggested by this evidence.

[5] Two miniatures only are obviously in Hermann's style, and these are identical in composition with two of the same subjects in Add. 16998, one of these an Annunciation copying that in Royal 2 A. XVIII.

convincing as spatial form and was certainly influenced by such architectural settings as are found in Hand A's miniatures in the Missal (*e.g.* fols. 6vo, 93 and 138vo). Here, then, seems to be an artist of comparable ability with Hand A, formed in a different stylistic tradition, but influenced by Hand A's realism, setting the style for a new phase of English illumination.

It is not, however, in Hermann's own work, important though it is, that the influence of the Carmelite Missal is most clearly apparent, but in that of the closest follower of Hand A[1], namely, Hand A[3], who associated himself, perhaps after the departure of his master, with Hermann in the illumination of the big Bible and certain other manuscripts under Hermann's supervision. Thus the Hand A modelled style was carried over directly from the Missal into the main stream of the developing English new style, giving it a richness and vigour which Hermann's work in its earlier stages lacked. The extreme sensitiveness and delicacy of Hermann's modelling, in less skilled hands, easily deteriorated into the ineffectual, badly drawn forms of, for example, the so-called Beaufort Master who painted a number of miniatures preceding the Annunciation in Royal 2 A. XVIII and who also collaborated with Hermann in the Bodleian manuscript, but not in the Bible. Hermann's style under the influence of the Carmelite Missal compositions and modelling, is sometimes difficult to distinguish from that of the mature Hand A[3]. Two figures on fol. 109vo of Roy. 1 E. IX (Pl. LIIIc), though almost identical in position with Hermann's on fol. 2, are more robust in modelling and less sensitive in feeling; they seem to retain something of the vigour and sparkle of Hand A's style.

Hand A[3] collaborated in another signed manuscript of Hermann's, the Chichele Breviary mentioned above, in the historiated initials on fols. 4vo, 26vo, and 55 (Pl. LIIIb). Hand A[3]'s copy of the Beaufort Annunciation on fol. 4vo of this manuscript shows his heavier modelling and stronger colouring, which is very similar to that of Hand A[1] in the Missal, and these qualities contrast markedly with the first miniature in the Breviary which is signed by Hermann.[1] Two other miniatures are also copied from initials in Roy. 1 E. IX: the Nativity (fol. 26vo) from that on fol. 254vo in the Bible, perhaps by his own hand; and the Baptism (fol. 55, Pl. LIIIb) from the initial with the same subject on fol. 262vo in the Bible, probably by Hermann.[2]

Hand A[3] collaborating with Herman, represents only one current in the stream of the new style. Hand A[2] and another identified illuminator, John Siferwas, a Dominican friar, with whom he apparently collaborated on the Sherborne Missal (see above) represents the other main current. Hand A[2] was identified, it will be remembered, in the Gregory manuscript (Roy. 20 D. V., Pl. LIVa); he is also found, I believe, in the Gospel Lectionary (Brit. Mus. Harl. MS. 7026), made for Lord Lovell (d. 1408) and containing the well-known portrait of him with the artist, John Siferwas. Fol. 9 (Pl. LIVb) shows the loose modelling and exaggerated hands of Hand A[2]. He worked on the big Bible also (*e.g.* fol.

---

[1] Reproduced *Bull. de la Soc. franç. reprod. de man. à peint.*, 1925, Pl. XLI; also Kuhn, *loc. cit.*, Fig. 15.

[2] On fol. 229 of the Bible is the motto: 'omnia leuia sunt amanti' in a French inscription, only partly legible. On stylistic grounds, I should not attribute this miniature to Hermann but to Hand A[3] or possibly some other assistant. A miniature at the top of the same column, however, seems to be closer to Hermann. Other miniatures with inscriptions in I E. IX are on fols. 126vo (in German in the scroll of the initial shaft), 136 (in Latin on Jerome's robe) and 145 (in German on the background). Fol. 136 could be by Hermann; the inscription is: 'Laus deo patri sit', repeated.

154vo Pl. LV) and may have done the strongly coloured, monotonously repeated figure in part, at least, of the miniatures in Marco Polo's *Livres du Graunt Caam*, added to the Alexander Romance (Bodl. MS. 264). One of these miniatures (fol. 220) contains the words, 'Johannes me fecit' in gold lettering. His facial style becomes stereotyped, with red spots on nose and chin, and with large red mouths. The figures have little originality, and the gestures and expressions are all much alike. A tendency to exaggerate certain facial types is characteristic.

The decoration of the Siferwas manuscripts, both the Sherborne Missal and the Lovell Lectionary,[1] is more lavish than that in the Carmelite Missal, though it has many of the same motifs, such as the small gold leaves on hair-line stems and the heavily shaded acanthus scrolls first seen in Hand A's miniatures. There are also fantastic variations of the simpler English motifs as found in the Missal. If the Siferwas decorative style derives from the Carmelite Missal, as seems likely, it rapidly goes to seed and becomes overloaded and crudely ornate, and even garish in its colouring.

The new style reaches its apogee in richness and variety in the Bedford Hours (Brit. Mus. Add. MS. 42131, 1414–1435) and the contemporary Hours of Elizabeth the Queen (in the Dyson Perrins Collection at Malvern). Several hands of varying skill collaborated with Hermann on these manuscripts, among them Hand A[3] who appears to have done some of the fine portrait heads.[2] The influence of the Siferwas style is evident especially in the Perrins manuscript, in the overloading of the designs and in a tendency toward coarseness in the figure types. It is also possible that fresh foreign influences such as French, Bohemian, and German may have combined here with the English style. From the second quarter of the fifteenth century, the style, though still florid in its decorative qualities, loses its keen interest in heavily painted figure modelling, and there is a return to the simpler drawing styles, possibly under the impetus of later Dutch manuscripts. Two very fine examples, Cambridge, Trin. Coll. MS. B. 10. 12, and Brit. Mus. Cott. MS. Faust. B. vi, Pt. 2, oddly enough, have much of the vividness, of Hand A's figure and facial types. The technique is coloured drawing as in the Empire and herald pictures in the Gelder *Wapenboek*. With the return to this linear technique the border decoration grows steadily thinner and poorer in amount and quality, and larger and coarser in form. In the last quarter of the fifteenth century, English work is largely replaced by manuscripts made wholly or in part in the Bruges school.

[1] A third manuscript, identified on stylistic grounds by Mr Francis Wormald as by Siferwas himself, though not signed, is Cambridge Trin. Coll. MS. B 3.7, Stephen Langton, *Glosses on the Pentateuch*, from Glastonbury. It appears to be early, before Siferwas came into contact with the Dutch elements of decoration as found in Hand A of the Missal. The sources of Siferwas' style do not concern us here, but it is interesting to note that this style also apparently does not come out of English sources. The closest Continental parallels which I have found are in a manuscript of *Ci nous dit*, MS. II 7619 Bibl. Roy., Brussels. See Lyna, F., 'Les Miniatures d'un MS. du "Ci nous dit" et le Realism Préeyckien', in *Scriptorium I* (1946–7), pp. 106–18 and Pl. 9. Its provenance is Artois. The form of the illustrations, which are in small framed miniatures, suggests that of the Gregory Sermons (Brit. Mus. Roy. 20 D.V.) and also those in the early manuscripts by Hermann. The miniatures seem to be by two hands, one of which is close to Siferwas in the proportions of the figures, the heavy voluminous draperies, and especially in the remarkable heavy modelling of the features. The colours are strong and rather crude, and the work is obviously rough and without any sign of influence from the more refined French style of the late fourteenth century.

[2] Three are reproduced in *Burl. Mag. LXV*, 1934, 'The Early English School of Portraiture', by P. J. Shaw, Pl. III. One of these (a *D* with 'Girls' heads', actually angels) I would attribute to Hermann. The *E* seems to me to be by Hand A[3]. Most of the stylistic attributions in the text of this article, as well as the identification of Hermann, are without foundation.

The disappearance of Hand A of the Carmelite Missal from the English scene led to an almost fruitless search for later examples of his work elsewhere. Though the influence of his fine modelling technique may be found in many Dutch manuscripts of the earlier part of the fifteenth century,[1] only one miniature has come to light thus far which I believe could be attributed to his own hand. This is one side[2] of one of three leaves, now in the Louvre (Cabinet des Dessins R.F. 2023, verso) which originally formed part of the ill-fated Milan-Turin Hours, begun for the duc de Berry in the late fourteenth century and completed under a variety of circumstances in subsequent years. This page (Pl. LVI) representing a group of confessors (a cardinal, an archbishop, a bishop, and representatives of the four mendicant orders) was apparently the last to be painted before the manuscript was divided in 1413.[3] The technique is that of Hand A in the Missal, with strongly modelled faces and little interest in draperies, and the figures themselves are so close to some in the Missal and also to the bishops in the *Wapenboek* Empire miniature that I have little hesitation in attributing them to the same hand. The circumstances of the illuminating of this early part of the Milan-Turin Hours at the court of the duc de Berry, and the contacts with many different artists, together with the later date, could account for what differences there are between this style and that of the Missal. This is a completely competent, mature piece of work which shows moreover, I believe, the influence of sculptured figures carved at Dijon by Claus Sluter, particularly the figures of the mourners on the tomb of Philippe le Hardi, begun in 1385 and finished in 1411. The imposing solidity of the figures, the heavily hanging drapery folds, and above all, the realism of the faces could, it seems, have resulted at this early date only from contacts with this amazingly realistic Burgundian figure style.

After the division of the manuscript of the Milan-Turin Hours in 1413, one part, including this leaf, went to Count William of Holland, where the miniatures attributed to Hubert van Eyck are believed to have been painted. It is tempting to imagine that Hand A of the Carmelite Missal in his mature years might have been their painter. In any case, without indulging in any such conjectures, the Dutch artist of the Missal unquestionably comes closer to furnishing an explanation of the early Van Eyck style than any other known artist of the late fourteenth century.

[1] One of the earliest and most important of these is a Carthusian Breviary made for Reinald IV, Duke of Gelder (died 1423), who succeeded his brother William as Duke in 1402. (Pierpont Morgan Library MS. 87.) The earlier pages properly folioed and now misbound at the end of the manuscript contain historiated initials recalling in decorative pattern and figure types Hand A's initials in the Carmelite Missal, but lacking their competence and brilliance. Several other artists collaborated in the decoration, one of whom (found in a great part of the first half of the manuscript) also worked on the Prayer Book of Marie of Gelder, wife of Reinald, dated 1415 (Berlin, Staatsbibl. MS. 42), and on other manuscripts of the Utrecht School.

The identification of the arms in MS. M.87 was made by Miss Meta Harrsen keeper of Manuscripts in the Pierpont Morgan Library. I am indebted to Miss Harrsen and to Professor Panofsky for bringing this manuscript to my attention.

[2] The recto of this leaf represents martyrdoms with much the same type of executioner as is found in the altarpiece of the martyrdom of Saint Denis begun, according to documentary evidence, by Jean Malouel and completed by his successor as court painter, Henry Bellechose. (Louvre, Paris.) I find it difficult to attribute the miniature of the Martyrs to the artist of the Confessors, in spite of some similarities in colouring and modelling technique. The Martyrs miniature is attributed by Kuhn (*loc. cit.*, p. 147) to Hand B as distinguished by Georges Hulin (de Loo), See *Heures de Milan*, Brussels and Paris, 1911, pp. 16–17. M. Hulin himself attributes both miniatures to his Hand C (1409–13). *Ibid*, pp. 18–19.

[3] For the history and reproductions of this manuscript, see Durrieu, Cte Paul, *Les Heures de Turin*, Paris, 1902.

5

Descriptions of the Miniatures in the Carmelite Missal

Fol. 6vo, fragment 4/93. HOLY SATURDAY[1]   PLATE I

Initial *D* ('Deus', for collect). A tonsured priest in alb and blue chasuble stands alone before an altar in a romanesque chapel. It is the moment after the *Kyrie* of the Litany, which precedes the mass of Holy Saturday, and while the *Gloria in excelsis* is being sung by the choir of four (probably, though not certainly) Carmelite friars in white surplices, the bell is rung for the first time since Maundy Thursday, by a youth clad in scarlet tunic and hose. The altar contains only an open book, a missal (?). At the left of the altar is a wooden cupboard, probably the aumbry for the sacrament. Two votive figures, the one on the right clad in tan, the other in vermilion, kneel at the foot of the altar steps.

The architecture inside and out is of terra-cotta colour, and the ceiling is blue; both are shaded deeply to suggest space. The black and white tiled floor is covered with a thin red wash, which is lighter in the foreground. The initial is grey, strongly shaded with white and black.

The very beautiful girl's head as the centre of a flower in the upper corner of the initial has no apparent connection with the subject of the picture. Her hair is yellow, shaded with brown; the flower is red on the outside and blue inside.

Folio 7vo, fragment 4/43. EASTER   PLATE II

Initial *R* ('Resurrexi', for introit). Two scenes from the Easter story according to the gospel for the day, Mark 16. 1–7. Above, the three Holy Women, Mary Magdalene, Mary the mother of James, and Salome, each carrying a jar of ointment (vs. 1). The scene is a garden, indicated by green grass and trees; the tomb is a mediaeval stone sarcophagus with a lid on which is inscribed a cross with a long shaft and beneath it, three transverse strokes, perhaps symbolizing the three nails of the crucifixion. The sun is rising (vs. 2) in a blue cloud. The words spoken by the women on arriving at the tomb are given on the scroll: 'quis reuoluet nobis lapidem etcetera' (vs. 3). The women are clothed in gowns and mantles of different colours: vermilion with lake pink mantle lined with blue; pink with blue mantle lined with vermilion; blue with vermilion mantle lined with pink.

---

[1] The titles given for the miniatures usually are those of the masses which they illustrate.

In the lower scene the same three women appear in different order (*e.g.* the one clothed in blue mantle is on the left); on the scroll are the words of the angel addressed to them: 'Nolite expauescere ihesum queritis surrexit non est hic' (vs. 6). The angel, clothed in an alb and with vermilion wings, is seated on the edge of the sarcophagus, the lid of which has now been taken off and laid on the ground, top uppermost, showing again the cross and the three transverse marks. A diaphanous white cloth (the graveclothes left by the risen Christ) hangs over the edge of the tomb. There seems to be no reason for the shift in position either of the women or of the trees in the background, except to produce a better balanced composition in the miniature as a whole.

In the margin, close to the initial, is an ostrich; in the curves of its neck and also scattered about it are golden balls. This may be merely a decorative feature, but there may also be some symbolism: the ostrich which hatches its eggs in the sand was interpreted as a symbol of the resurrection.

The two curves of the right side of the initial letter contain (above) a pink monochrome grotesque; (below) a blue monochrome angel of the feathered seraph type who repeats the position and gesture of the angel in the miniature. Is there an implication of malicious mimicry here, or are the figures merely decorative? The latter interpretation is perhaps suggested by the manner of terminating the initial by elongating the leg of the angel into a stem which is held in the beak of a long-legged bird.

In addition to the historiated initial introducing the Easter mass, on the following leaf (fol. 8) there are nine small letters beginning verses of the same gospel lesson which is illustrated by the large initial. These small letters contain tiny scenes from the Easter story. (1) The three women arrive at the tomb (initial *E*, 'Et valde mane una sabbatorum . . .', Mark 16. 2); (2) the women confer about the removal of the stone (initial *Q*, 4/444, 'Quis revolvet nobis lapidem . . .', vs. 3); (3) the lid of the sarcophagus is lifted (initial *E*, 4/453, 'Et respiciens viderunt revolutum lapidem . . .', vs. 4); (4) the women wonder at the removal of so large a stone (initial *E*, 4/435, 'Erat quippe magnus valde . . .', vs. 4); (5) the angel appears to the women (initial *E*, 'Et introentes in monumentum viderunt juvenem sedentem . . .', vs. 5); (6) the angel addresses the women (initial *Q*, 'Qui dicit illis', vs. 6); (7) and (8) the angel tells the women that Christ has risen (initial *N*, 4/454, 'Nolite expavescere . . .', and initial *S*, 'Surrexit . . .', vs. 6); (9) the angel reascending into Heaven, gives the women parting instructions (initial *S*, 4/447, 'Sed ite . . .', vs. 7).

Fol. 21vo, fragment 4/44. ASCENSION   PLATE III

Initial *U* ('Uiri galilei', written in mauve and red decorative letters, introducing the introit). Two scenes illustrating the gospel and epistle for the day. Above, Christ sending the apostles forth to preach, as indicated by the words on the scroll (Mark 16: 15): 'Euntes in mundum predicate euuangelium omni creature'. The eleven apostles are seated on two sides of an oblong table; Judas is absent unless, indeed, it is he who is represented with red beard and clothed in a long red gown, lying full length on a branch of decoration outside the initial, looking away from the scene.

Below, Christ enthroned beside God the Father, both in pink gowns and blue mantles, within an aureole of clouds; the eleven disciples at the left, in a landscape, are looking upward, while on the right, the two 'men in white' with red and blue wings, are speaking to them in the words on the scroll (Acts 1. 11): 'Uiri galilei quid statis aspicientes in celum.' The disciples are dressed like the women in the Easter miniature.

The significance of the two-humped camel standing on a small patch of green in the margin is not clear.

Fol. 27vo, fragment 4/45. PENTECOST   PLATE IV

Initial S ('Spiritus', for introit). One scene in two registers. Below, in a green landscape at right, Christ holding a scroll with the words: 'Sipiritus (sic) sanctus quem mittet pater in nomine meo ille uos docebit omnia' (John 14. 26, from the gospel for the day). The first of the eleven disciples (five are indicated only by small segments of gold haloes seen between those of the six) receives the message from Christ by touching the end of the scroll. Christ points upward with His right hand to God the Father blessing, who is seated above on a throne surrounded by a cloud of red monochrome angels, and flanked by the sun and the moon in blue clouds. From under the beard of God the Father issue eleven gold rays ('tongues of fire', Acts 2. 3, from the lesson for the day), and in their midst a downward flying dove symbolizes the Holy Spirit. The dove is represented a second time in the small letter p of the word 'spiritus'. All the figures are clad in mantles and gowns of blue, pink, or red.

There are two beautiful monochrome angels, one pink, one blue, in the crossbar of the initial, and two curious grotesques are incorporated in the bar of the marginal decoration.

Fol. 36vo, fragment 4/61. TRINITY   PLATE V

Initial B ('Benedicta', for introit). Two separate scenes with a single significance as indicated by the use of the cross to join them. Above, God the Father in blue mantle and gold cruciform halo, seated on a brown and gold throne holds the cross on which hangs the dead Christ, Second Person of the Trinity; the Third Person, the dove of the Holy Spirit, is missing (see above, p. 47), though it seems to be suggested by the pattern made by the forked beard of God. Pink, blue and red angels surround the throne, on the four corner posts of which are four golden figures (of prophets or evangelists?). The foot of the cross touches the rim of the baptismal font in the scene below, where a tonsured priest is baptizing an infant by immersion. A scroll fastened to the cross bears the words of baptism: 'In nomine patris et filii et spiritus sancti amen.' The priest wears an alb with red apparels. The godfather with his hand on the child's head, is in a red and blue motley gown; beside him is the godmother, also with her hand on the child's head, and a server holds the service book. The romanesque baptistery is grey with a blue roof and is set in a green landscape; the font is grey stone.

Fol. 38, fragment 4/40. CORPUS CHRISTI   PLATES VI and B

Initial C ('Cibavit', for introit). Two separate scenes. Above, the Last Supper, with Christ blessing the bread and wine in the institution of the Holy Sacrament. Christ's words are inscribed on two scrolls: 'Accipite et comedite hoc est corpus meum' and 'Hic calix nouum testamentum est in meo sanguine' (1 Cor. 11. 24–25).

Below, the elevation of the Host in the celebration of the mass. The scene illustrates some details of the ceremony as prescribed in the Carmelite Ordinal (Sibert, Rubric xli, pp. 81 f.): the two Carmelite servers (in brown gowns and scapulars and white mantles), the soft corporal over the chalice, and the fourfold elevation candle held by the kneeling server at the left of the altar. The two male lay figures kneeling at the left may be benefactors.

For an explanation of the Carmelites and the white dogs in the corners of the miniature, see above, pp. 49 ff.

Fol. 68vo, fragments 4/89 and 4/38. DEDICATION OF THE CHURCH   PLATES VII and A

Initial *T* ('Terribilis', for the introit). A single scene representing that part of the dedication ceremony which took place outside the building, namely the procession which encircled the church three times, stopping on each round at the principal entrance, where the Bishop knocked on the door with his crozier and said, 'Aperite portas principes vestras . . .' (*Leg. Aur.*, ed. Graesse, 1890, p. 851). The procession in the picture consists of (1) an acolyte in pink carrying a gold processional cross, accompanied by two other acolytes; (2) two tonsured choristers with a scroll containing musical notation and words (illegible); (3) a prior in a red cope carrying a crozier; (4) a bishop in blue cope and gold mitre filling his holy water sprinkler from a pail; (5) five fashionably dressed laymen, the first walking alone clad in a long scarlet gown and carrying a rosary, and followed by the others in pink, blue, white and dark green walking in pairs. During the procession around the church, the bishop sprinkled it with holy water for which the *Legenda Aurea* gives three reasons, the first of which is illustrated here, namely to drive out the devil who is seen in great consternation walking on the ridge of the roof preparing to jump off and fly away. In a blue cloud in a golden mandorla formed by two branches of the decoration is a half-length figure of Christ blessing. He wears a white gown and has a diamond-shaped rayed halo, and carries a golden globe in His left hand. The initial letter shaft is filled with blue monochrome angels, and supported by two seated figures, one in red, young and mischievous looking, the other in dark green, older and with a very fine, serious face, whom one would like to believe were the illuminator and his apprentice.

No explanation appears for the dromedary-like creature in the margin who carries on its back a golden column topped by a gold figure bearing shield and pennon, and encircled by a scarlet acanthus scroll. It may be purely decorative and whimsical, or it may suggest a mediaeval idea of the idolatrous East: the figure on the column resembles the idols represented as falling down in pieces at the approach of the Holy Family into Egypt, as, for example, in the Broederlam altarpiece wings at Dijon.

Fol. 90, fragment 4/48. CONVERSION OF PAUL   PLATE VIII

Initial *L* ('Letemur', for introit). Saul riding with his companions has been thrown prostrate, his horse falling under him (Acts 9. 1–22, epistle for the day). The vision of Christ appears in a red cloud in the upper right corner of the picture. The scene is dramatic and also has a tinge of Eastern atmosphere as suggested by the types of costumes worn, especially by the two figures nearest him: the man in the peaked hat and the one with his hair in braids and a band around his head. Saul's mantle and hose are deep blue, his gown is rich vermilion, his horse grey. The man with braided hair wears a dull green tunic embroidered at shoulder and waist. The man in the peaked hat has a soft pink tunic with enormous bag sleeves and exaggeratedly long cuffs covering the hand, such as were fashionable in the late fourteenth century. The second horse is bright chestnut; the landscape is very dark green with coloured flowerets in the foreground. The initial letter is blue monochrome and contains a shaded acanthus scroll and a mask with a leaf in its mouth. The acanthus scroll in the border changes colour each time it turns over.

Fol. 93, fragment 4/18. PURIFICATION OF THE VIRGIN   PLATE IX

Initial *S* ('Suscepimus', for introit). In the centre of a gothic chapel (representing the temple) is Mary with the Child; she holds out the naked Babe to the high priest Simeon, who, with closed eyes, reaches out his covered hands to receive Him. Behind the priest is Joseph, and accompanying the Virgin are four women, one of whom carries a basket with the offering of doves—two according to the gospel (Luke 2. 22-32) but three here. Two lay figures are entering the porch of the chapel, and another clad in a golden mantle stands in front of the altar. Cf. p. 90.

The colouring is particularly brilliant and varied: the Virgin is clad in a deep blue mantle, and both she and the Child have golden haloes. Simeon is in white; Joseph has a cap and gown of soft grey-blue, the same colour worn by the figure on the left of the two in the porch; the colour here is shaded with brown and has a shimmering texture. The companion to this figure is in an orange mantle. The woman with the doves has a dark green mantle over a gold gown. The architecture is largely grey shaded with white and darker grey. The barrel roof and dome are blue, the vaulting inside is red but the walls are dark green. The porch is brown with a terra-cotta tiled roof, and inside has a dark green ribbed barrel vault. The black and white tiles are washed over with red which is pale in the foreground and becomes darker further back. The scroll wrapped round the tree is blue lined with vermilion. The tree grows out of a patch of dark green ground behind the grotesque animal which holds a corner of the initial in its mouth. The hermit and his hut held in the curves of the many-coloured acanthus scroll are charming suggestions of Eastern atmosphere, or perhaps of Carmelite origins.

Fol. 99, fragment 4/8. ANNUNCIATION   PLATE X

Initial *R* ('Rorate', for introit). The Virgin in a gown of strong pink and a blue mantle lined with orange colour, kneels at a yellow *prie dieu*, her hands folded across her breast. The angel Gabriel, barefoot, and with the six wings of a seraph, points to the scroll with the angelic greeting which he holds in his left hand: 'Aue maria gracia plen(a) dominus tecum.' The Virgin's reply is written on the book open before her: 'Ecce ancilla domini fiat mic(hi)' (Luke 1. 26).

Gabriel's feathers are dark blue-grey; around his neck is a white amice, and attached to his girdle is a white kerchief and a silver messenger's pouch marked with a red cross. The head of God the Father appears in a yellow tabernacle surrounded by a frill of pink, blue and orange clouds. Two musical angels with instruments (a rebeck and a harp) are dressed respectively in blue dress and pink wings, and pink dress and blue wings. The kneeling Carmelite wears a rusty black habit under his white cloak.

The colour is heavily shaded, also in the border, and hot in tone, but the effect is rich though rather heavy.

Fol. 100, fragment 4/84.

RICHARD, BISHOP (OF CHICHESTER) and CONFESSOR (d. 1253)   PLATE XIa

Initial *D* ('Deus', for collect). Richard de Wyche, Chancellor to Edmund Rich, Archbishop of Canterbury (see Pl. XXIIb). He wears a pink cope decorated with a pattern of three white dots, with a blue orphrey. He holds a blue book in his left hand and carries a crozier in his right. His mitre is gold washed over with red. The background is vermilion with darker red arabesques; the initial is pink and blue, and the leaf motifs are heavily shaded as in the preceding miniature.

Fol. 100vo, fragment 4/82. AMBROSE, Bishop (of Milan), Doctor of the Church, and Confessor   PLATE XIb

Initial *D* ('Deus', for collect). He is seated with an open book in his lap, teaching two ecclesiastics (a Carmelite and a novice) and a lay man and woman who might be bene-factors (cf. Pls. XV and XXXIII). Ambrose wears a pink chasuble over a blue dalmatic and an alb with blue apparels. His mitre and crozier are gold. The Carmelite habit is rusty black as in the Annunciation.

Fol. 100vo, fragment 2/101. SIXTUS I, Pope   (Not reproduced)

Initial *D* ('Deus', for collect). He is dressed in pontifical robes and wears the triple tiara. The miniature has been ruined by repainting. See p. 137.

Fol. 113, fragment 4/1. NATIVITY OF JOHN THE BAPTIST   PLATE XIIa

Initial *D* ('De', for introit). The scene illustrates the gospel for the day (Luke 1. 57-68). Elizabeth is sitting up on a couch with a pink coverlet, receiving from the hands of a young woman the naked child John. Zacharias sits on the foot of the couch writing on a scroll the name of the child: 'Ioh(annes) est nomen e(ius)' (vs. 63). Elizabeth wears a blue gown and white wimple; Zacharias also is in a blue gown, and wears a pink hood. The young woman attendant wears a pink gown and a loose white veil held by a gold band across her forehead. The kneeling Carmelite, as usually, holds a blank scroll; his habit is rusty black.

Fol. 118, fragment 4/78. MARTIN (Bishop of Tours)   (Not reproduced)
Translation and Ordination

Initial *D* ('Deus', for collect). Two tonsured clerics in surplices are reading prayers before a rich golden shrine, flanked by two pairs of candles. The shrine presumably con-tains the relics of Saint Martin whose body was stolen from Poitiers by citizens of Tours. (*Leg. Aur.*, p. 748 f.). The colours are strong hot pink, vermilion, and harsh blue.

Fol. 118vo, fragment 4/26. OCTAVE OF THE APOSTLES PETER AND PAUL   PLATE XIIb

Initial *S* ('Sapientiam', for introit). Two scenes from the gospel for the day (Matt. 14. 22-33). Above, Christ is walking on blue and white streaked water toward a yellow boat in which are three of the Apostles; Peter is in the bow, holding a scroll inscribed with the words which he addressed to the Master: 'Domine iube me uenire a (*sic*) te super (aquas)' (vs. 28). Below, the arrangement of the scene is reversed: Christ is walking on the water in the extreme left corner, while Peter, having left the boat (now on the right side) is also walking with his feet in the water, toward the Master. The scrolls in the hands of Christ and Peter indicate their conversation as follows: Peter, 'Domine saluum me fac' (vs. 30); Christ, 'Modice fidei qua(re) dubitasti etcetera' (vs. 31). The colours are chiefly hot pink and strong blue.

Fol. 130, fragments 4/59, 4/31, 4/14. LAWRENCE, Martyr   PLATE XIII

Initial *C* ('Confessio', for introit). Eight scenes from the life and miracles of Lawrence, five in the initial letter and three in medallions. A fourth medallion contains a kneeling Carmelite holding a blank scroll.

The story follows the *Leg. Aur.* (pp. 488–92). It begins in the medallion at the top of the border, where the pope, Sixtus II, is being led away to prison by a centurion for refusing to render to the Emperor Decius money entrusted to him for charity. Lawrence, his archdeacon, addresses him by means of the inscription on the scroll: 'Domine quid faciam de thesa(uriis).' The answer is shown in the second medallion: the treasure chest is open and overflowing with gold pieces which Lawrence is distributing to a crowd of men and women. But the day of reckoning comes speedily. Decius in his determination to secure the treasure, causes the arrest of Lawrence; he, on the last of the three days of grace he has requested before accounting to the Emperor for the treasure, appears before Decius and his prefect Valerian followed by a crowd of the poor among whom he has distributed the money. His words, on the scroll, are 'Hii sunt thesauri ete(rni)'. Next follow the inevitable consequences, in two scenes: Lawrence is taken, bound, and put in prison and ordered to be burned, bound on a gridiron over a hot fire. After suffering this horrible torture for some time, Lawrence remarks: 'Iam uersa et manduca quia,' or, in the gruesome words of the Legend, 'assasti unam partem, gira aliam et manduca.'

The remaining three scenes (two in the initial, the third in the border medallion) deal with two incidents in the story of the Emperor Henry II and his wife Cunigunda, which in the Golden Legend forms part of the story of Lawrence. The first related that the Emperor and his wife had taken vows of celibacy, but at the instigation of the devil, Henry was led to suspect that Cunigunda had broken her vow, and he was persuaded to put her to the test of treading on hot coals to prove her innocence; thus she is represented in the lower scene (left) in the initial. In the Legend (p. 495), the Empress calls upon Christ and walks on the coals without burning her feet; in the miniature, she calls upon Lawrence to aid her in her trial in the following words: 'Sanctus Laurencius adiu(ua me).'

The other incident from the story of Henry is illustrated in two pictures; in the right lower corner of the initial a hermit (a Carmelite!) leans out of his window and says to a devil on the wing: 'Adiuro te dic michi quo uis (*sic*)'; the devil (who looks ridiculously like an American Indian) replies: 'Ad obitum herod (*sic*)', which, it seems, must be an error on the part of the illuminator for 'Ad obitum hērici (henrici), (see above, p. 52); in the medallion, is the weighing of the Emperor's soul, with the devil sitting in the scales, and Lawrence standing by with the chalice given by Henry ready to throw it in to make weight on the Emperor's side.

The colour scheme is blue, vermilion, orange, and lake pink; the colours are clearer and less unpleasantly strong than in the preceding miniatures. Contemporary costume is used for the participants in the scenes.

Fol. 131, fragment 4/92. ANNUNCIATION TO THE VIRGIN OF HER DEATH   PLATE XIV*a*

Initial *S* ('Salve', for introit of the Vigil of the Assumption). Small red and blue initial *a* joining the *S*, with Carmelite praying. In the upper scene, an angel in red with blue wings gives the Virgin the palm which is the emblem of her approaching death; in the lower, at the left, John the Evangelist enters her room summoned by the angelic message, and at the right he is again represented receiving from the Virgin the palm with which he is to prevent the desecration of her body by the Jews (*Leg. Aur*, p. 505 f.). (See below, miniature of the Assumption.) The Virgin wears a pink kirtle and blue mantle lined with red, and a golden crown.

Fol. 131, fragment 4/86. HIPPOLYTUS   PLATE XIV*b*

Initial *D* ('Da', for collect). This saint is closely connected with Lawrence, since it was Lawrence who converted and baptized Hippolytus, and Hippolytus who buried the remains of Lawrence after his martyrdom. Hippolytus was harnessed to the feet of unbroken horses and dragged over rocky ground through thorns and thistles until he was dead (*Leg. Aur*., p. 502). A soldier holds in one hand a sword, in the other a severed head, presumably one of Hippolytus' brothers who were beheaded before his eyes as part of his martyrdom. The colours (chiefly pink and blue) are rather strong but fine and clear.

Fol. 132vo, fragments 4/58, 4/49, 4/68.
DEATH AND ASSUMPTION OF THE VIRGIN   PLATE XV

Initial *G* ('Gaudeamus', for introit). In the initial are six incidents from the story of the Virgin's death and assumption (*Leg. Aur*., pp. 504 ff.): (1) at the extreme left, angels are bringing together the disciples to be with the Virgin before she dies; (2) below, left, the Virgin is on her deathbed, beside her are seven disciples; (3) right, the funeral of the Virgin, showing four disciples carrying the bier, and John (palm in hand) and other disciples forming the cortege; one of the Jews who tried to seize the Virgin's body is falling off head downward, the other climbing on the bier has his hands fixed to it; (4) centre, twelve disciples (two in the initial framework facing towards centre) gathered round the closed tomb; (5) above, Christ crowning the Virgin; (6) the Virgin dropping her girdle into the hands of Thomas who, according to the legend, came too late to witness the Assumption and doubted what had happened until he received the girdle from the hands of the Virgin in heaven.

In four medallions of the border, incidents from a miracle of the Virgin are represented (*Leg. Aur*., pp. 513 f.). (1) A knight is bargaining with the devil to sell his wife for gold; (2) the knight persuades his wife to accompany him to his rendezvous with the devil; (3) on the way she stops to pray to the Virgin in a wayside chapel, while her husband waits outside holding the horses; (4) the Virgin, impersonating the wife (whom she has put to sleep in the chapel) accompanies the knight to the place of rendezvous where she is recognized by the devil who, furious at the deception, flees in terror from the power of the Virgin, while the knight falls on his knees in gratitude to her for delivering him from his nefarious bargain. The conclusion of the story (not represented in the Missal unless implied by the kneeling man and woman in the border) is that the knight subsequently receives even greater wealth through the help of the Virgin than the devil had promised him.

The costume is contemporary fourteenth century dress throughout, even for the Virgin. The colours are the usual pink, red, orange, and ultramarine blue of the fine clear quality used by this artist, but the miniature has been smudged, perhaps through damage by water.

Fol. 133vo, fragment 4/85. LAWRENCE with Emblems of his Martyrdom

(Not reproduced)

Initial *B* ('Beati', for collect of the Octave). The saint holds in his right hand the gridiron on which he was burned, and in his left the two-pronged fork with which the fire was stirred. He is dressed in a blue dalmatic as in the miniature with scenes from his life.

Fol. 135vo, fragment 4/83. LOUIS, King (of France) and Confessor   PLATE XVII*a*

Initial *D* ('Deus', for collect). Richly dressed in a blue ermine-lined robe, he carries in his right hand a sceptre and in his left a red book. This picture was formerly thought to be a portrait of Richard II; though the artist may have made the king resemble Richard, the identification could never have been taken seriously owing to the halo! On the style, see above, p. 92 f.

Fol. 136vo, fragment 4/81. AUGUSTINE, Doctor, Bishop (of Hippo) and Confessor

PLATE XVI*a*

Initial *A* ('Adesto', for collect). Three ideas connected with Saint Augustine are suggested by this picture: (1) the traditional composition by him, in collaboration with Saint Ambrose, Bishop of Milan, of the beautiful hymn beginning, 'Te deum laudamus', which, the Golden Legend relates (p. 553) was written by these two men, each contributing alternate lines; the scrolls read: 'Te deum laudamus te dominum [confitemus]' and 'Te eternum patrem: omnis ter[rae] vene[ramur]'. (See John Julian, *A Dictionary of Hymnology*, revised ed., London, 1907, pp. 1120 f.). (2) The consecration of the saint as Bishop of Hippo (*Leg. Aur.*, p. 554). (3) Reference to the so-called Rule of Saint Augustine followed by the Friars Austin, one of whom is represented adoring the patron of his Order.

Fol. 136vo, fragment 4/46. DECOLLATION OF THE BAPTIST   PLATE XVI*b*

Initial *G* ('Gloria', for introit). Four scenes taken directly from Mark 6. 17–29, the gospel for the day. (1) John the Baptist denouncing Herod for marrying Herodias, his brother's wife (vs. 18); (2) Herod's birthday party at which Salome, daughter of Herodias, pleases the king so much by her dancing that he grants her any wish she may make (vss. 21–23); (3) Salome receives the head of the Baptist on a silver platter from the executioner who has cut it off, in fulfilment of her wish (vss. 27–28); (4) two disciples of the Baptist place his head and body together in a tomb, contrary to the statement in vs. 29 that the head and body were buried apart to prevent any chance of John's resurrection.

An additional detail taken from the Golden Legend is faithfully pictured in the framework of the initial, the incident of the punishment of Salome: 'while she was walking over ice, the ice gave way under her and she remained in a continual state of drowning' (*Leg. Aur.*, p. 573). Salome half immersed in water is gesticulating frantically over the head of the Baptist. The kneeling Carmelite holds the usual blank scroll. The gold is exceptionally fine, and the red and blue strapwork in the initial is richly shaded.

Fol. 138, fragment 4/50. GILES   PLATE XVII*b*

Initial *I* ('Intercessio', for collect). The hermit saint is seated before his hut fondling the doe, while the hunter all in red, ruefully fingers the bow that has just loosed the arrow which wounded Giles (*Leg. Aur.*, p. 583). The saint is dressed in a black hooded mantle; red drops of blood issue from the arrow wound in his knee. The dark green of the landscape and the soft pink of the initial make a fine colour contrast. The faces are wonderfully modelled, and also the soft body of the doe. This is unquestionably one of the most touchingly beautiful miniatures in the Missal.

Fol. 138vo, fragment 4/13. BIRTH OF THE VIRGIN   PLATE XVIII

Initial *G* ('Gaudeamus', for introit). Anna, in deep blue gown and white wimple, is sitting propped up in a bed handsomely furnished with dark green curtains and a grey embroidered cover; she is reaching out to take the swaddled child (a girl, with long hair!) who is held by one of the four attending women. A low wooden stand with a candlestick is the only other furniture in the room. In this scene there is none of the activity usually found in representations of this event; it seems, in fact, more a devotional than a narrative picture. Everything is quiet and orderly; the three coifed women in orange, light blue and pink stand by with thoughtful faces, while Anna, as she reaches out for the child, has a far-away look on her face, as though, in fact, she were saying (to quote the *Protevangelium*), 'My soul is magnified this day.'[1]

There is a sense of space in the room, in spite of the crowding of the figures into the foreground, and this space is further increased by the empty porch at the left. The architecture is painted entirely in tones of terra-cotta, inside and out, except for the light blue roofs. The foreground is dark green with red and blue flowerets growing in the grass; the initial is soft shaded pink. The musical angels in the branches of the border are dressed in red, blue, and pink mantles. The whole composition both in drawing and in colour is conceived as painting rather than as illumination; the modelling of the faces is carefully and beautifully done in white and pink on a greenish flesh base. The head of Anna is particularly fine in its modelling and shows this artist's characteristic style to best advantage.

Fol. 140, fragment 4/72. EXALTATION OF THE CROSS   PLATES XIX*a* and C

Initial *N* ('Nos', for introit). The Emperor Heraclius riding with his knights, clad in contemporary (*i.e.* late fourteenth century) armour; at the top of the picture, against the stippled gold ground, is a scarlet cloud from the midst of which an angel leans out holding the cross (*Leg. Aur.*, p. 607). Obviously the artist was overwhelmingly interested in the panoply of the scene and in the differentiation of the many types of faces and dress in the noble company, which formerly was thought to represent King Richard II with his knights. The red-gowned prophet in the margin surrounded by blank scrolls, and the similar figure,

[1] James, M. R., *The Apocryphal New Testament*, Oxford, 1924, p. 41.

perhaps of a patriarch, holding an open book, may be intended to suggest a connection with Jerusalem, traditional early home of the Carmelites. The youth in blue in the lower scroll seems to be purely decorative. The colour is brilliant with much red and terra-cotta used for tunics, horses and initial, but the large amount of steel-blue armour tones down the warmer colours. The Emperor is clad in a scarlet tunic and white hose; his mantle is deep blue, and his imperial bonnet is terra-cotta red. The trappings of his horse are terra-cotta. The ground is the usual dark green dotted with coloured flowerets.

On the armour and costume, see above, pp. 55 f.

Fol. 143vo, fragment 4/60. MAURICE AND HIS COMPANIONS — PLATE XIX*b*

Initial *D* ('Deus', for collect). The story of the famous Theban legion who, when called into service to fight for the Emperor of Rome, vowed not to kill Christians, and who themselves were nearly all killed in consequence (*Leg. Aur.*, pp. 629 f.), was difficult to illustrate. Maurice is on the left, fully armed with his helmet on the ground in front of him. Opposite him a youthful figure (the standard bearer?) clad in a long blue tunic girt with a jewelled sword belt; his blue cap also lies on the ground. Behind him on the right side are two beardless figures and behind Maurice on the left are two figures with beards. All are nimbed and all are praying. Above the heads of the two principal figures is the hand of God stretched out in blessing.

Fol. 143vo, fragment 4/77. CLEOPHAS — PLATE XIX*c*

Initial *L* ('Letabitur', for introit). The Cleophas incident is told in Luke 24. 13–18, but the illustration is not very clear. Cleophas carrying a pilgrim's staff in his left hand and a book in his right, is about to enter the city (of Emmaus); the porter has opened the gate to him. Cleophas wears an orange gown with short sleeves over a blue tunic and hose. A pink hood is topped by his pilgrim's hat. He has a pink halo.

Fol. 152vo, fragment 4/55.
ALL SAINTS, with the CORONATION OF THE VIRGIN — PLATE XX

Initial *G* ('Gaudeamus', for introit). The Virgin in a soft pink mantle is seated on a wide gold throne behind which are three scarlet angels, and above these, a band of blue monochrome angels. Beside the Virgin, God the Father in a deep blue mantle and cruciform halo crowns her with His right hand and with His left supports the crucifix; a downward-flying dove halfway between the head of the Father and that of the Son on the cross, represents the Third Person of the Trinity. (See above, pp. 48 f., for the iconography.) On each side are saints, male at the left of the throne, female at the right. These are, for the most part, not individually recognizable, except almost certainly (by their facial types) Peter, Paul, and Andrew in the front row. The Baptist is not in a prominent place as might be expected. The female saints also carry no attributes, but the first one, who is crowned, is probably Catherine. Below the central figures is a group of singing angels, gathered round a music scroll, on which the word 'gloria' can be read. Other angels with musical instruments are in the margin; the initial letter is filled with monochrome angels in pale, terra-cotta red. Below the initial is a *bas de page* scene, representing a woman (with a distaff?) hunting a stag who has turned on the two pursuing dogs. There seems to be no connection between this and the subject of the miniature.

Fol. 159, fragment 4/52. MARTIN, Bishop (of Tours) and Confessor   PLATE XXI

Inital *D* ('Deus', for collect). Three incidents in the life of this popular saint are represented in the miniature (*Leg. Aur.*, p. 742). (1) Below, left, Saint Martin on horseback divides his fur-lined mantle with a cripple; (2) right, the saint is perhaps resurrecting a dead youth (*ibid.*, 744) (as in the window at Bourges: see Amédée Pigeon, 'Un Vitrail de la Cathédrale de Beauvais', in *Gaz. des Beaux Arts*, 3e Per., xiv, 1895 [11], p. 242). The young man is clad in red, and is standing on a grey cloth which appears to be a shroud, almost suggesting the form of a body under it. (3) Above, the consecration of Martin as Bishop of Tours. The vestments in this scene are all richly embroidered. The initial is a deep blue on a red field decorated in the corners with white or gold arabesques.

Fol. 159vo, fragment 4/75. BRICE, Bishop (of Tours) and Confessor   PLATE XXIIa

Initial *D* ('Da', for collect). The story of Martin and Brice his archdeacon, is told in *Leg. Aur.*, pp. 751 f. The bishop in gold mitre and rayed nimbus carries an archiepiscopal cross in his left hand and blesses with his right. He wears a vermilion robe over a white gown. The initial is blue.

Fol. 160, fragment 4/64.
EDMUND RICH, Archbishop of Canterbury, Confessor (d. 1242)   PLATE XXIIb

Initial *D* ('Deus', for collect). The saint wears a blue robe over a white gown, and a white mitre. He is teaching five bishops and a company of lay men and women.

Fol. 160vo, fragment 4/74. EDMUND, King (of East Anglia) and Martyr   PLATE XXIIIa

Initial *D* ('Deus', for collect). Three archers are in the act of shooting King Edmund who stands with his hands bound behind him. (For this story, see Carl Horstman, *Nova Legenda Anglie*, Oxford, 1901, 1, pp. 326 f.) He is nude except for a thin white loincloth; his body already pierced by arrows stands out sharply against a dark wood behind him. The contrast between the delicate, dignified face of Edmund and the heavy coarse faces of his executioners is striking.

Fol. 160vo, fragment 4/79. CECILIA, Virgin and Martyr   PLATE XXIIIb

Initial *D* ('Deus', for collect). In the Golden Legend story of the martyrdom of Cecilia (p. 776), before she was beheaded she was placed in a boiling cauldron whence she issued without any injury. In the miniature, the saint stands in a circle of flames which may be a variant on the traditional story. For artistic reasons, this artist may have preferred to represent her thus rather than as a nude figure half immersed in a cauldron (cf. scenes from the life of Cecilia in the Uffizi Gallery, Florence). The patterns of the flames are carried up by the gold arabesques on the red background. The saint is clad in a deep blue mantle and wears a large red halo with gold rays.

Fol. 161, fragment 4/70. CLEMENT, Pope and Martyr   PLATE XXIVa

Initial *D* ('Dicit', for introit). In a chapel with a belfry and a closed door (but an open wall) containing an altar, stands Clement holding in his left hand an anchor, symbol of his martyrdom (*Leg. Aur.*, pp. 786 f.). Water (unmistakable with boats and enormous fish) surrounds the chapel except for a path on which Clement's worshippers are walking out to his shrine on the anniversary of his death. A variation of the Golden Legend account is the fact that here Clement is not in his tomb but very much alive and apparently welcoming his visitors.

Fol. 161, fragment 4/87. CHRYSOGONUS, Martyr .... PLATE XXIV*b*

Initial *A* ('Adesto', for collect). A Roman martyr, beheaded under Diocletian, according to the story told briefly in the Golden Legend (p. 789). He is represented in the scene of his beheading with his eyes bound. The high throne on which the Emperor is seated is solidly represented by the use of planes of light and dark grey. The soldier wears a complete suit of chain mail, and over it a full-sleeved jacque.

Fol. 161vo, fragment 4/71. CATHERINE (of Alexandria), Virgin and Martyr ... PLATE XXV

Initial *O* ('Omnipotens', for collect). Two scenes from the latter part of her life: above, her disputation with the doctors; below, the miracle of the breaking of the wheel on which she was to have suffered martyrdom (*Leg. Aur.*, pp. 793 f.). She wears a blue mantle over a white, full-sleeved gown, and on her bushy golden-yellow hair she has a crown indicating her royal rank.

Fol. 162, fragment 4/88.
SATURNINUS, Bishop (of Toulouse) and Martyr .... PLATE XXVI

Initial *D* ('Deus', for collect). Dressed in blue chasuble and white mitre and gloves, and carrying a crozier in his left hand, he blesses with his right. In the border sprays are four little grotesque animals which may have been intended by the artist to suggest a facet of the life of this saint. It is related in the Golden Legend (pp. 797 f.) how, on his entrance into the heathen city of Toulouse, all the devil-gods ceased to respond when invoked by the inhabitants. Then one of the heathen said to the others that unless Saturninus were killed, they could never again get anything from their gods. The newly elected bishop, therefore, was bound to the feet of a bull which was driven over the edge of a precipice. The grotesques may, as in other cases, be merely decorative, but it seems possible that, since more of them accompany this miniature than any other in the Missal, they may also represent some of the devils in the story. In the margin below the miniature, two centaurs are fighting. The initial is grey, the background red with gold arabesques, and the field on which it is placed, very beautifully stippled gold.

Fol. 162, fragment 4/76. LINUS, Pope and Martyr .... PLATE XXVI

Initial *P* ('Preces', for collect). Clad in red pontifical robes over an alb, and wearing the three-tiered papal tiara, and carrying an archiepiscopal cross. The initial is pink and the background is blue.

Fol. 162, fragment 4/33. THE CALLING OF PETER AND ANDREW .... PLATE XXVI

Initial *D* ('Dominus', for introit of the Vigil of Andrew). The incident is from the gospel for this day (Matt. 4. 18–22). Peter is in the prow of the boat and Andrew is behind him, drawing in his net. Christ stands on the shore and talks to them. Christ is dressed in a gown of taupe colour and is barefoot; Peter is in red, and Andrew is in blue. The boat is yellow shaded with brown. The characteristic round, short-bearded face of Peter and the elongated head and long beard of Andrew as seen here are recognizable also in the front row of the saints in the All Saints miniature (Pl. xx).

At the bottom of this page is a marginal scene (fragment 4/65) illustrating further in a naïve and charming way verse 19: two youths have cast their net and caught three fish, the number perhaps symbolizing the Trinity. The decorative initials on this page are blue, gold, and pinkish tan.

Fol. 163, fragment 4/73. MARTYRDOM OF ANDREW   PLATE XXVIIa

Initial *M* ('Michi', for introit of mass for the day). Two scenes following closely the Golden Legend (pp. 16–17). On the left, the trial of Andrew at which he argued that the Crucifixion was a mystery, not a punishment. He was condemned to death by being crucified, and on the right he is shown being bound on the cross with ropes, so that the torture might be prolonged. The cross is the saltire form; its curious appearance in relation to the ground is due to faulty perspective. Andrew is recognizable in type, and is clothed in a blue mantle; he wears a halo. The initial is vermilion heavily shaded with brown. The landscape is the usual dark, bluish green.

Fol. 165, fragment 4/54. ANDREW   PLATE XXVIIb

Initial *P* ('Protegat', for collect of the octave). Andrew bound on the cross, alive but suffering. Two of the executioners are tightening the cords binding his hands to the cross. The type of Andrew is recognizable as in the other miniatures representing him.

Fol. 164, fragment 4/69. ELIGIUS (LOY), Bishop (of Noyon) and Confessor
PLATE XXVIII

Initial *E* ('Exaudi', for collect). The grey-haired saint in red chasuble, apparelled alb, and white mitre, holds his crozier in his left arm and offers a golden saddle to the King (of France) in blue ermine-lined robes. The picture combines two incidents in the Golden Legend story (p. 952) in which Loy, a skilled goldsmith, was given gold to make the King a beautiful saddle. From the amount of gold judged sufficient for one saddle, he made two, carrying one to the King who was pleased and paid him well for it, and keeping the other in his own house. After some little time, Loy brought the second saddle to the King, who was even more amazed to find that two had been made from material intended for one. When asked by the King how he could do this, Loy replied: 'Bene . . . ex gratia Dei.' Loy became famous at court as a goldsmith and renowned for his charity to the poor; he was later made Bishop of Noyon.

Fol. 164, fragment 4/37. BARBARA, Virgin and Martyr   PLATE XXVIII

Initial *C* ('Concede', for collect). Barbara is standing beside a tower obviously conceived as of natural size set in a landscape, rather than as a symbol held in her hand as is more usual. Barbara wears a blue mantle over a red gown, banded at the hem with ermine. On her hair is a chaplet of red roses and in her hand the palm of martyrdom. The tower shows the three windows which, as Barbara explained to her father, represented the persons of the Trinity (*Leg. Aur.*, p. 900).

Fol. 164vo, fragment 4/91. NICHOLAS, Bishop (of Myra) and Confessor   PLATE XXIX

Initial *D* ('Deus', for collect). The picture follows fairly closely the Golden Legend story (p. 23) of the poor man who received from Nicholas dowries for his three daughters, which permitted them to find husbands instead of living as prostitutes. Nicholas is seen handing in a bag of gold at the window of a room where the father is lying in bed. The first daughter stretches out her hand to receive her dowry. The others are awaiting their turn, one looking rather eagerly toward Nicholas, the other with her hands piously held in prayer, toward her dying father. The faces of all the figures in this miniature are exquisitely modelled; the flesh tones are rather dark, especially the face of the sick man. Outside in the margin kneels a charming figure of a young man holding a long-handled green besom. The figure is drawn and shaded in delicate browns. There is evidence of a correction in the drawing of the left leg and perhaps of an erased scroll. The building and its furnishings are interesting. The architecture is grey and the stepped roof with recessed arches is shaded lighter and darker. The centre arch is open and has a wooden, hinged shutter which stands ajar. The bed has dark green curtains and cover, and is highlighted at the near corner. Both building and bed are set at an angle to the foreground, as is the low wooden stand at the foot of the bed, containing an empty candlestick of blue-grey (pewter?); a shelf under the window contains a ewer (also of pewter?). The girls are dressed plainly in red, blue and pink. Saint Nicholas wears a blue chasuble, an alb, and a white mitre, and carries a crozier. The initial is light red shaded with white, and is one of the most carefully and delicately painted of the scrollwork initials. The colour and design of both sides of this leaf are rich yet restrained, the strong, fine brilliance of the miniatures being set off by the blue, tan and gold of the smaller decorative initials.

Fol. 165, fragment 4/51. CONCEPTION OF THE VIRGIN   PLATE XXX

Initial *G* ('Gaudeamus', for introit). Four separate scenes in the lives of Joachim and Anna, in a continuous spatial composition. (1) Above, the rejection of Joachim's offering in the temple. Joachim and Anna both carry a dove in the left hand, extending the right toward the priest. He holds out his left hand in a gesture of refusal, while with his right he accepts a dove from one of two women on his right. (2) Below, in a heavily wooded landscape, Joachim and two shepherd boys (one playing on a pipe) are keeping their flocks; Joachim is listening intently to an angel who speaks to him out of the clouds in the shaft of the initial. (3) At the extreme left, is the same landscape (perhaps intended to represent here the garden where Anna saw the nest of swallows in a laurel tree); she is seen listening to an angel who addresses her out of a cloud in the shaft of the initial. (4) Between the two scenes, Anna and Joachim meet at the Golden Gate.

The principal details are taken from the story as told in the *Protevangelium Jacobi*,[1] but there are some differences, such as the presence of Anna in the temple with Joachim, which seems to be an Eastern idea[2] and further points to the Eastern origin of the cult of Anna and its early adoption by the Carmelite Order.

[1] James, *op. cit.*, p. 39 f.; see also *Leg. Aur.*, p. 587 f.
[2] Cf. Beda Kleinschmidt, O.F.M., *Die Heilige Anna*, Düsseldorf, 1930, p. 31; see also p. 39 and Fig. 15.

Some additional interesting material is introduced into this subject as represented in the Missal. Outside the initial, in the lower right corner is a fierce lion with a large bone in its mouth, crouching beside a sleeping lamb or sheep; in the upper right corner, is a boy holding in each hand one of the strands which terminate the initial letter; and in the opposite corner is an animal suggesting a panther. In the margin is a drawing of two birds: above, a yellow bird of prey with a large, blue eye and a strong, hooked beak (perhaps an eagle); below, a large, long-legged white bird standing on one foot, perhaps a crane or a stork. Between these two birds is a scroll with an inscription which though apparently legible, after many attempts by different experts in handwriting, has proved to be unreadable, except for a word or two, as *est* which appears to be the second word. It may be concerned with the significance of birds which are mentioned in a prophecy of Jeremiah (8. 7): 'Milvus in coelo cognovit tempus suum; turtur et hirundo et ciconia custodierunt tempus adventus sui.' The birds might be identified as milvus (bird of prey) and ciconia (stork), but precedent for the use of this passage in connection with the Conception has not been found. Another passage from the prophecies of Isaiah (11. 6) might explain the animals and the child in the corners of the initial field: 'Habitabit lupus cum agno et pardus cum haedo accubabit; vitulus et leo et ovis simul morabuntur et puer parvulus minabit eos.' The panther (pardus), leo et ovis (lion and sheep) and the child, though not very little, are identifiable. The first verse of this chapter in Isaiah beginning 'Egredietur virga de radice yesse' is used as the alleluia versicle of the grail of the Conception mass.

This is the last of the miniatures which I can attribute to Hand A¹ in the Missal (see above, Chapter III). The colour is magnificent, and the composition of the two miniatures on the page, together with the small tan, blue, and gold initials is essentially a composition in colour. In the Conception miniature, the balance of red and blue in the draperies of Joachim and Anna is carefully worked out in relation to the deep green of the landscape, the grey of the architecture, and the soft pink of the monochrome angels in the initial. The blue of Anna's mantle carries down into the tunic of Andrew (fragment 4/54), and the grey of the architecture in the Conception is repeated in the initial of Andrew. The page must have been one of the richest and most beautiful in the whole Missal, and could be considered the *chef d'oeuvre* of this artist. In view of the fact that he does not explain his subjects by means of texts on scrolls, as do the other artists of this manuscript, it is not inconceivable that the inscription contains a signature and/or a date.

Fol. 166, fragment 4/67. LUCY, Virgin and Martyr   PLATE XXXIa

Initial *E* ('Exaudi', for collect). This 'virgin of the Lord' (*Leg. Aur.*, p. 31) is shown harnessed to a yoke of oxen which, pull as hard as they could, were unable to move her that is, shake her faith. In the Legend, not one yoke of oxen but a thousand, and in addition, a thousand men were set to try to move her, but to no avail: 'virgo domini immobilis permansit.' The source of her strength and steadfastness is symbolized by the dove of the Holy Spirit on her halo.

Lucy is in a blue gown and has flat, yellow hair, and a pink halo. The near ox is terra-cotta in colour, the far one white with black spots. The initial is painted in flat red, with no plasticity in the design. The ground is dark green with many pink and white daisies growing in it.

Fol. 166, fragment 4/39. LAZARUS, Bishop (of Marseilles?) and Confessor PLATE XXXIb

Initial D ('Deus', for collect). The resurrection of Lazarus as related in John 11. 34–44, the gospel of the day. The scene is very simple, the only persons present being Christ, and Mary and Martha, the two sisters of Lazarus. The tomb is a stone sarcophagus from which Lazarus, clad only in a thin transparent shroud, is about to arise. Christ is barefoot, wears a blue gown and carries in His left hand a globe; he has a pointed, rayed halo tooled in the gold of the background. Martha and Mary are dressed in vermilion and orange mantles, and Martha wears a wimple. The initial is soft pink beautifully shaded, but the corners of the field are filled with flat blue and red paint, possibly unfinished as to design; the lack of shading in the draperies betrays either an inferior or a learning hand (see above, pp. 93 f.). The faces are modelled better than the Lucy, but are less vivid than in the preceding miniatures in Hand A style.

Fol. 192, fragment 4/80. A MATRON   PLATE XXXIIa

Initial D ('Dilexi', for introit of the Common for a matron). A single figure clad in a mantle with a peaked hood, and a wimple, holding a rosary in her right hand and turning the pages of a book which lies open on a reading desk. In the book can be read the opening words of the introit psalm (Ps. 44. 2) of this mass: 'Eructauit cor meum uerbum bonum.'

Fol. 193, fragment 4/66. SEVERAL VIRGINS   PLATE XXXIIb

Initial U ('Uultum', for introit of the Common for several virgins). Five young women, nimbed, are praying to God whose head with cruciform nimbus appears in a cloud in the upper corner of the initial. Four of the virgins wear diadems; one, a crown. This is perhaps Catherine since she is identical with the standing figure with a wheel in the Trinity miniature (Pl. XXXIII). The others are not identifiable individually.

Fol. 193vo, fragment 4/90.

THE TRINITY WITH THE VIRGIN AS INTERCESSOR   PLATES XXXIII and D

Initial B ('Benedicta', for introit). In the upper part of the picture, God the Father and Christ the Son are seated on a rainbow, while the Dove of the Holy Spirit flies downward between them, with the rays of the Spirit streaming from its head. Below, the Virgin, clothed in a long, rose-coloured dress and a mantle lined with ermine, stands between a kneeling man and woman, each accompanied by a patron saint, only Catherine with her wheel on the left being identifiable. The saint behind the woman carries a cross and may be Cristina or possibly Margaret. In the corners of the initial are the four symbols of the Evangelists, each with a text taken from the appropriate gospel. For an explanation of the meaning of this miniature, see above, pp. 46 f.

The colour is very finely balanced, the deep blue of the mantles of God and Christ is carried down to the dress of the votive figures below by means of the mantle of the Virgin in the centre. The gold is especially brilliant and the tooling in groups of four dots may be intended to suggest the starry firmament. This is undoubtedly the *chef d'oeuvre* of Hand C in the Missal.

Appendix

A. THE METHOD USED IN THE RECONSTRUCTION OF THE MISSAL

The process of reconstructing the manuscript has evolved its own method on the basis of a succession of adaptations to the various kinds of fragments to be placed, together with the necessity of dealing with a variety of problems as they successively arose. The point of departure in the initial stages of the work was a group of twenty-two historiated initials, the subjects of which were certainly identified at the outset by their pictorial features. These, together with the portions of decoration which could be shown to join them (as demonstrated by a partial preliminary reconstruction of photographs of these cuttings), were carefully removed from the volumes and temporarily placed in folders. As each fragment was taken out, a permanent identification number was written on its back, consisting of the serial number which had already been given to the fragment, even while in the scrapbook, preceded by a 4 for Add. 29704 and a 5 for Add. 29705, and (later) a 2 for Add. 44892. The page numbers in the scrapbooks on which the various fragments were mounted, were disregarded in the new numbering. Thus a fragment which had been number 1 of 29704 became in the permanent series 4/1; whereas number 1 of 29705 became 5/1.[1]

Fundamentally, the method used in the reconstruction consisted of two distinct processes: (1) the deduction, from data collected from the twenty-two fragments first identified, of a body of criteria, cumulative and constantly subject to revision; (2) the application of these criteria to unidentified fragments. These two aspects of the reconstructive process naturally did not remain separate; on the contrary, they became increasingly interdependent as the work progressed. The best way of presenting clearly such a complicated method as was finally evolved is to go back to the beginning of the work and describe its various chronological stages in order of development.

Identification of the subjects of the first group of miniatures automatically assigned to them their places in the Missal, since there is little variation in the order of most of the feasts, even in different ecclesiastical uses. The masses thus identified by the pictures illustrating them, arranged in missal order, were as follows:

1.	Initial *U*	Ascension	*Temporale*	fol. 21vo	4/44[2]
2.	*S*	Pentecost		27vo	4/45

[1] A concordance of these numbers with the manuscript folios on which they are now found is available for use in the British Museum.

[2] Some observations regarding the numbers of the fragments may be of interest. First, it will be noted that all the miniatures are preceded by the numeral 4, since they were all collected at the beginning of scrapbook 29704. Second, the cuttings were not for the most part placed in the scrapbooks in the order

3. Initial	T	Dedication of Church	Temporale		68vo	4/89
4.	L	Conversion of Paul	Sanctorale	Jan. 25	90	4/48
5.	S	Purification		Feb. 2	93	4/18
6.	R	Annunciation		Mar. 25	99	4/8
7.	D	Birth of Baptist		June 24	113	4/1
8.	C	Lawrence		Aug. 10	130	4/59
9.	D	Hippolytus		Aug. 13	131	4/86
10.	G	Assumption of B.V.M.		Aug. 15	132vo	4/58
11.	G	Decollation of Baptist		Aug. 29	136vo	4/46
12.	I	Giles		Sept. 1	138	4/50
13.	G	Nativity of B.V.M.		Sept. 8	138vo	4/13
14.	D	Martin of Tours		Nov. 11	159	4/52
15.	D	Edmund King and Martyr		Nov. 20	160vo	4/74
16.	D	Clement Pope and Martyr		Nov. 23	161	4/70
17.	O	Catherine of Alexandria		Nov. 25	161vo	4/71
18.	M	Andrew		Nov. 30	163	4/73
19.	C	Barbara		Dec. 4	164	4/37
20.	D	Nicholas		Dec. 6	164vo	4/91
21.	E	Lucy		Dec. 13	166	4/67
22.	D	Lazarus		Dec. 17	166	4/39

The study of the above miniatures disclosed also evidence for a further identification of the nature of the original missal. In fragments 4/8, 4/1 and 4/46 a little kneeling figure appears in the corner of the initial, clothed in the dark gown and white cowled mantle of the White Friars or Carmelites. Other miniatures revealed similar figures introduced in some cases even in the miniature itself. So, it appeared, the new Missal was Carmelite.

After putting the twenty-two historiated initials in order so as to form the skeleton of a missal, the next step in the reconstruction was to identify the text which the initial letter introduced. For this purpose, two excellent printed editions of missals which were provided with well-arranged liturgical indexes were used at first: Dr J. Wickham Legg's edition of a manuscript Missal written for Westminster Abbey, London, in 1383–4[1]; and the no less valuable edition prepared by F. H. Dickinson[2] of the printed Sarum Missal published together with a Calendar. Obviously the usefulness of the Westminster Missal for purposes of identifying fragments of text in the prospective Carmelite Missal was limited because of the difference in the feasts peculiar to the Benedictine and the

in which they were cut out of the original manuscript, as is shown by the fact that the numbers of the fragments when restored to their proper order in the Missal do not run consecutively as when in their scrapbook order. It is apparent, therefore, that the original manuscript must have been completely cut up (or, at least, all the pages containing miniatures) before the arrangement of the cuttings was begun. There are a few exceptions to this difference in order: the Pentecost picture followed that of the Ascension both in the Missal and in the scrapbook; and the pictures of Clement and Catherine, which were consecutive in the scrapbook, are now mounted on the two sides of the same leaf in the Missal. The fragments of border decoration which join these miniatures were scattered throughout both scrapbooks.

[1] The so-called Lytlington Missal. The edition here referred to was published by the Henry Bradshaw Society under the title: *Missale ad Usum Ecclesie Westmonasteriensis*, 3 vols., London, 1891, 1893, 1896.
[2] *Missale ad Usum Sarum*, Burntisland, 1861–83.

Carmelite rites; however, for the *Temporale*[1] and for the more common masses of the *Sanctorale*, especially for those of the English saints, it was found invaluable. The Sarum Missal represents the rite most commonly used in England in the fourteenth century.

The ideal source for the identification of the Carmelite text would have been another complete missal of the same rite, use, and date; but, unfortunately, no such manuscript was known. The best substitute, therefore, was the Carmelite Ordinal of Sibert de Beka,[2] which, by the time the new Missal was written, had been adopted generally throughout the Order. The extremely close dependence of the Carmelite Missal on the Ordinal is indicated by the fact that in the new Missal were found fragments of rubrics which correspond word for word to those in the Lambeth copy of Sibert. The outstanding disadvantage of using an ordinal as the basis for reconstructing a missal is obvious: the ordinal is a book of instructions covering every phase of the religious devotions in a conventual house, arranged in the most convenient order for ready reference. The masses form only a portion of these devotions; hence much material extraneous to a mass-book is included in an ordinal. Moreover, an ordinal usually gives only the cues for the various parts of the mass, and the Lambeth manuscript of Sibert omits even these in the case of secrets and postcommunions. Thus the Lambeth manuscript text had to be constantly supplemented from other sources for the identification of many fragments of missal text.

From the cues in the Sibert ordinal, however, the particular part of the mass introduced by all except one of the initials listed above could be readily identified. Thirteen out of the twenty-two were found to introduce the introit of the mass; eight introduce the collect; one (4/37 with a picture of Saint Barbara) could not be found either in the mass for this saint as given in Westminster or in Sarum; the Lambeth manuscript of Sibert does not contain the special mass for her. When later Carmelite sources became available, this initial *C* was found to begin a special collect for Barbara introduced into the rite in 1321. In two cases further confirmatory evidence was found in bits of text on the fragments themselves: 4/18 contains a portion of the mass heading which had not been cut off from the initial. The text (with a few letters interpolated) reads as follows: '(Mis)sam totum duplex offici(um)', after which follows immediately the large initial with the first letter of the 'officium', that is introit, of this mass as found in Sibert. In the case of the other text fragment found on 4/44, the whole of the first two words of the introit, 'Uiri galilei', are given with the historiated initial.

One of the twenty-two historiated initials first identified was found in Sibert to introduce the collect of the mass for Saint Lazarus, a feast which does not occur in the Westminster and Sarum Missals, but among missals of English use is peculiar to the Carmelite rite. In this first group of identified fragments, therefore, two types of variation distinguish-

---

[1] The *Temporale* contains the feasts of movable date depending on the date of Easter; they normally comprise the first part of a missal. The *Sanctorale* contains the feasts of fixed date as listed in the Calendar; they follow the *Temporale*. The *Commune Sanctorum* contains masses and collects for saints having feasts of different ranks, to whom an individual mass is not assigned in the missal, as well as votive masses for different occasions. The *Commune Sanctorum* comes last in the usual order of the missal.

[2] Compiled by Sibert de Beka *ca.* 1312; manuscript copy of *ca.* 1320 in Lambeth Palace Library, MS. 193. Printed and edited with an introduction by Fr Benedict Zimmerman, O.C.D., as *Ordinaire de l'ordre de Notre-Dame du Mont-Carmel* ('Bibliothèque Liturgique' [Ulysse Chevalier, Paris, 1910], XIII). For greater convenience the printed edition has been used in preference to the manuscript itself which, however, was deposited in the British Museum for many months to be consulted on questionable points.

ing this Carmelite Missal from that of other rites are represented: the use of special and characteristic collects for feasts common both to Carmelite and to other rites, as that for Saint Barbara; and the introduction of special and characteristic feasts, as that of Saint Lazarus. A third outstanding variation between the Carmelite Missal and other rites is the division of the masses between *Temporale* and *Sanctorale* so that the latter begins with the mass of Saint Maur. The rubric at the beginning of the *Sanctorale* in Sibert's Ordinal reads as follows:

'Quia supra in Temporali actum est de festis quibusdam quae scilicet eveniunt a Nativitate Domini usque ad crastinum octavarum Epiphaniae, idea consequenter illum ordinem continuando incipiendum restat a festo sancti Mauri quod immediate festa prae-dicta sequitur, ut sic ipsum Sanctorale ad festum Nativitatis Domini terminetur . . .'[1]

Thus in the Carmelite liturgical year, the first mass of the *Sanctorale* is that of Saint Maur (Jan. 15) and the last is that of Saint Thomas the Apostle (Dec. 21); all the special feasts between Dec. 21 and Jan. 15 are included in the winter portion of the *Temporale*[2] with the other feasts of variable date. The usual arrangement in missals of other rites is to begin the *Sanctorale* with either the Vigil of Andrew (Nov. 29) or the day of Saint Silvester (Dec. 31). The discovery of this fundamental difference in the arrangement of a Carmelite Missal, as stated in Sibert, was very important in planning the general layout of the manu-script to be reconstructed.

All the data thus far collected from a study of the preliminary group of twenty-two identified historiated initials have been concerned with the verification of the parts of the mass introduced by these initial letters, and with their position in the order of a Carmelite Missal. The next point to be determined in regard to these miniatures was their exact position on the page.

From a careful preliminary study of all the cuttings while still in the scrapbooks, a number of facts about the layout of the page in the original manuscript had been dis-covered, including rough measurements of its dimensions. One detail thus early observed was of fundamental importance in establishing criteria governing the placing of fragments on the page: the fact that the text was written in two columns separated by a centre margin measuring, as shown on several different fragments, 4 cm. Any fragments, there-fore, which showed on the left side both rulings of the centre margin could be placed immediately in the right hand text column; any which showed a single ruling and a margin measuring more than 4 cm. could be placed in the left column. Sometimes one of the centre margin rulings had been cut off (as in 4/52); but the position of the initial in the right column is none the less clearly indicated by the fact that two letters at the ends of lines of the left text column can be seen on the fragment. One more observation about the width of mar-gins: those of fragments 4/89 and 4/50 (both measuring more than 4 cm. and therefore left column initials) show a very great difference in width, though the border decorations which fill the margins are in exactly the same style. It appeared, therefore, that, as usual, there was a considerable difference between the width of the inner and the outer side margins of the pages as originally planned: the miniature 4/89 having a wide left (outer)

---

[1] Sibert, p. 206. In text passages quoted from this printed edition of the Lambeth manuscript, the modernized spelling of the Latin as used there has been retained.

[2] Since no fragments of this part have been identified it may be assumed that it did not form part of the manuscript when it was cut up.

margin, must have been on the verso of the leaf; the initial 4/50, having a narrower left margin (but still measuring more than 4 cm.), must have been on the recto of the leaf, where the left margin is the inner one, and is partly included in the binding. These tentative calculations were confirmed by later evidence.

Several of the identified initials show evidence in the form of top or bottom margin lines for their exact position on the page. One (4/50) is definitely placed in the bottom corner of a left hand column; another (4/37) belongs in the right column, one line from the bottom, as shown by the lower margin lines on the attached decoration. Fragment 4/8 was clearly in the bottom corner of a column and could be placed in the left column of the recto of a page because the margin at the left is wider than a centre margin and not so wide as a verso outer margin. A number of other initials in the group likewise could be placed definitely when the decoration which originally joined was added, since these fragments often show top or bottom margin lines.

From the number of identified miniatures showing some evidence for their position on the page, four on two different folios have been selected to illustrate in detail the four different positions possible. The diagram on page 122 shows these positions marked out on the recto and verso of the leaf, and at the same time demonstrates the relation, in terms of text space, of any initial to the fragment of text on its reverse.

Let us examine each of these four positions in turn.

Position *A*. Left column of the recto of the leaf: Saint Giles, Sept. 1 (4/50). The *I* introduces the collect of his mass: 'I[ntercessio . . .]'; on the reverse of the fragment is a portion of the epistle of the mass for the Nativity of the Virgin, Sept. 8. Between these two points in the Missal three whole columns of text intervene. Since space must be allowed for the remainder of the mass for Giles (secret and postcommunion, and, possibly, cues for the other parts of the mass), cues for the morning mass of the Nativity of the Virgin, collects for a commemoration of Adrian (whose feast is celebrated on the same day) the introit of the Nativity mass, with a very large historiated initial, the collect and all the first part of the epistle (the fragment found on the back of the Giles picture coming at the very end of this passage), three columns are not too much; hence Position *A* is verified.

Position *B*. Left column of the verso of the leaf: Birth of the Virgin, Sept. 8 (4/13). The large *G* introduces the introit of the mass: 'G[audeamus . . .].' On the back of this fragment are the latter part of the postcommunion of the mass of Giles (in which his name occurs), and the '*Ite missa est*', with music, and '*Deo gracias*', which close the mass; and the heading of the mass of the Nativity, with the beginning of rubrics for the celebration of the morning mass if the feast comes on Sunday. Between the heading of this mass and the first word of the introit (found on the miniature side), there is only one column of text, and this would be enough for the three collects for Adrian and also for cues if given.

To sum up the evidence furnished by an explanation of the positions *A* and *B*, we find (1) that an initial in the left column of the recto of a leaf has text on its back which comes three columns further on in the missal, and usually must be sought for, therefore, in a later mass; (2) that an initial in the left column of the verso of a leaf has text on its back which will be found in the mass immediately preceding that introduced by the initial, as the intervening space is only one column. The exact position of a fragment within either of these columns (that is, whether top, middle or bottom of the column) has no effect on this calculation, since the spatial relation between the text on the one side and that on the other side is constant.

Initials in Positions C and D, that is, in right hand columns of text, were difficult to place on the recto or verso of the leaf because in either case they would have on the left side the centre margin which is always the same width. Only after the text on the backs of these fragments had been identified could the question of position be settled.

Position C. Initial C with the miniature of Barbara, Dec. 4 (4/37), introduces the collect for her mass: 'C[oncede . . .]'; the text on the back was identified unmistakably as the postcommunion of Sabba, Dec. 5, in which his name occurs. The text follows the initial in this case, as in position C on the diagram, the intervening space between initial and text being one column.

Position D. Initial D with miniature of Nicholas, Dec. 6 (4/91), introduces the collect of his mass: 'D[eus qui beatum . . .]. On the back of this fragment are parts of the secret, preface and communion of Andrew (Nov. 30). Thus the text in this case precedes the initial, and the Nicholas miniature fragment can be placed in position D, on the verso of the leaf. The intervening space between text and initial in this case is three columns.

To recapitulate: An initial in Position A will have text on its back to be found three columns further on, that is in a mass considerably later than the one of which the initial is a part.

An initial in Position B will have text on its back to be found one column further back, that is, probably in the mass immediately preceding.

An initial in Position C will have text on its back to be found one column further on, that is, probably in a later part of the same mass.

An initial in Position D will have text on its back to be found three columns further back, that is, in a mass perhaps considerably earlier than the one of which the initial is a part.

Before demonstrating the application of the principles thus found to govern the relation of the initial to the text on its back, one further detail should be discussed, namely, the basis for calculating the amount of text in a column as indicated by the fragments on the backs of the cuttings.

Let us take, for example, the three larger cuttings described in the preceding paragraphs: one of these (4/13, Nativity of the Virgin) has on the back, six lines of text; Nicholas (4/91) has five lines. The text lines on other cuttings were seen to number three or four. Since the page was ruled and the text written before the illuminated initials were put in, they occupied the space measured by an exact number of text lines; thus we describe the initials as six-line, five-line, and so forth. The width of each text line was found to vary slightly between 1·7 and 1·8 cm. The Barbara fragment not only gives us the number of text lines on the back of the initial but, because it retains its fragment of border which shows a bottom margin line, it also shows that the initial was placed one line from the bottom of the column. The number of lines in a column could be estimated by totalling the measurements of several fragments (initials and pieces of decoration) which could be pieced together and joined without a gap; for example, 4/229 and 4/213 (fol. 106vo) which together showed a length of 47·3 cm. and no sign of bottom margin lines. Dividing this total length by 1·75 (as the average width of a single line) it was calculated that there were

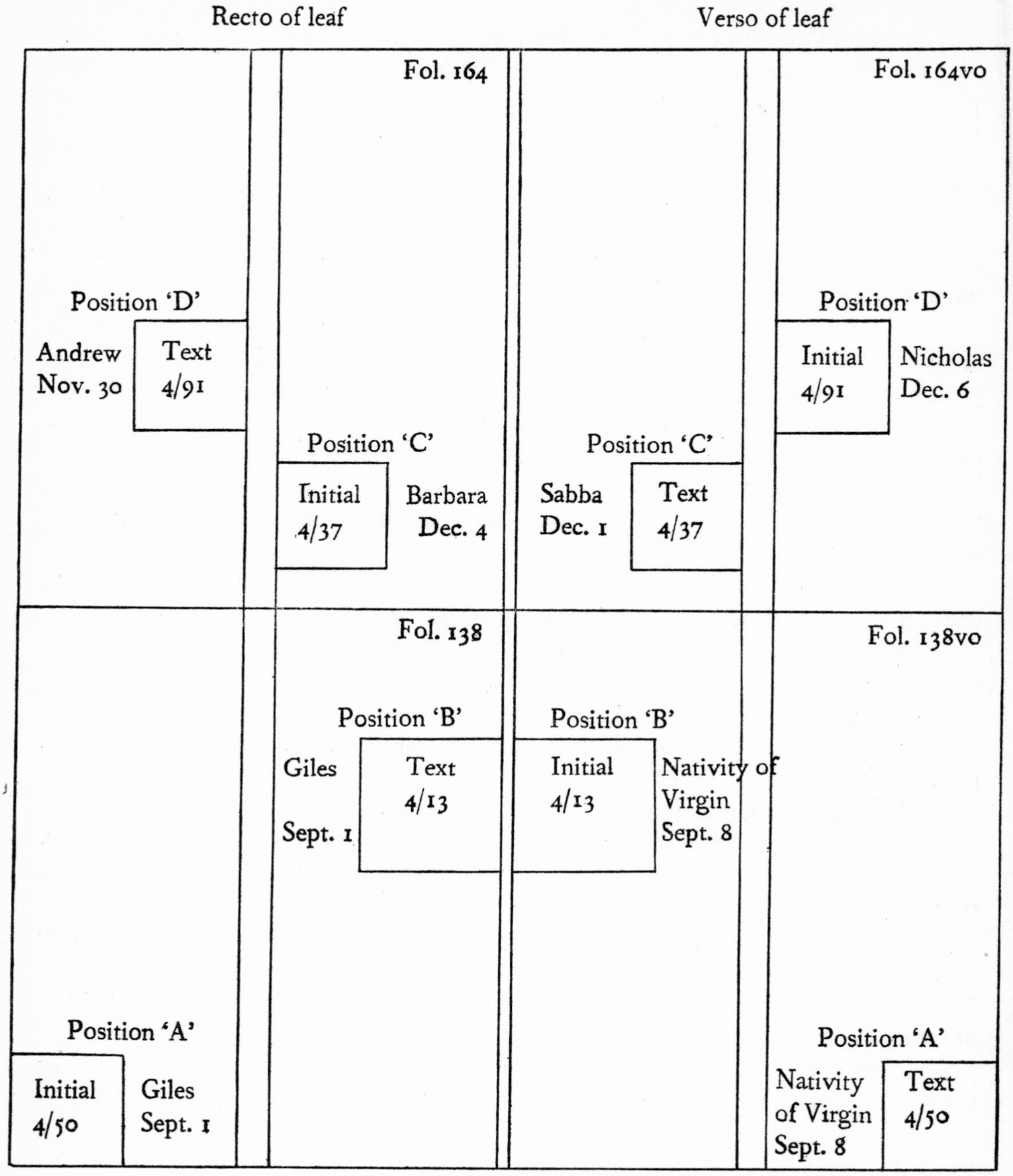

Recto of leaf   Verso of leaf

Fol. 164

Fol. 164vo

Position 'D'

Andrew | Text
Nov. 30 | 4/91

Position 'D'

Initial | Nicholas
4/91 | Dec. 6

Position 'C'

Initial | Barbara
4/37 | Dec. 4

Position 'C'

Sabba | Text
Dec. 1 | 4/37

Fol. 138

Fol. 138vo

Position 'B'

Giles | Text
  | 4/13
Sept. 1 |

Position 'B'

Initial | Nativity of
4/13 | Virgin
  | Sept. 8

Position 'A'

Initial | Giles
4/50 | Sept. 1

Position 'A'

Nativity | Text
of Virgin | 4/50
Sept. 8 |

Diagram showing the relation of the text on the backs of fragments placed in different positions on the page, to the text introduced by the initial letter. For reproductions of fols. 164 and 164vo showing positions C and D, see Pls. XXVIII and XXIX.

at least 27 lines in a column. Later, a small initial joining these two fragments added two lines making the number 29.

The number of words in a single line could also be estimated on the basis of the fragmentary text passage on the back of any cutting. For instance, on the back of the Nicholas (4/91 on fol. 164vo, Pl. XXIX) is part of the secret for Andrew, beginning 'Sacrificium nostrum' and ending (on the fragment) with these lines:

'[. . . conciliet] UT CUIUS HONORE
[sollemp] NITER EXHIBETUR MERITIS
[efficiatu] R ACCEPTUM. PER DOMINUM.'

The words in brackets are not on the fragment and must be inserted to complete the passage.

Although the number of words in different lines varies because of the use of abbreviations and contractions, a rough calculation of the number of lines required for a given passage in the reconstructed Missal could always be made on the basis of the parts of lines on the fragment itself.

A more accurate and much quicker method of calculating the amount of text intervening between an initial and the text on the back was to count it out in some missal containing the full liturgical text in lines comparable in length to those in the new manuscript. Admirably suited to this purpose was the 1504 edition[1] of the Carmelite Missal which, though smaller in scale, was found to contain in a single line almost the exact number of words as were calculated to be in a line of the new Missal. It was necessary, therefore, only to estimate the number of lines of text intervening between any given initial and the text on the back of it in order to judge where to look in the 1504 Missal for the passage sought.

Having established these fundamental principles governing the spatial relation of the text on one side of a fragment to the illuminated initial on the other, the next step was to apply them to identified initials whose positions on the page were either not in any way indicated or were uncertain, by trying out each fragment in positions *A, B, C,* and *D* successively and searching for the fragment of text where it might be expected in the missal order. As there were only four possible places in which to look, the search was not interminable and in every case resulted in the finding of the text on the backs of the twenty-two identified historiated initials and in the subsequent accurate placing of these fragments in the correct column and on the correct side of the leaf.

Such of these fragments as had any indication of top or bottom margin lines were now ready to mount on the large sheets of hand-made imitation vellum paper, which had been ruled according to the measurements calculated on the basis of marginal lines shown

---

[1] *Missale Factum ad Usum Fratrum Carmelitarum* Venice, 1504. A copy of this edition, which is rare, was very kindly lent for use in reconstructing the new Missal by the Very Reverend Brocard Taylor, O. Carm., Prior of the Carmelite College of Pius XI, Rome. It was deposited in the British Museum for many months and, although not available during the initial stages of the reconstruction, it proved most valuable for the identification and placing of the more difficult fragments which had been left until the end. It was also very useful for the final checking. If this book had been available at the beginning, such small errors as were found later, in calculations of the positions of the fragments first mounted, would doubtless have been avoided. A photostatic copy of this Missal was made while it was in the Museum and is now permanently available there.

on different fragments. However, it was thought wiser not to mount any fragments until it was certain that all the evidence had been collected for these measurements.

To this end it was necessary to undertake to identify the remaining historiated initials, the subjects of which were not self-explanatory (as single figures of bishops and other saints, and some scenes not readily recognizable) and also the many large decorative initials which gave no indication as to which mass they introduced. With these fragments nothing could be done before they were removed from the scrapbooks, since it was essential to examine the text on the backs. When this had been done, it was frequently found that a proper name or some other word at once gave a clue as to where to look for the text fragment; in such cases, when the passage had been identified, the initial on the other side of the fragment could be found, usually with very little difficulty, by applying in reverse the principles governing the four possible positions of any fragment on the page. Instead of starting with the identified initial and counting out the intervening text space between it and the text fragment, this fragment itself, following the clue of a suggestive word contained in it, was sought for and the initial on the other side of the cutting was located in relation to this passage.

In many cases, however, there was no certain clue in the text passage and, since the number of fragments was considerable, some systematic method had to be devised for saving time in searching for them. First, in order to avoid handling the fragments themselves more than was absolutely necessary, and in order to collect all the textual evidence in usable form, it was decided to copy off on slips of paper all the data contained on each cutting: the number, the letter, its size, and any indications of its position on the page as shown by margin lines were noted on one side of the slip; the text fragment was copied in lines on the other. A specimen slip, showing both sides, would appear as below:

INITIAL SIDE			TEXT SIDE
4/165	*B*	5-line	ua domine propici-
Top corner, left column, verso			acione et beate marie
			cis semperque uirginis
			intercessione ad perpe-
			atque presentem hec o-

The text fragments copied on the slips, when studied as a whole, were seen to fall into three groups, each of which proved to be handled best in a different way.

1. Those which gave some indication of the part of the mass from which they came, such as rubrics, parts of headings, portions of the names of the different parts of the mass (as *Oracio*, *Secretum*, etc) or words recognizable as always belonging to certain parts of the mass, as 'alleluia' (indicating a grail), forms of the personal pronoun, as 'nos', 'nobis', 'tu', 'tibi', and so forth, indicating one of the prayers, as also the words (or their abbreviations) '*Per dominum*' or '*Per*'. Of such fragments, those which gave any slightest hint of a likely place to look, were undertaken first, and many of them were identified by running through the full text of a missal, looking exclusively at the part of the mass indicated, for words found in the fragments. For instance, if a number of fragments showed indications of coming from grails, all the grails in the complete missal would be scanned for combinations of words such as were found on any of these fragments. Although some fragments

were identified in this way, a good many were not; this remainder was eventually turned over to the third group, as described below.

2. Biblical passages could usually be recognized as such by their phrasing. These were sought for, word by word, in Dutripon's excellent *Concordance* of the Vulgate Bible. Any single whole word in the fragment could be looked for, but it worked much more quickly and surely if at least a portion of what preceded and what followed the word sought for in the *Concordance* were also given, so that time would not be wasted in looking up the wrong passages in the Vulgate itself. Passages which seemed to fit the fragmentary text and were verified in the Vulgate could then be looked up once more in the 'Index of Biblical Passages', in the Dickinson edition of the Sarum Missal, in order to find out for which masses this particular epistle or gospel passage was used; each mass in turn was then looked up in a complete missal and the initial on the other side of the text fragment was sought as introducing the part of a mass in one of the positions which would allow the requisite amount of space to intervene between initial and text. This process of identifying text and initial was clearly much more complicated than the more direct method of following a clue as to the identification of the passage; but it proved more successful than might be imagined, and became more workable with increased use.

3. The remainder of the fragments, namely those which gave no indication whatsoever as to what they were (to which, unsolved puzzles from the other groups were eventually added) were carefully indexed, each whole word or recognizable portion of a word (except prepositions, conjunctions, and other very common words) being written on a separate slip and the slips arranged alphabetically. If more than one text fragment used the same word, the number of each fragment in which it was found was noted on the index slip of that word. The original text fragment slips were then arranged in numerical order, all the 4 numbers forming one series and all the 5's another.

With the index at hand for quick reference, and the text slips in order, I began at the beginning of the missal (the Legg edition of the Westminster Missal because that happened to be available for use outside the Museum) and read as slowly and carefully as possible, alert for any word remembered as being in the alphabetical index. It was surprising how many passages were identified in this way even at first, and as the reading progressed and the words in the index became more clearly fixed in my mind, the search became even more fruitful. The difficulty to be guarded against in using the Westminster text was possible variation from the Carmelite use. Always, however, the fragment was only tentatively placed unless the initial could be certainly identified in some Carmelite source, and unless its position could be accurately determined. If there was more than one possible place for a passage, all were noted even though one seemed to fit better than another.

In addition to identifying a considerable number of initials by this method, the first reading of the missal text suggested an important fact about the probable contents of the new Carmelite Missal. Not one single fragment was identified in that part of the *Temporale* containing masses from Advent to Easter Saturday. It had been noted already that no identified historiated initial came earlier in the Missal than Easter Sunday (4/43, representing the Three Maries at the tomb, with a portion of the Holy Saturday gospel lesson on the back). Nevertheless it seemed possible that some of the larger decorative initials, at first unidentified, later might have been found to fit into this earlier part of the book. The fact that they apparently did not was significant as indicating that this part was probably altogether lacking in the original Missal at the time it was cut up. A second reading of the text for further identifications, therefore, could begin with the Holy Saturday mass, instead of with that of the first Sunday in Advent. This shortened the 'combing' process greatly. Increased familiarity with the words in the index and several successive readings of the complete text yielded more and more satisfactory results. Finally, however, it seemed that the possibilities of this method had been exhausted and that the remaining unidentified larger fragments (which were comparatively few) might be left for a later stage in the work, since already sufficient material was identified and placed to justify the actual mounting of some of it on the sheets.

To return for a moment to an earlier phase of the reconstruction, namely, the removal of these larger decorative initials from the scrapbook in order to identify the text on the backs by the method just described, it may be interesting to note the first of many instances in which the style of decoration played an important part in the placing of the fragments. Some of the larger initials of particularly delicate workmanship and colouring had been separated from the others as being slightly different in style. This distinction was justified, when these initials were taken out of the scrapbooks, by finding that the text on the backs was written in a different liturgical hand, which was larger and slightly stiffer in type; the ink on these fragments was almost black, in contrast to the paler brown ink used on most of the other fragments thus far seen. At first it seemed possible that these fragments might come from a different manuscript, not the Carmelite Missal. Then it was observed that to one of the finest of the large initials, a T, could be joined a small e spelling the word 'Te' which begins the Canon of the Mass: 'Te igitur . . .' (Pl. XXXIV). This was, indeed, an exciting discovery, for on the basis of similarity in the style of other initials to this T, and of identity of hand in the text found on them, this group of fragments could now be identified as belonging to the Canon and Prefaces of the Missal, fourteen pages of which (fols. 70–83) were eventually reconstructed.

In the meantime, in order to vary the somewhat monotonous and purely mechanical labour of searching for text fragments, a beginning was made on the reconstruction of the Calendar pages of the Missal. The fragments of Calendar entries were easily recognizable. They consisted of six KL monograms, all in the same style (which was slightly different from that of the other large decorative initials), and a number of entries or parts of entries —single lines only, often with the initial letter missing, but with the entry perfectly comprehensible. One side, at least, of all these fragments was written in gold letters, thus indicating the probable reason for their having been saved from the original manuscript.

The KL letters were assumed at first to come from six double leaves which, with one leaf, recto and verso, for each month would have contained the twelve months of the Calendar; this, however, was proved untrue when the 'verses' for the months[1] were identified on the backs of the fragments. The January KL is missing, but the verse for that month is found on the back of another fragment containing a KL which, therefore, must be for February and belongs on the verso of this first, or January, page. There is no KL

---

[1] 'The Almanac, each month headed with one of the verses relating to the unlucky or "Egyptian" days, two apiece, counted one from the beginning and the other back from the end of each month.' Christopher Wordsworth and Henry Littlehales, *The Old Service-Books of the English Church*, London, 1910, p. 89.

and no verse for either March or April; hence the leaf containing the entries for these two months must be lost, as is also that for the months of September and October. These two lost leaves, in the normal arrangement of the Calendar, would make up the two halves of a double leaf, including, altogether, four months. Thus it is evident that only two double leaves out of the three necessary for the twelve months of the whole Calendar have survived: the middle one of the three (as laid one on top of the other to form the quire) has been lost. May and June have *KL* letters, and likewise July and August; but on the November-December leaf (which contains more entries than any of the others) only one *KL* seemed to have survived, that for December.[1] The verses for the months, which are on the backs of the *KL* letters, are written in crimson ink.

The Calendar entries can be accurately placed on the page according to the known dates of the feasts; recto and verso of the leaf usually are clearly indicated by the order of the entries, one in December, for instance, occurring on the verso of the leaf, while one in November is on the recto of the same leaf. The mounts for the Calendar fragments had to be ruled both vertically and horizontally in order to calculate more exactly the places for the various entries; the rulings are continued from the margins as they appear on the *KL* fragments.

Before leaving the subject of the Calendar, one more interesting little problem may be described. One of the finest text fragments, apparently from the Calendar, was a single line written in blue letters, containing the words: '[. . .] rum abraham ysaac et iacob.' When this cutting was taken out of the scrapbook there seemed no doubt that it could be placed on the October page, since the feast of the Patriarchs occurs in the calendar of Sibert on October 6. When the text on the other side of the fragment was examined, however, it was found to be the heading of the feast, 'Germanus remigius uedast et', which occurs on October 1. Since two entries from the same month could not in this calendar layout be on opposite sides of the same leaf, it was obvious that the pretty blue text fragment did not belong in the Calendar after all. When the page with initials introducing the masses for these two feasts was reconstructed, it was found that the headings for them came in exactly the same position on opposite sides of the same leaf. The fragment therefore was fitted into its correct place there and adds much to the decorative appearance of the page (fol. 146).

After nearly seven weeks of work devoted exclusively to the identification and placing of the larger initials according to the methods thus far described, evidence showed the contents of the partially reconstructed Missal to be as follows:

(1) Four leaves of the Calendar out of the six which originally made up the gathering: March–April and September–October lacking.

(2) The summer portion of the *Temporale*, from Easter Eve to Advent and in addition, the Dedication of the Church and the Prefaces and Canon of the Mass.

(3) The *Proprium Sanctorum* or *Sanctorale* containing the offices of saints from Marcellus, January 16 (the mediaeval Carmelite Missal, as noted above, began the *Sanctorale* with Maur, January 15, but this feast was not yet identified among the fragments) to Lazarus, December 17 (Thomas the Apostle, December 21, which should end the *Sanctorale* was also unidentified).

---

[1] The November *KL* was found later in the third scrapbook; see p. 137.

(4) The *Commune Sanctorum*, with fewer masses than were identified in the other parts of the Missal, but showing evidence of the usual common masses of martyrs, confessors, virgins, and others, some votive masses beginning with that of the Trinity, a table of collects for various occasions, together with many of the prayers, cues of which are given in this table, and a mass and another table of cues of prayers for the dead.

The number of identified pieces comprising this skeleton layout was nearly 300, consisting of initials of three to six lines and the fragments of decoration which joined them. About sixty of the larger initials were still unidentified, and none of the smaller ones had been undertaken as yet. It was while considering whether it would be worth while to attempt to place these hundreds of smaller initials that I took occasion to examine another manuscript Carmelite Missal, MS. 123 in the John Rylands Library at Manchester.

This book, which is the only manuscript of a complete Carmelite missal known to exist in England, unfortunately is not of English use. Though two English saints are entered in the Calendar (Richard of Chichester and Edmund, King and Martyr) the masses for them are not included. From indications furnished by the style of decoration as well as from the presence of a full mass of high rank for Saint Justina of Padua, it would appear that the manuscript was made in north Italy. The date is late fourteenth or early fifteenth century.

But in spite of its probable Italian provenance, there was no choice but to make use of this manuscript as an early Carmelite Missal text, and I set to work collating it with the reconstruction. As regards the *Temporale*, the results were most satisfactory, all the identifications proving correct in this part. In the *Sanctorale*, however, the collation was less satisfactory, partly because fewer fragments had been placed definitely in this portion of the reconstruction, partly because the Manchester Missal was not of English use. Moreover, some fragments of text which had been thought to be identified correctly but which could not be placed certainly, since they could be used equally well in one of several different masses, could not be found in the Manchester Missal without a laborious search of the entire text. Permission could not be obtained at this time for the Manchester manuscript to leave the John Rylands Library[1] and it was not practicable to remain in Manchester merely for the purpose of continual reference to this Missal when the other liturgical material was in the British Museum. It was necessary, therefore, to devise some means of systematizing the contents of at least the Proper and Common of Saints in this manuscript in order to make them available for use in the successive stages of the reconstruction. The best way to do this seemed to be to transcribe a synopsis of each mass, giving cues for all the parts except the collects which, because of possible variants, had to be copied in full. The transcription was done on the typewriter, in duplicate. One copy was afterwards cut up into the different parts of the masses (as collects, secrets, postcommunions, offertories, and so forth); these were grouped and arranged in alphabetical order and pasted on large sheets of paper so that they could be read through quickly when a fragment of text in any known part of the mass was being looked for. The second copy was retained intact for purposes of collation with the Sibert ordinal and other Carmelite sources which were eventually accumulated.

Two such Carmelite sources had already, in fact, been placed on deposit in the British

[1] Later, however, the manuscript was sent to the Museum and a complete photostatic copy was made.

Museum for use in the construction; although they were secured at different times, it may be well to speak of them together in order to suggest their relative importance as regards both the Manchester manuscript and certain printed Carmelite missals also used in the course of the reconstruction. These are a late fourteenth century Carmelite Breviary and short missal from Oxford[1] and a complete Carmelite Missal dated 1458 from Kilcormuck (King's Co., Leinster) Ireland, now in Dublin.[2]

The Oxford Breviary is clearly of English use and nearly contemporary with the new Missal; it was found, therefore, to be the most reliable of all available sources for the masses which it contains, namely the principal masses of the *Temporale*, some forty masses from the *Sanctorale*, and the greater part of the *Commune Sanctorum*, with the exception of the general collects. In addition to these masses, which are given in full and which include one of the most characteristic Carmelite feasts, that for the Three Maries (May 25), the Breviary gives the collect for the office of the day, which is also the collect of the mass. This manuscript was also very useful for the wording of the Litany, the Prefaces and Canon of the Mass, the Calendar, and the text of the *Commemoratio Animarum* which precedes the mass for All Souls (November 2) in the Carmelite rite.

The Kilcormic Missal furnishes a better text of a complete Carmelite Missal than Manchester, and contains masses for many English (and Irish) feasts in use only some sixty years after the new Missal was written. Most of these we know from the Sibert Ordinal and the Oxford Breviary to have been in use also in the fourteenth century; the text of the Kilcormic Missal, therefore, was of the greatest value for identifying and verifying the actual wording of most of the masses represented in the fragments of the new Missal.

The value of the printed Missal of 1504 in spacing out the text has been described; further use of this Missal was for verifying rubrics, which proved to be taken almost word for word from those in the Sibert Ordinal, and even to bear the same numbers. Though not of English use, this printed Missal was also helpful for the masses in both the Proper and Common of Saints, especially for the feasts peculiar to the Carmelite rite. Another printed Carmelite Missal, an edition of 1640 formerly in the British Museum,[3] was less useful because of its having been printed after a great many reforms had taken place in the Carmelite rite. In certain cases, however, the Missal of 1640 alone among Carmelite sources agreed with the wording in the reconstructed Missal.

This collection of Carmelite source material was ultimately of immense value for the collation of the text, but it was not all brought together until the reconstruction had reached an advanced stage. In the meantime, there was the problem of mounting the identified fragments on the new pages. When it came to the point of settling upon the sheets to be mounted first, doubts seemed to arise on every side. In the first place, were the estimated measurements of the text and margin spaces certainly correct? Although all the fragments which showed maximum widths of margins had been measured and remeasured, there was still the possibility that some as yet unsuspected combination of fragments might prove these calculations to be inaccurate. Once mounted on the sheets, it would be difficult to

---

[1] University College, MS. 9. Deposited in the British Museum for study and photostating.

[2] Trinity College MS. 82. This Missal was written, according to the colophon, at the Carmelite convent of 'kyllcarmayc' in 1458. It is here spelled Kilcormic.

[3] Burned in the second world war.

make adjustments in the positions of the fragments, for the plan was to inlay them in the paper in such a way that both text and initial side would be permanently visible. To add to this hesitance about undertaking the mounting on one of the two reconstructed pages which furnished the best evidence of the length of the text column (fol. 120, Pl. XXXVI, containing two large left-column initials which seemed to constitute the total length of the column, though they did not actually join) the text was still only tentatively identified and, because of disagreement with Manchester in one of the principal text fragments, could not be verified as constituting part of the mass of Saint Margaret (July 20). There remained as reliable evidence of the approximate length of the text space, only the first Canon page (fol. 78, Pl. XXXIV); on this the fragments of decoration could be joined together without a break, and the total length was found to measure 50·1 cm., but no bottom margin showed. However, it was decided to accept the measurements of this page, mark out the places for the certainly identified fragments on the pages where they belonged, and send the first pages to be mounted, after a final check had once more verified all the evidence.

As soon as these first pages came into the hands of the expert craftsman in the Museum bindery, to whom the delicate task of inlaying the fragments had been entrusted, another problem arose which threatened the validity of the system so carefully evolved for identifying and placing the fragments on the pages. This was the question of whether, in certain instances, all the fragments laid out for mounting on any single page showed the same side of the vellum uppermost. It is true that this point had been considered in placing the cuttings on the pages, and it was believed that no mistake had been made, even though in some cases the vellum differed markedly in the fragments on the same side of the leaf. However, the binder was an expert in the handling of skins and it did not seem possible that he could mistake the hair and flesh side of the vellum. Eventually, the question was settled by means of a powerful microscope which, in each of the cases questioned, showed unmistakable hair marks on one side and their absence on the other.

The outcome of this technical problem was most satisfactory not only because it verified the identifications already made, but because it emphasized the importance of examining very carefully the vellum of each fragment before finally accepting its identification and location on any leaf. Later, with increased experience, the evidence of the general appearance of the fragment, and especially of the vellum, was found to be valuable in two ways: sometimes the colour and texture of the vellum of the cutting to be placed was so similar to that of other fragments already placed that the unplaced piece seemingly had to belong with them and not elsewhere; and usually, when all the other evidence was in, it was found to do so. On the other hand, it sometimes happened that fragments of vellum very dissimilar in appearance actually did come from the same original page, the difference being due partly to the unavoidable variations in such large skins as would be required for the leaves of so great a book, partly to changes in the vellum of individual cuttings, either because of the action of the paste with which they were mounted in the scrapbooks, or (in a few cases) because of having been for many years exposed to light while exhibited in the Museum.

On no one of the pages first sent to be mounted was a fragment included which could not be definitely placed on the basis of margin lines. This certain evidence of position was lacking, however, in a great many of the finest fragments already identified; thus their positions on the page could only be guessed at. The problem of trying to decide what to do about mounting these fragments finally led to the consideration of the possibility and advantages of including the many hundreds of two-line initials which still remained in the scrapbooks. A large number of these, it was observed, had top and bottom margin lines, definitely placing them on the page. It seemed possible that if they could be identified and their exact positions in relation to the larger fragments could be established, many of the latter could themselves be placed with a good deal more certainty. It was clear, moreover, that the great number of the smaller initials (many of which were very beautiful in colour and design) would both help to fill up the pages and considerably increase their beauty; it was not foreseen (as later proved to be true) that these small fragments with their minute text passages would add much to the liturgical contents of the reconstructed Missal.

Before describing the modifications of method necessary for dealing with the two-line initials, one further detail of the reconstruction technique should be mentioned. This is the 'dummy book', which was made for the purpose of keeping a record of the placing of all the fragments. On each page of this book (corresponding to a leaf of the Missal) the position of the fragments was marked out to scale in accordance with the text on the backs. A typical page from this dummy book appeared as on p. 132 below.

The dummy sheets were kept in missal order, *Temporale, Sanctorale*, and *Commune Sanctorum*, and numbered in separate series, as T–1, S–1, C–1, and so forth. As new fragments were identified and added to the Missal pages, the slips representing them (see p. 124 above) were attached to the dummy sheets.

The need for a more systematic method of handling the material became imperative when the placing of the many two-line initials was undertaken. When removed from the scrapbooks, these proved to be more numerous than estimated; actually there were over six hundred of them. The pile of slips representing them was bulky and difficult to use. Moreover, while some text fragments showed specific indications of the place where they might be looked for in a missal text, most of them were so small that there was not room on the reverse for more than one or two words at most, and sometimes there was not even one whole word, but only the beginnings and endings of words. Ultimately, the distinction of certain differences in style among the two-line initials was used, in the absence of any other primary basis, for dividing up these hundreds of fragments into manageable groups.

The outstanding features differentiating the styles of these initials were: (1) the range of colours used in the grounds on which the gold initials were placed; and (2) the patterning of the gold in the initial letters themselves. An initial which was stippled with a pattern of foliated and spiral motifs against a blue and tan ground seemed to represent one main type; and an initial decorated with circles and groups of dots, against a crimson and blue ground, the other. On the basis of these distinctions, both the initials and the slips representing them were separated into two groups. Then the slips of each group were arranged alphabetically according to the initial, all the *A*'s, for example, remaining together, while the fragments also were placed in separate folders, one for each letter. Thus all the *A* slips could be examined quickly and the fragment corresponding to any given slip could readily be found.

From the resemblance of the stippled leaf and scroll patterns in the gold initials of the blue and tan group to patterns used on the gold field of the larger initials already

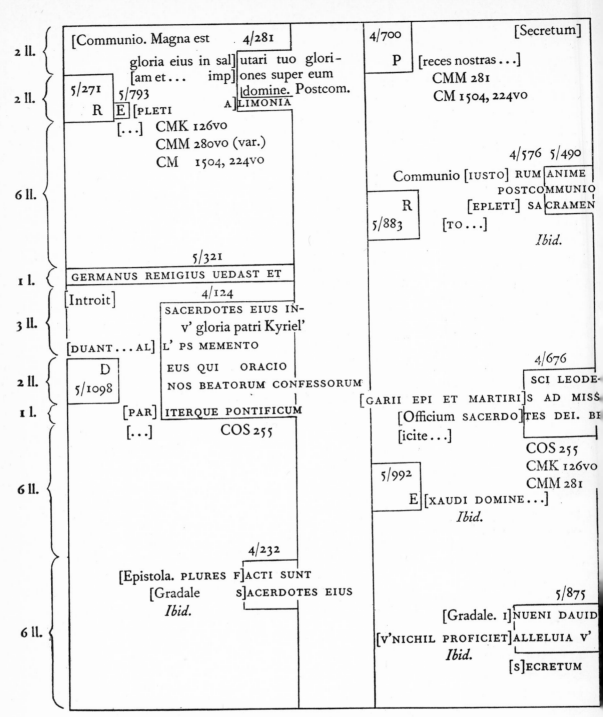

TYPICAL PAGE FROM DUMMY BOOK

Key to the abbreviations of sources used as evidence for the identification: CMK—Kilcormic Missal; CMM—Manchester Carmelite Missal; CM 1504—printed edition of Carmelite Missal of 1504; COS—Sibert Ordinal, ed. by Zimmerman. Text in brackets is not on fragment but is supplied from these or other sources.

placed in the *Temporale*, and also from a correspondence of the colour scheme and even of the motifs employed in these two types of initials, it appeared that the blue and tan letters also might come from the *Temporale*. This hypothesis was supported by the observation that two of the crimson and blue two-line initials were included on the same fragment with some border decoration which joined large initials in the *Sanctorale* or *Commune*. If there was any consistent distribution of the small initials throughout the manuscript, it seemed that the blue and tan ones should be found in the *Temporale* and not in the *Sanctorale*.

The method of searching for these small initials followed an order exactly the reverse of that used for the larger ones. With the dummy sheets of the *Temporale* at hand and also the slips of the blue and tan group of small initials, the text of the *Temporale* in the Westminster Missal was once more carefully read to discover which initials would be needed to introduce the principal parts of any given mass (other than the introit or the collect, one of which was always introduced by one of the large initials). At first it was not certain which parts of the mass would be likely to have illuminated two-line initials, but by trying out a few and identifying the text on the backs, it soon appeared that these smaller letters, at least in the *Temporale*, were used principally for collects (if a large initial introduced the introit), secrets, and postcommunions, and occasionally epistles. This observation somewhat simplified the search for text passages. The method was the following: if a large initial had been identified for the introit of a mass and an *A* was needed for the collect (which always began not many lines below the introit initial), a calculation would be made of the amount of text intervening between the fragment on the back of the introit initial and that which should be found on the reverse of the required *A*. Then a search was made among the *A* slips for one with the estimated portion of this required text passage on the back. To illustrate further: if the introit initial had on the reverse a passage from the beginning of the gospel lesson, the collect initial would have a passage from the same gospel some six or eight lines further on; if the estimated portion of that gospel lesson were carefully scanned, almost any fragment of it, no matter how few words it contained, could be recognized. It was a method which became more fruitful the more it was used, for practice gave experience in calculating the right places to look for the text fragments. Within a very short time, in fact, some two hundred of the small initials had been placed in the *Temporale*.

However, quite a number of these blue and tan initials remained unplaced and it began to appear that they must be looked for elsewhere, especially since those which were left over seemed to be slightly inferior in workmanship and in pigments, and to differ somewhat in the patterns used on the gold. The possibility suggested itself that the same style might continue into the early part of the *Sanctorale*. This, in fact, proved to be true, and most of the remainder of the blue and tan initials were placed in the first gathering (eight leaves) of the *Sanctorale*. The last leaf on which initials in this style could be placed was that containing the mass of Saint Valentine (February 14, fol. 95), that is, the verso of the eighth leaf in the *Sanctorale*.

A modification of the method just described of identifying text fragments on the basis of style was to try to 'force in' initials where the appearance of the vellum or the style of decoration, or the type of hand and of ink in the written text showed a striking resemblance to these features on any given page. Often a variation in the form of the text passage on the back of one of these initials was found, which, when identified, confirmed the placing of the initial. Sometimes the forcing would not work: for even in some striking instances of similarities in external features, if the fragment of text could not be identified from any source, eventually the initial must be left out. A typical example of such failure to force an initial into a certain place was one which looked right both as to illuminated letter and text on the back, except that in the middle of the latter was an almost invisible bit of rubric, indicating that the textual passage for some reason was interrupted at that point. Since the text fragment had been identified as part of a gospel passage which would be written continuously in black ink, the presence of the tiny spot of red showed that there was something wrong with the identification. The same portion of the gospel to which the text fragment belonged was frequently used also as grail and as offertory. It was certain, therefore, that the fragment must be placed where one or other of these parts of the mass and not the gospel passage was required. For many months this particular fragment remained 'homeless', until some new evidence from a different source showed its correct place to be already occupied by another initial, which, as it happened, might fit equally correctly in either of two positions, whereas the fragment with the tiny bit of red in the text could obviously fit only in the one. This and one other similar case[1] seem to be the only occurrences of such a misplacement in the whole process of reconstruction.

The experience gained in the use of the new method evolved for the placing of this first group of small initials, served to make the identification of the remainder of the two-line letters easier. After the eighth leaf of the first gathering of the *Sanctorale*, the style of the large initials, both historiated and decorative, was seen to change abruptly. The new style in the historiated initials was easily recognizable by the strong, heavy colouring, blue and red being used in great abundance, and in particularly rich, heavy tones. Some of the two-line initials used a similar type of colour, both in the ground of the letter and in the motifs of the border decoration. Other characteristics of this group are the shaded forms of the motifs and the use of very heavy black lines for spray stems and for outlining the motifs. The initials of this type were easy to sort out from the others, and with few exceptions were quickly fitted into their places by identifying the text on the back, as in the *Temporale* group. They were found to be confined to the second gathering in the *Sanctorale*.

A third distinct style was located in the last gathering of the *Sanctorale* on the basis of one fragment, the text of which contains the name of Edmund, King and Martyr (November 20). A distinguishing characteristic of this style, as of the one last described, is the colouring which, like that of the *Temporale* and of the first gathering of the *Sanctorale*, is blue and tan, the latter colour, however, of a strong yellowish tint instead of pinkish as in the earlier blue and tan group. The gold is patterned as in the second *Sanctorale* (blue and crimson) style, with circles and dots instead of foliated and scroll patterns as in the *Temporale* group. The motifs and designs of this third group are different from either of the other two thus far placed. There were comparatively few fragments in this group and they were nearly all identified without difficulty.

But even after these three groups had been segregated and placed in their respective

[1] On fol. 16, an *S* (5/437) was mounted, which seemed to fit both as to the initial and as to the text on the back. However, it appeared later, while placing a fragment from the third scrapbook, that another *S* in exactly the same style with text fragment coming a little earlier in the mass, fitted better because it allowed more space for missing text. The incorrect *S* was not removed from the page.

parts of the Missal, more than half of the two-line initials remained to be fitted into the greater part of the *Sanctorale* and the *Commune*. The style of this large group resembles that of the second gathering in the *Sanctorale* except that the shades of blue and red are much paler, and the pigments are used much less heavily, and the motifs are flat, not shaded as in the second gathering. No consistent differentiation of illuminators' tricks or of details of style in this large group could be detected; hence the group had to be handled as a whole, with noticeable increase in the difficulty of identifying the text and also in deciding on the correct positions, since many text fragments could belong equally well to more than one mass. Eventually, however, nearly all of these were placed. The unforeseen possibility of finding a great many of the fragments in the *Commune*, where all the alternative forms of collects, grails, communions, and so forth were introduced by illuminated initials, many of which were found actually to join, reduced the number to be identified and simplified the search for them. Some single leaves in the *Commune* contain more fragments than those in any other part of the Missal (cf. fols. 182 and 182vo, Pls. XXXVII and XXXVIII).

The explanation and significance of the various styles distinguished in the foregoing paragraphs have been given fully in Chapter III above; it is only their obvious importance for the actual reconstruction, which amounted almost to indispensability for the placing of this great number of small initials, that should be emphasized here.

Before leaving the matter of the two-line initials, two additional points should be noted. First, the method of placing on the page the identified two-line initials which show no indication of margin lines. Most pages, luckily, had at least one initial certainly placed and on the basis of this, the position of the others could be counted out, as had previously been done in identifying the text fragments on the backs. For this purpose the 1504 edition of the Carmelite Missal was again used with great advantage. The fact that there was often a fair number of these small initials on the same page made it even easier to place them, since there were fewer lines to calculate between them. It was observed, moreover, that a fragment one line from the top or bottom margin showed the ruling for this margin across the attached spray. Inversely, initials with sprays showing no lines crossing them were taken to be not less than two lines from the corner. Initials without sprays, and some few coming in the middle of a column, without margin lines, were the most difficult of all to place. Often, however, it was found that a bit of the design of a spray which had joined it in the original manuscript, overlapped from one fragment to another, or that the cut edges of two fragments fitted together, or that there was some other minute detail which indicated the position of a fragment. The number and variety of these indications were legion; an enumeration of them would be tedious and pointless. However, the fact to be remembered in regard to the reconstruction is (as stated often already) that some kind of positive evidence always was used in identifying and placing the fragments.

The difficulties of identifying the two-line initials were as nothing compared with those of trying to fit in the long, narrow initial *I*'s (shaped like *J*'s), usually introducing the gospel lesson (In illo tempore . . .). Since they are always situated in the margin, outside the text space, only rarely do they have identifiable fragments of words on the reverse side. These few scraps of text (where they do occur) could not furnish any clue to the placing of the initial *I* until it had been tentatively placed on other grounds, such as noticeable peculiarities of style, of vellum, of pigments, or of ink in the script. When a possible position had been found for any particular *I*, its correctness in that place could usually be verified by the recognition of even such small fragments of text as might occur on the reverse (where the letters had run over the margin slightly) as belonging to a text passage which was known to be in that place. Sometimes a rubric or part of a heading in red could be recognized on the back and this furnished the required evidence.

An interesting example of the placing of an *I* on somewhat thin evidence (which was afterwards verified) was that of the *I* of the 'In principio', the beginning of the Creation story which is the first of the five prophecies following the ceremony of the Blessing of the Paschal candle. The first prophecy is immediately preceded, in the missal text, by the 'Exultet iam angelica', which, in the new Carmelite Missal, was written out in full in tiny script, with the music (*Temporale*, fol. 1). The *E* of the 'Exultet' was identified as having a fragment of the text of the second prophecy on the back. The front of the fragment with the *E* shows the ends of the red lines ruled for the musical notation. An initial *I* with similar red lines and fragments of music on the back was tried in the proper place for the *I* of the 'In principio'; it seemed to be right, for the fragmentary music could be identified as a part of the 'Exultet' music. Positive confirmation of the identification was furnished by a small *N* which was found to join the *I* and had on the reverse another tiny fragment of music from the *Exultet* completing that on the reverse of the *I*. This *N* was one of the many one-line initials, drawn with the pen in brown or coloured inks, with which whole pages of the scrapbooks were filled. In only a few instances, however, could they be placed.

There was still another way of placing the *I*'s in certain cases. On some fragments, it was noticed, there were offsets of the decoration, produced on facing pages while the Missal was still intact. The gold dots, particularly, used in groups of three, four, or five in the sprays, could frequently be matched with their offsets, and fragments could thus be placed with certainty. The *I*'s lent themselves especially well to this method of placement, since their decorative sprays with the characteristic gold dots were usually still attached to the initial letters. The *I*'s added extremely little to the text of the reconstructed manuscript but contributed greatly to the beauty of the pages (Pl. XXIX).

The placing of the smallest initials of all (such as the *N* mentioned above) had not at any time been considered as a serious possibility; but the chance identification of a few of them led to a closer examination of their styles and of the subjects of those having pictures. One series of nine was seen to illustrate the Easter gospel story and therefore could be placed; the initials introduce the verses of the biblical passage, and the small amount of text to be found on the backs forms part of the latter portion of the Easter mass, which is on the other side of the leaf (fol. 8, Pl. II).

Another one-line letter (4/443 on fol. 27vo), a tiny *P* with a beautiful drawing of the dove of the Holy Ghost, was identified as the second letter of the word 'Spiritus' which begins the introit of the mass for Pentecost, thus joining a fine historiated initial *S* (4/45, Pl. IV). The three letters of text on the back complete the fragmentary first word on the back of this large initial.

Doubtless a great many more of these smallest letters could be identified and placed if indefinite time were available; it is even possible that some further important and interesting textual evidence might be found among them. But in any case, even though identified, because they are so small and without indications of exact position, it would be very difficult if not impossible to find the exact place for them on the pages. These and all other unplaced fragments have been returned under their original numbers to the scrapbooks from which they were lifted.

Almost at the very moment when it had been decided that the reconstruction of fragments from the two original scrapbooks had reached the degree of partial completeness beyond which it would be impracticable to proceed, the other Hanrott scrapbook of cuttings from the same Missal appeared. On its acquisition by the British Museum (as Additional MS. 44892) there was no question but that these fragments also, as far as was possible, must be incorporated into the reconstructed Missal.

Only one historiated initial was contained in this new scrapbook—a *D* (2/101, fol. 100vo) with the figure of a pope who was identified by the text on the back as Sixtus (April 6). The miniature has been terribly repainted[1] but enough of the style can be seen to prove that it belongs with 4/82 on the same page. Aside from this initial, the *KL* for November in the Calendar, and several fragments of decoration which, on stylistic grounds, clearly belonged in certain recognizable places, the fragments that seemed most likely to be identifiable were some sixty two-line initials. These were removed and separated into styles as described above, and then fitted into the vacant places in various parts of the Missal where these initial letters were found to be missing. The results were most satisfactory, all having now been placed. Not only do these fragments help to fill up the pages, but in some cases they supply the exact additional textual evidence needed for confirming the presence of certain masses already thought to have been recognized in the Missal but not quite certainly identified. The most important of such instances are the masses of Erkenwald and Mellitus, both significant London feasts.[2]

[1] The story goes that later Hanrott children were allowed to paint in the scrapbook on rainy Sunday afternoons. Many of the small pen-drawn initials also are daubed over with water colour paint.

[2] The Glasgow scrapbook contains forty-seven of these two-line initials, apparently taken from all parts of the Missal.

APPENDIX

B. Some Materials for a Study of Low Country-Burgundian Sources of Influence on English Style, *ca.* 1400

The Broederlam Altarpiece Wings at Dijon[1] and the Beaufort Annunciation[2]

The architectural setting for the Beaufort Annunciation together with the arrangement of the figures is too close to the Broederlam Annunciation to be accidental. It is not copied but adapted from this representation, with much more use of ornamental pattern in the background and almost no suggestion of space. This is a French characteristic; the patterns on the *prie-dieu* and canopy, and in the background are painted with great precision and delicacy, and with a balance of colour in the surface patterns which is neither English nor Italian. The architecture in the Beaufort Annunciation as in the Broederlam panel in part, is white shaded with grey; the detail of the structure with projecting buttress-like forms and sculptured ornament, even to the scroll patterns, is very close in the two Annunciations. Evidence that the Beaufort miniature originally may have been painted without the spray decoration is found in the fact that the sprays at the bottom of the page spring from the drapery of the *prie-dieu* (therefore must have been put in after the donor figures were painted), and the spray at the left actually passes over the painting, as do some of the crestings at the top of the architecture. The relation of the donors to the architecture echoes that of Philippe le Hardi and Marguerite of Flanders carved by Claus Sluter at the two sides of the portal of the Chapel of the Chartreuse of Champmol (Dijon) in the last decade of the fourteenth century. And finally the curious polygonal shape of the architecture with the standing figures of prophets in the upper part cannot help recalling the form of the famous Well of Moses with the prophet figures carved by Sluter for the cloister of the Chartreuse, and painted by Jean Malouel, painter and valet de chambre of the dukes of Burgundy from 1397 to 1415 (see below). In this work he was assisted by a Herman of Cologne in the years 1401–3.[3] Malouel had special reason for thorough familiarity with Broederlam's altarwings: he was one of a commission appointed by Duke Philippe to examine and pass upon these panels when finished in 1399 in order to determine whether the contract had been properly fulfilled and the work should be paid for.[4] It seems possible that Malouel painted the Beaufort Annunciation miniature.

On the possible identification of Herman of Cologne with Hermann Scheerre, illuminator, see below.

The Gelder Documents

Malouel is one of several French spellings of Maelwael which appears on his seal attached to a receipt for his salary, 24 March, 1398.[5]

The name Maelwael (Maelwail, Mailwail) is entered a great number of times between 1386 and 1397 in the Household Accounts of William Duke of Gelder, now in the

---

[1] Reproduced, Fierens-Gevaert, Hippolyte, *Histoire de la peinture flamande*, Paris and Brussels, I, 1927, Pl. XVI.

[2] Brit. Mus. Royal MS. 2 A. XVIII, fol. 23vo, Pl. LI.

[3] Archives départementales de la Côte-d'Or. Quoted by Dehaisnes, Chrétien, *Documents et extraits divers concernant l'histoire de l'art dans la Flandre, l'Artois et le Hainaut*, Lille, 1886, I, p. 797.

[4] *Ibid.*, p. 720, note 1.

[5] *Ibid.*, p. 777.

APPENDIX

Rijksarchief in Gelderland, at Arnhem (unpublished)[1] for payments made for various kinds of heraldic work. Three of the earliest of these are the following from the Rekeningen van den Landrentmeestergeneral van Gelre, A. 1, a (1386):

Fol. 11. Item Willem Maelwael van mijns Heren steeckgetouwe ende sheren van Ghemen ende van x speeren mit gulden loveren xxvi aud scild ende van mijns Heren helme ii aud scild r(ijns).

> Inde habet in Novimagio vigilia Mathie xx aurea.
> Item idem crastino Oculi[2] in Arnhem x aurea.
> Item idem per filium ejus feria tercia post Palmarum vii aurea x placken.

Fol. 26. Item Willem Maelwael van enen steecgetouwe quod habuit dominus Johannes de Velde (word illegible) xiii clypea antiqua r(enensia).

> Inde habet viii aurea die Ascensionis Domini per dominum Joannem filium ejus.
> Item idem per H(ermannum?) filium Dominica crastino Laurencii v aurea.

Fol. 30vo. Item Willem Maelwael van ii trumpwympelen van goud ende ii trump-wympelen, geneyet van zyndael xvi aurea renensia.

> Inde habet viii aurea per Joannem filium ejus feria sexta post Viti.
> Item idem in Novimagio viii aurea die Margarete.

Herman Maelwael is mentioned with increasing frequency in the Gelder documents, sometimes in connection with his father, Willem, more often in later years alone. Particularly interesting is the item in the account of 'Extra-ordinaris uitgaven' for 1389–90 (fol. 60): Herman Mailwail, five nobles for banners, pennons, and other things for the journey to England; on fol. 72 of the same account, the heralds Herman die Coningk and Gelre receive new clothes for the English journey (cf. p. 86, above).

Finally, in the account of 1388–9 (fol. 35) payment is made to 'Herman den maelre tot Colne van werke de he tot Colne then Predikeren van mijns heren wegen in Goids eer dair gemaickt heeft'.

There are three especially interesting angles to the items quoted above. (1) A family named Maelwael, father and two sons, were employed on heraldic work required by

---

[1] The first item containing a reference to 'Johannes', son of Willem Maelwael (see fol. 26 below) I discovered by chance during a short visit to Arnhem in 1936. The accounts fill many volumes and cover, with gaps, the period between 1382 and 1398. They are written very clearly on paper, in a mixture of old Dutch and Latin, much abbreviated and contracted. The items published here for the first time have been selected for their bearing on the particular problem of artistic relations between England and the Low Countries and Burgundy in the late fourteenth and early fifteenth centuries. There are many other items referring to heraldic work by Willem and Herman Maelwael and also information about other work, as embroideries and goldsmith work, done for the Duke of Gelder and his household. The documents were examined cursorily for me before the war by Dr J. A. Van de Ven, Archivist at Utrecht, formerly at Arnhem, who copied out many of the more interesting items, especially those containing the name of Maelwael. The account books are still intact and it is hoped that eventually a thorough study may be made of pertinent items with a view to their precise interpretation and their implications for art. Pending this study, it has seemed worth while to include here some of the more striking items, in their original form and without annotation (because the exact meaning of some of the terms used is not always clear), as a sample of additional source material to be exploited when opportunity arises for further research.

[2] The Monday after the third Sunday in Lent.

William Duke of Gelder of whom Froissart[1] tells us, 'the more he increased in age the greater was his love for tilts, tournaments, and rich amusements, and he was more attached to the English than to the French which he showed as long as he lived.'

In this environment Jean Malouel got his early training. He is not mentioned in the Gelder documents after July, 1386–7, from which it would appear that he did not remain in Gelder. He is known to have been in Paris in 1396–7, working for Queen Isabeau de Bavière, 'drawing designs for ornaments of gold and coats of arms of gold and divers colors'.[2] In December, 1397, he was appointed court painter to Duke Philippe le Hardi.[3] In 1399 he was paid for painting the arms of Burgundy on shields.[4] In 1403 he made 'harnois de joustes' for the wedding of Antoine de Bourgogne at Arras, and in 1405–6 for the weddings of the Dukes of Touraine and of Angoulême at Paris and at Compiègne.[5] Payments of his salary occur regularly in the archives until 1415, when on May 23 his successor, Henri Bellechose, was appointed.[6] Malouel's work for the Duke was not all heraldic; there are references to various panel paintings which he had undertaken, and in the inventory of Duke Philippe (1404), a large altarpiece of wood is mentioned, with Our Lady in the centre, the two Saints John and Saint Peter and Saint Andrew, painted by Malouel.[7] If this painting were ever identified, and in its original condition, we should know what Malouel's style was; otherwise, there is only the traditionally attributed tondo of the Trinity-Pietà in the Louvre,[8] and the Martyrdom of Saint Denis, also in the Louvre, which we know to have been finished by Malouel's successor, Henri Bellechose.[9] These facts are some of the materials for a study of Malouel which, in the light of the new Gelder documents, now seems more than ever worth while attempting.

One of the most frequently quoted Malouel documents concerns the ransom in 1400 of his two nephews who were imprisoned in Brussels on their way home from Paris to Gelder 'where they were born'.[10] These boys, Herman and Jacquemin, were almost certainly sons of Jean's brother, Herman.

(2) In 1390 William Duke of Gelder made a journey to England, taking with him his two heralds, Herman die Coningk and Gelre. A herald Gelre, it will be remembered, perhaps this same person, wrote the later poems in the *Wapengedichten en Wapenboek* which contains a coat of arms and two miniatures here attributed to Hand A of the Carmelite Missal (see above, pp. 83 ff.). The herald Gelre is mentioned again later in the Gelder documents; Herman die Coningk is not. Is it possible that he, or (if he was not an artist), someone associated with him or with Gelre herald went to England with the Duke's party and stayed to work on the Carmelite Missal? Both Richard and John of Gaunt were patrons of the Carmelites, and John of Gaunt had Carmelite confessors.[11]

If William of Gelder had in his train a gifted artist, it would have been most natural

---

[1] *Op. cit.*, XIII, pp. 15 and 30 f.

[2] *Nouvelles Archives de l'art français*, 1878, pp. 167 f. Champeaux, A. de, 'L'Ancienne école de peinture de la Bourgogne', *Gaz. des Beaux-Arts*, 3e Per., XIX (1898), T. 1, p. 42.

[3] Dehaisnes, *op. cit.*, p. 759.   [4] *Ibid.*, p. 780.

[5] Archives départementales de la Côte-d'Or, B. 1519; Laborde, Léon Cte de, *Les ducs de Bourgogne*, Paris, 1849–52, I, p. 17.

[6] *Ibid*, p. lxix.   [7] Dehaisnes, *op. cit.*, p. 840.

[8] Paul Durrieu, *Mon. et Mem. Piot* (Acad. des Inscriptions et Belles Lettres), XXIII, 1918, p. 79.

[9] Champeaux, *loc cit.*, p. 131, n. 1.   [10] Dehaisnes, *op. cit.*, pp. 790 f.

[11] William de Teynham, John Badby, Walter Dysse, and John Kynyngham. See Sheppard, L. C., *The English Carmelites*, London, 1943, p. 43.

for him to be invited to collaborate on the magnificent Carmelite Missal then in process of making.

(3) Herman of Cologne, paid by the Duke of Gelder for work he did in Cologne in 1388–9, was probably known to Jean Malouel while both were in Gelder, long before Herman assisted Malouel in painting the Well of Moses in 1401–3. Later (1419), Herman of Cologne worked for Isabeau de Bavière in Paris.[1]

The illuminator Hermann who, there seems little reason to doubt, was Hermann Scheerre, first appears in English documents in 1407 when he witnessed the will of one Peter of Cologne who left all his goods to 'Brother Herman of Cologne, of the Order of Carmelites'.[2] A manuscript undoubtedly illuminated by Hermann Scheerre (Brussels Bibl. Roy. 4862–9), a copy of the Carmelite Calendar of Nicholas of Lynn, contributes another small bit of evidence on his Carmelite connections. The date 1407 and the approximate dates of the manuscripts attributed to him on grounds of style, signatures, or mottoes, would fit nicely between the dates when Herman of Cologne was working in Dijon and 1419 when he was in Paris; if Hermann Scheerre were in Dijon in 1401–3 he would have had the opportunity to acquire the Beaufort Annunciation miniature (see above), which so greatly influenced his style in England. The latest of the Hermann manuscripts, made for the Duke of Bedford between 1414 and 1435 (Brit. Mus. Add. 42131) seems to show some French influence, especially in the colouring of the miniatures, such as is found in the other magnificent book made for the Duke (Brit. Mus. Add. 18850) illuminated in Paris *ca.* 1425. It is possible that while the Duke was regent of France, or perhaps even before, Hermann had come into contact with French artists who may have collaborated with him in the Bedford Hours (in which his name appears in two line endings), particularly in the full page miniatures, some of which do not seem to be in his characteristic earlier style.

This is all the evidence that has yet come to light regarding the possible identification of Hermann Scheerre with Herman of Cologne. Admittedly it is inconclusive, but it may perhaps furnish some indication of the direction which further research might take in the solution of this important but puzzling problem.

[1] *Nouvelles Archives*, p. 180. Durrieu in Michel, *Histoire de l'Art*, III, 1, p. 150.
[2] Archdeaconry of London, Reg. I, fol. 185vo. The will is dated 22 September, 1407. It is published in full in *Burl. Mag.*, LXI (1935), p. 40.

Selected Bibliography

*Books and Manuscripts Bearing on Special Phases of the
Reconstruction or Study of the Carmelite Missal*

The Missal Fragments before and after the Reconstruction

British Museum. *Catalogue of Additional Manuscripts*. London, 1854–75.

—— *Schools of Illumination*. Part IV: English 1350–1500. London, 1922.

—— *Guide to the Exhibited Manuscripts*. Part III. London, 1923.

*Catalogue of the Antiquities and Works of Art, Exhibited at Ironmongers' Hall, London, in
the month of May, 1861*. Compiled by a Committee of the Council of the London
and Middlesex Archaeological Society, with numerous illustrations. Part II, London,
1863. Part III, 1867.

Hanrott, P. A. *Sales Catalogues*, Evans, 5 August, 1833 and 28 January, 1857.

Rickert, M. 'Reconstruction of an English Carmelite Missal', *Burlington Magazine*, LXVII
(1935), 99–113.

—— 'Reconstruction of an English Carmelite Missal', *Speculum*, XVI (1941), 92–102.

Shaw, Henry. *Alphabets, Numerals and Devices of the Middle Ages*. London, 1845.

Tite, Sir William. *Sales Catalogue*, Sotheby, 18 May, 1874.

The Reconstruction of the Text

Analecta Ordinis Carmelitarum, Vol. X, Fasc. VII. Rome, 1940.

Cabrol, Fernand, et Leclerc, Henri. *Dictionnaire d'archéologie chrétienne et de liturgie*. Paris,
1907–

Gordon, G. A. *Manuscript Missals, The English Uses*. 'Sandars Lectures', Cambridge,
1936. Typescript copy in British Museum, Add. MS. 44920.

Leroquais, Victor. *Les bréviaires manuscrits des bibliothèques publiques de France*. 6 vols.
Paris, 1934.

—— *Les sacramentaires et les missels manuscrits dans les bibliothèques publiques de France*.
4 parts. Paris, 1924.

Magennis, Fr. E., O. Carm. *The Scapular and Some Critics*. Rome, 1914.

Maskell, William. *The Ancient Liturgy of the Church of England*. 3rd ed. Oxford, 1882.

Missale ad Usum Ecclesie Westmonasteriensis. Edited by J. Wickham Legg for the Henry
Bradshaw Society, London. 3 vols. 1891–7.

Missale ad usum insignis et praeclarae Ecclesiae Sarum. Edited by F. H. Dickinson. Burntisland, 1861–83.

SELECTED BIBLIOGRAPHY

Missale Factum ad Usum Carmelitarum. Venice, 1504. Photostatic Copy in the British Museum (London, 1936). 3 vols.

Missale Ordinis Fratrum Beatiss. Dei Genetricis Mariae de Monte Carmelo Antiquae Observantiae Regularis. Rome, 1640.

Sibert de Beka. *Ordinale ad Usum Fratrum Beatae Mariae Montis Carmeli*. Lambeth Palace Library, MS. 193. Published by Fr. Benedict Zimmerman, O.C.D.: *Ordinaire de l'Ordre de Notre-Dame du Mont-Carmel* (Chevalier, Ulysse, 'Bibliothèque Liturgique', XIII), Paris, 1910.

Simpson, W. Sparrow. *Documents Illustrating the History of St. Paul's Cathedral*. 'Camden Society Publications', N.S. XXVI. London, 1880.

Villiers de St. Étienne, Cosmè de. *Bibliotheca Carmelitana*. 2 vols. Orleans, 1752. Photographic facsimile with introduction by Fr. Gabriel Wessels, O. Carm., Rome, 1927.

Wessels, Fr. Gabriel, O. Carm. *Acta Capitulorum Generalium Ordinis Fratrum B.V. Mariae de Montis Carmeli*. Vol. I (1318–1593). Rome, 1912.

Zimmerman, Fr. Benedict, O.C.D. *Monumenta Historica Carmelitana*. Paris, 1907.

MANUSCRIPTS

Dublin, Trinity College Library, MS. 82 (B.3.1). Carmelite Missal. Dated 1458.

Manchester, John Rylands Library, MS. 123. Carmelite Missal. Early fifteenth century.

Oxford, University College Library, MS. 9. Carmelite Breviary and Short Missal. Late fourteenth century.

ICONOGRAPHY AND COSTUME

Boutell, Charles. *Monumental Brasses and Slabs*. London, 1847.

—— *Monumental Brasses of England*. London, 1849.

Gay, Victor. *Glossaire archéologique du moyen-âge et de la renaissance*. Paris, 1889–1928.

Horstman, Carl. *Nova Legenda Anglie*. 2 vols. Oxford, 1901.

Jacobus da Voragine. *Legenda Aurea*. Edited by Th. Graesse. 3rd ed. Breslau, 1890.

James, M. R. *The Apocryphal New Testament*. Oxford, 1924.

Kelly, F. M., and Schwabe, R. *A Short History of Costume and Armour chiefly in England*. 2 vols. London, 1931.

Macklin, H. W. *The Brasses of England*. London, 1907.

Netter, Thomas, of Walden (ascribed to). *Fasciculi zizaniorum magistri Johannis Wyclif cum Tritico*. Edited by Walter Waddington Shirley. 'Rolls Series', London, 1858.

Planchè, James Robinson. *A Cyclopedia of Costume*. London, 1876–9.

Post, Paul. *Die französisch-niederländische Männertracht ... im Zeitalter der Spätgotik 1350 bis 1475*. Halle, 1910.

Valentin Carderera y Solano. *Iconografia Española*. Madrid, 1856–64.

STYLE

Blokland, A. Beelaerts van. *Beyeren quondam Gelre*. 'Koninklijk Nederlandsch Genootschap voor Geslacht en Wapenkunde'. The Hague, 1933.

Bouton, Victor. *Wapenboeck, Armorial de 1334 à 1372 ... précédé de poésies héraldiques par Gelre, héraut d'armes*. Paris, 1881–6.

Byvanck, A. W. *La miniature dans les Pays-Bas septentrionaux*. Paris, 1937.

SELECTED BIBLIOGRAPHY

Byvanck, A. W., and Hoogewerff, G. J. *La miniature hollandaise dans les manuscrits des 14ᵉ, 15ᵉ, et 16ᵉ siècles.* 3 vols. The Hague, 1922–6.

Durrieu, Cte Paul. *Les heures de Turin.* Paris, 1902.

Dvořák, Max. 'Die Illuminatoren des Johann von Neumarkt', *Jahrbuch der kunsthistorischen Sammlungen des allerhöchsten Kaiserhauses,* XXII (1902), 35–126.

Gaspar, C., and Lyna, F. *Les principaux manuscrits à peintures de la Bibliothèque Royale de Belgique.* (Soc. franç. de reprod. de manuscrits à peintures). Paris, 1937, I, 372–7.

Herbert, J. A. *Illuminated Manuscripts.* London, 1911.

—— *The Sherborne Missal.* Roxburghe Club, Oxford, 1920.

Hoogewerff, G. J. *De Noord-Nederlandsche Schilderkunst.* The Hague, 1936. Vol. I.

James, M.R., and Millar, E. G. *The Bohun Manuscripts.* Roxburghe Club, Oxford, 1936.

Marle, Raimond van. *The Development of the Italian Schools of Painting.* Vols. V, VII, The Hague, 1925, 1926.

Millar, E. G. *English Illuminated Manuscripts of the XIVth and XVth Centuries.* Paris and Brussels, 1928.

Robinson, J. A., and James, M. R. *The Manuscripts of Westminster Abbey.* London, 1909.

Schlosser, Julius von. 'Die Bilderhandschriften Königs Wenzel I', *Jahrbuch der kunsthistorischen Sammlungen des allerhöchsten Kaiserhauses,* XIV (1893), 214–317.

Vogelsang, Willem. *Holländische Miniaturen des späteren Mittelalters.* Strassburg, 1899. (Studien zur deutschen Kunstgeschichte, 18).

Index

INDEX

The Plates

I. Carmelite Missal, fol. 6vo: Holy Saturday
(Initial actual size; detail enlarged)

II. Carmelite Missal, fols. 7vo and 8: Easter

(Large initial introducing the introit of the Mass; small letters beginning the verses of the gospel; approximately four-fifths actual size)

III. Carmelite Missal, fol. 21vo, reconstructed page from the *Temporale*
(*Approximately one-third actual size*): *Ascension*

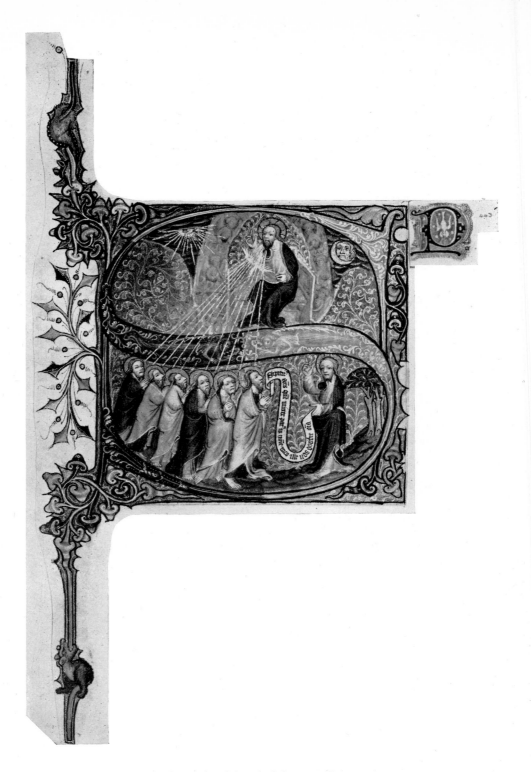

IV. Carmelite Missal, fol. 27vo: Pentecost
(*Four-fifths actual size*)

V. Carmelite Missal, fol. 36vo: Trinity Sunday

(Four-fifths actual size)

VI. Carmelite Missal, fol. 38: Corpus Christi Day
(*Four-fifths actual size*)

VII. Carmelite Missal, fol. 68vo: Dedication of the Church
(*Four-fifths actual size*)

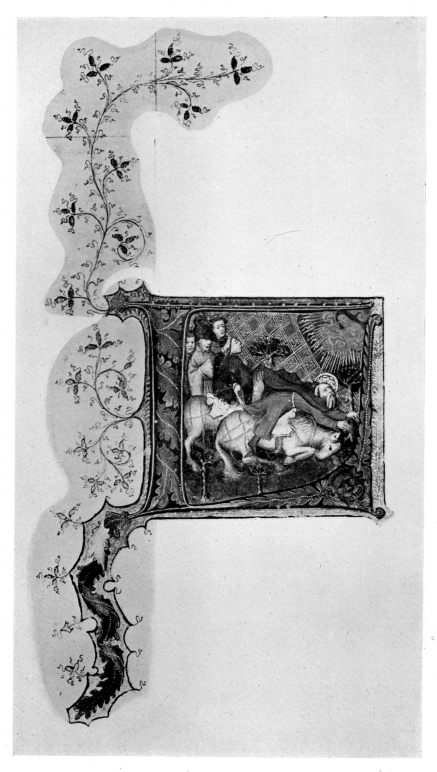

VIII. Carmelite Missal, fol. 90: Conversion of Paul
(*Actual size*)

IX. Carmelite Missal, fol. 93: Purification of the Virgin
(*This and all the following miniatures reproduced from the Missal, four-fifths actual size*)

X. Carmelite Missal, fol. 99: Annunciation

XI. (*a*) Carmelite Missal, fol. 100: Richard de Wyche, Bishop (of Chichester)

(*b*) Carmelite Missal, fol. 100vo: Ambrose

XII. (*a*) Carmelite Missal, fol. 113: Nativity of John the Baptist
(*b*) Carmelite Missal, fol. 118vo: Octave of the Apostles Peter and Paul

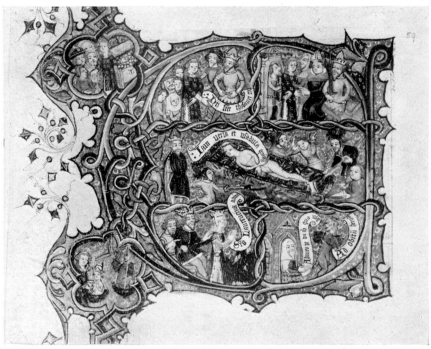

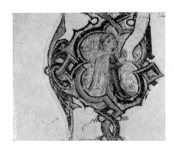

XIII. Carmelite Missal, fol. 130: Lawrence

XIV (*a*) Carmelite Missal, fol. 131: Vigil of the Assumption

(*b*) Carmelite Missal, fol. 131: Hippolytus

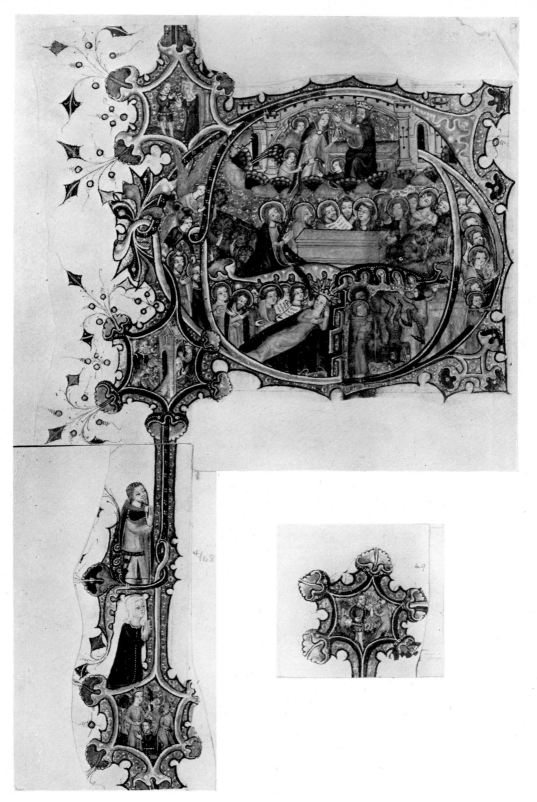

XV. Carmelite Missal, fol. 132vo: Assumption of the Virgin

XVI. (*a*) Carmelite Missal, fol. 136vo: Augustine, Bishop (of Hippo)
(*b*) Carmelite Missal, fol. 136vo: Decollation of John the Baptist

XVII. (*a*) Carmelite Missal, fol. 135vo: Louis, King (of France)

(*b*) Carmelite Missal, fol. 138: Giles

XVIII. Carmelite Missal, fol. 138vo: Nativity of the Virgin

XIX. (*a*) Carmelite Missal, fol. 143vo: Cleophas

(*b*) Carmelite Missal, fol. 140: Exaltation of the Cross

(*c*) Carmelite Missal, fol. 143vo: Maurice and his Companions

XX. Carmelite Missal, fol. 152vo: All Saints

XXI. Carmelite Missal, fol. 159: Martin, Bishop (of Tours)

XXII. (*a*) Carmelite Missal, fol. 159vo: Brice

(*b*) Carmelite Missal, fol. 160: Edmund Rich, Archbishop (of Canterbury)

XXIII. (*a*) Carmelite Missal, fol. 160vo: Edmund, King (of East Anglia)

(*b*) Carmelite Missal, fol. 160vo: Cecilia

XXIV. (*a*) Carmelite Missal, fol. 161: Clement, Pope
(*b*) Carmelite Missal, fol. 161: Chrysogonus

XXV. Carmelite Missal, fol. 161vo: Catherine (of Alexandria)

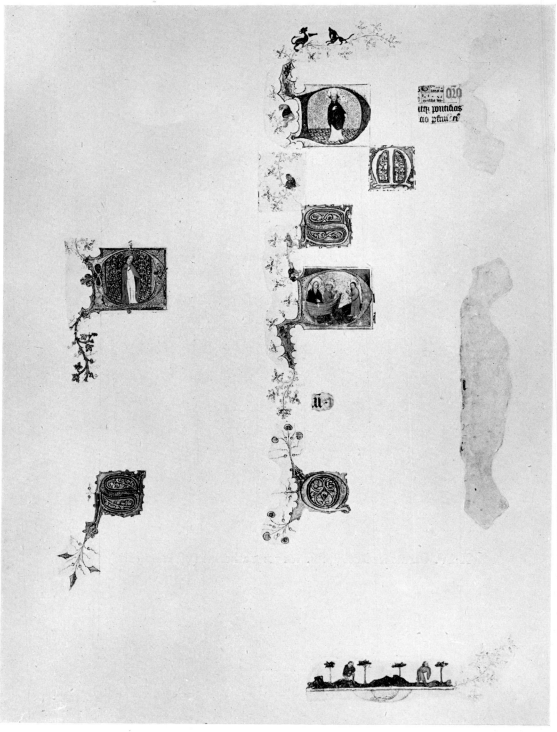

XXVI. Carmelite Missal, fol. 162, reconstructed page from the *Sanctorale*
(*Approximately one-third actual size*): *Linus, Saturninus and the Vigil of Andrew*

XXVII. (*a*) Carmelite Missal, fol. 163: Andrew, Mass for the Day

(*b*) Carmelite Missal, fol. 165: Andrew, Mass for the Octave

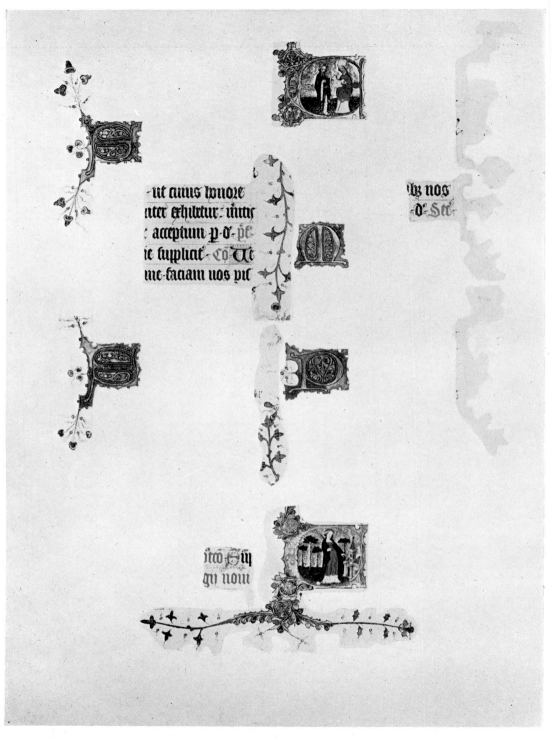

XXVIII. Carmelite Missal, fol. 164, reconstructed page from the *Sanctorale*
(*Approximately one-third actual size*): *Loy and Barbara*

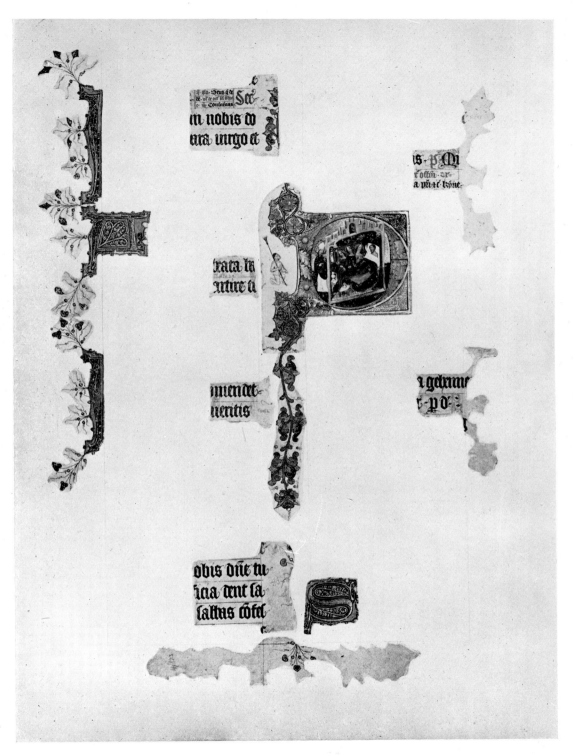

XXIX. Carmelite Missal, fol. 164vo, (verso of Plate XXVIII): Nicholas (of Bari)

XXX. Carmelite Missal, fol. 165: Conception of the Virgin

XXXI. (*a*) Carmelite Missal, fol. 166: Lucy
(*b*) Carmelite Missal, fol. 166: Lazarus

XXXII. (*a*) Carmelite Missal, fol. 192: a Matron

(*b*) Carmelite Missal, fol. 193: Several Virgins

XXXIII. Carmelite Missal, fol. 193vo: Votive Mass of the Trinity

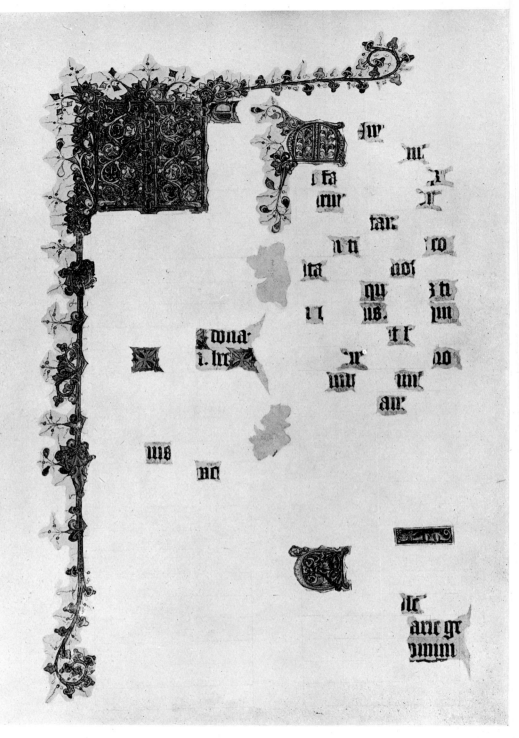

XXXIV. Carmelite Missal, fol. 78, reconstructed page from the *Ordo Missae*
(*Approximately one-third actual size*): Te [igitur] *beginning the Canon of the Mass*

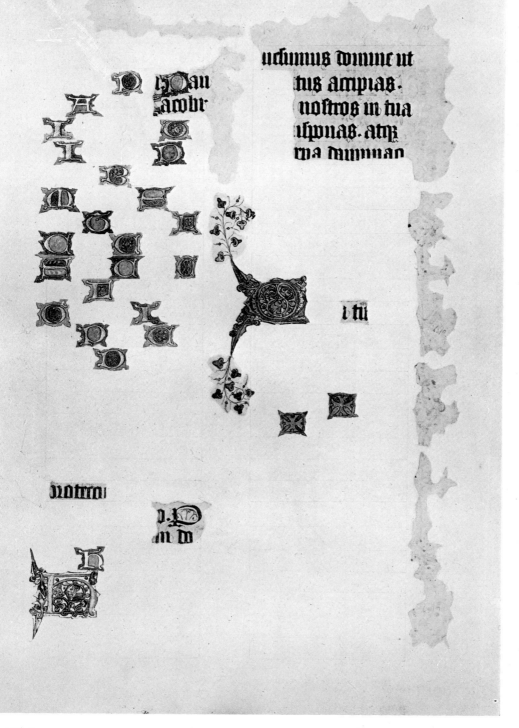

XXXV. Carmelite Missal, fol. 78vo (verso of Plate XXXIV): Canon of the Mass

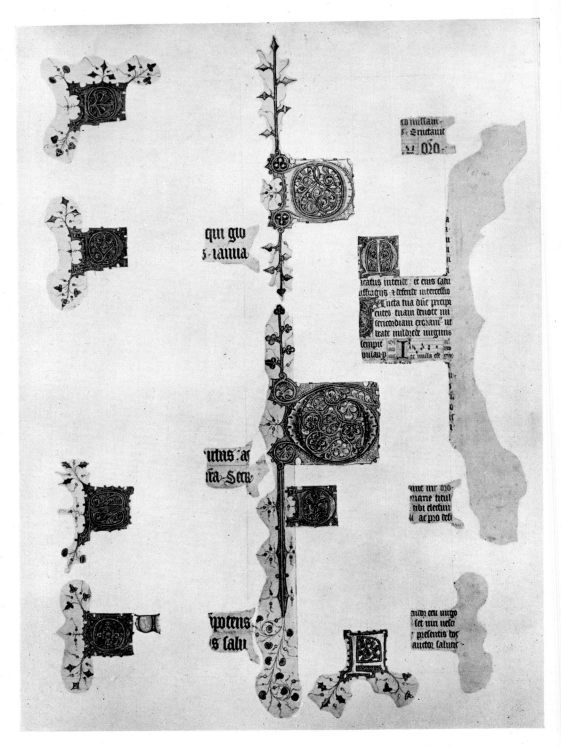

XXXVI. Carmelite Missal, fol. 120, reconstructed page from the *Sanctorale*
(*Approximately one-third actual size*): *Initial G beginning the introit of the Solemn Commemoration of the Virgin*

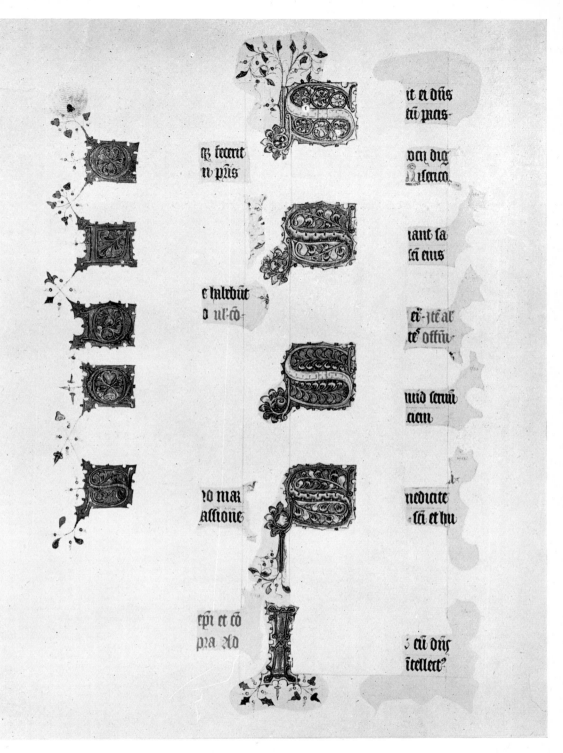

XXXVII. Carmelite Missal, fol. 182, reconstructed page from the *Commune Sanctorum*
(Approximately one-third actual size):
Initials beginning alternative offertories etcetera, *for the Common Mass of Several Martyrs*

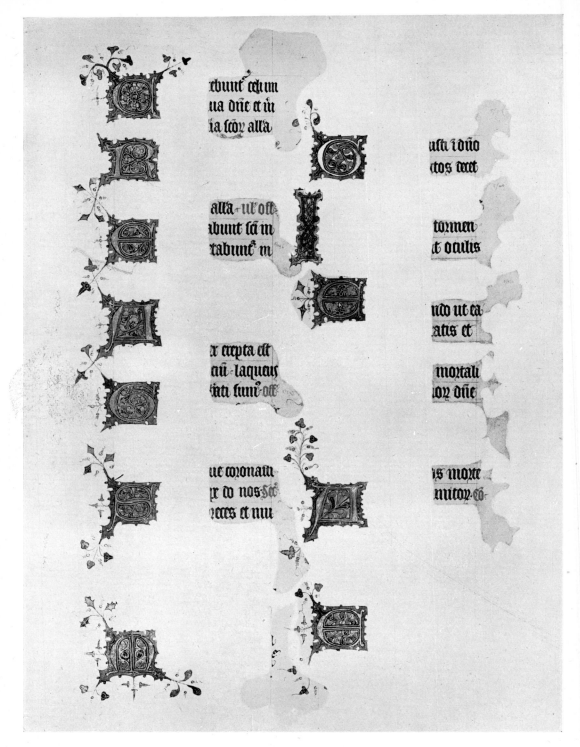

XXXVIII. Carmelite Missal, fol. 182vo (verso of Plate XXXVII):

Initials beginning alternative communions etcetera, *for the Common Mass of Several Martyrs, and introits for the Common Mass of a Bishop and Confessor*

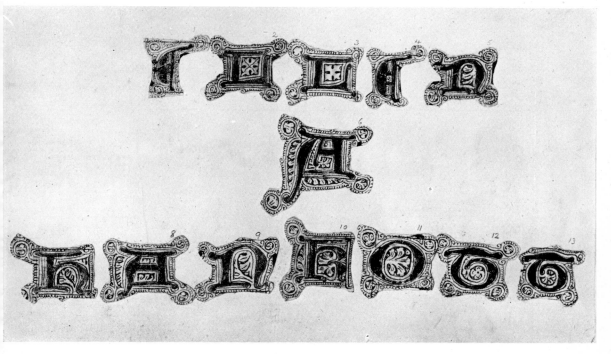

XXXIX. Hanrott 'Signatures' from the Scrapbooks in the British Museum

(*a*) and (*b*) Additional MS. 29704, page 139

(*c*) Additional MS. 44892, inside of front cover

(a)

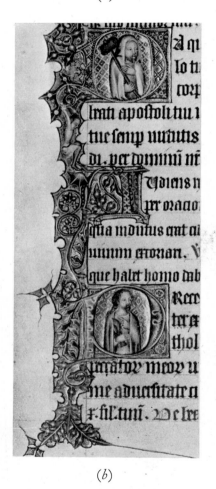

(c)

(b)

(d)

XL. Three Manuscripts Illustrating Early Phases of the English Style in the Carmelite Missal

(a) and (b) Psalter of Humphrey de Bohun. Vienna, Nazionalbibliothek, MS. 1826*, fols. 15vo and 153. Before 1372

(c) *Lancelot du Lac*, with the Arms of Mary de Bohun. British Museum, Royal MS. 20 D. IV, fol. 102vo. After 1380

(d) English Statutes. British Museum, Cotton MS. Nero D. VI, fol. 31. After 1386

XLI. (a) Psalter and Hours. Oxford, Bodleian Library, MS. Laud. Misc. 188, fol. 1.
Late XIVth century

(b) Psalter and Hours. British Museum, Additional MS. 16968, fol. 24vo. Late XIVth century

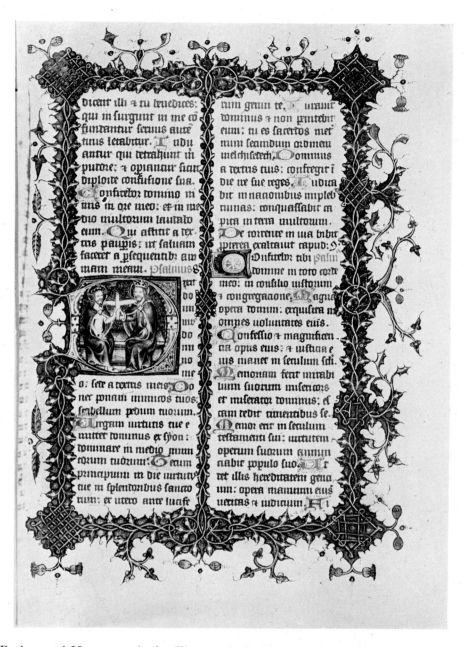

XLII. Psalter and Hours, made for Eleanor de Bohun. Edinburgh, National Library, Adv. MS. 18.6.5, Psalm 109. Before 1399

XLIII. William of Nottingham, Commentary on the Four Gospels. Oxford, Bodleian
Library, MS. Laud. Misc. 165, fol. 5. Dated 1397

XLIV. *Liber Regalis*. London, Westminster Abbey Library Manuscript, fol. 20. Probably
shortly after 1382

XLV. (*a*) Missal. Oxford, Trinity College, MS. 8, fol. 157. Before 1388

(*b*) English Statutes. Cambridge, St John's College, MS. A.7, fol. 1. After 1387

XLVI. (*a*) 'Gelder *Wapenboek*.' Brussels, Bibliothèque Royale, MS. 15652–56, fol. 15vo. 1377–93?

(*b*) and (*c*) Jacob van Maerlant, *Rijmbijbel*. Amsterdam, Koninklijke Akademie, MS. XVIII (deposited in the Royal Library, The Hague), fols. 101 and 130. Late XIVth century.

XLVII. 'Gelder *Wapenboek*.' Brussels, Bibliothèque Royale, MS. 15652–56, fol. 26. Before 1378?

XLVIII. 'Gelder *Wapenboek*.' Brussels, Bibliothèque Royale, MS. 15652–56, fol. 122. Before 1393?

XLIX. Durandus, *Rationale* (German translation). Vienna, Nazionalbibliothek, MS. 2765, fol. 1. Dated 1384

L. Missal. Oxford, Corpus Christi College, MS. 394, fol. 102vo. Dated 1398

LI. 'Beaufort Hours.' British Museum, Royal MS. 2 A.XVIII, fol. 23vo. 1401–10

LII. (*a*) Book of Hours. Oxford, Bodleian Library, MS. Lat. lit. f. 2, fol. 10. 1405–13

(*b*) Bible. British Museum, Royal MS. 1 E. IX, fol. 2. Ca 1410

LIII. (*a*) St Gregory, Homilies. British Museum, Royal MS. 20 D.V, fol. 41vo.
Late XIVth century

(*b*) Breviary of Archbishop Chichele. London, Lambeth Palace Library, MS. 69, fol. 55.
Before 1416

(*c*) Bible. British Museum, Royal MS. 1 E. IX, fol. 109vo. Ca 1410

LIV. (*a*) St Gregory, Homilies. British Museum, Royal MS. 20 D.V, fol. 98.
Late XIVth century

(*b*) 'Lovell Lectionary.' British Museum, Harley MS. 7026, fol. 9.
Before 1408

LV. Bible. British Museum, Royal MS. 1 E.IX, fol. 154vo. Ca 1410

Within the illustration:

mnes sancti confessores deuotio
nem debitam et in bonis openb3
occupationem assiduam et atten
tam.

LVI. Leaf from 'Milan-Turin Hours' of the Duc de Berry. Paris, Louvre, Cabinet des Dessins,
R.F. 2023, verso. 1404–13?